ANIMATED FILM

ANIMATED FILM
CONCEPTS, METHODS, USES

ROY MADSEN

INTERLAND PUBLISHING INC.
New York

Distributed by PITMAN PUBLISHING CORPORATION
New York   Toronto   London   Tel Aviv

□ Films from the National Film Board of Canada are invariably distinctive: each offers a refreshing cinematic concept, a deepening or broadening of educational opportunity, a perceptive insight into the problems and complexities of modern society. Each film reaches out to more than a hundred nations and influences a world audience of uncounted millions—to an effect of immeasurable good. This book is dedicated to the artists and animators of The National Film Board of Canada.

CONTENTS

FOREWORD

THE explosions of interest in film that have reverberated through the educational world in recent years have too much neglected one branch of the art—animation. Yet here, too, a chain reaction is beginning.

☐ Curiously, the animated film was long held by its own successes. The very young were so pleased with funny animals that went bang, zap, wham, and old advertisers so enamored of animated cereals that went snap, crackle, pop, that the medium seemed doomed to perpetual infancy.

☐ Yet many artists—including some of the world's most celebrated—have long recognized in the animated film an extraordinary opportunity for expression. And numerous educators have seen it as an educational tool of vast possibilities. Its domain includes the visible and invisible, the concrete and abstract. No other medium can so vividly clarify relationships of all sorts. It offers unexplored opportunities to the teaching of history, mathematics, physics, chemistry, geology—as well as to professional studies such as architecture, medicine, business, engineering.

☐ Problems of cost long seemed a stumbling block but are beginning to lessen. Animation equipment is finding its way into colleges and schools. Here experiments have shown not only that the young can make valuable animated films but also— perhaps equally important—that the experience of making them can open doors of knowledge and comprehension.

☐ Educators have reason to welcome the medium of animation, freed of its old chains.

Erik Barnouw, PROFESSOR
School of the Arts (Film Division)
Columbia University

INTRODUCTION

THE unique characteristics, techniques, and values of that special kind of motion picture known as the animation film, are thoroughly discussed and clearly illustrated in this volume. In a world which is in dire need of better communication between people at all levels, the potential of this exciting and challenging form is limitless because there is something fundamental and timeless about the animated image which attracts and engages human beings everywhere.

☐ As the author points out, the art of animation really began with prehistoric paintings of animals found on the walls of caves in France and Spain. These primitive but remarkably effective representations of the deer, bison, boar, and other creatures may have actually appeared to move and have life when seen by the light of the flickering fires in the caves of Altamira and Lascaux. Animal images seen by the light of a flickering television tube on any given Saturday morning, remind us that we are still the ancients in the art of communication and that we are still curiously attracted to such animal forms today.

☐ One of the very first animated films ever produced involved a dinosaur, and when sound came in it was a mouse who starred in the first musical cartoon. The bulk of commercial animation continues to feature birds and animals including an insane woodpecker, a loud-mouthed duck, a frustrated cat chasing an eternally illusive and particularly invincible mouse, a variety of talking dogs, roosters, chipmunks, coyotes, squirrels, beavers, and a conglomerate assortment of cross-breeds between animal and human forms. These cartoon-animals are so empathetic, and expressive of human emotions that we shall not soon see the end of anthropomorphic characters like Bugs Bunny or the incredible Road Runner created by Chuck Jones.

☐ At the same time, however, the art of animation is changing and multiplying in both form and content. In theatrical, television, educational, and industrial film production, the skill and imagination of the professional animator are becoming more highly valued because of the knowledge explosion and consequent need for economy of factual expression, compression of time and space, and the necessity for dramatizing and simplifying complex ideas and concepts.

☐ Much of our world, physically and psychologically, is increasingly abstract, nonverbal, and nonphotographable. The animation camera is a remarkable facility for showing not only what things are but also what they mean. Consequently, it is completely understandable that chemists, physicists, and biologists should be among the first to seize upon and explore the technique of animation as a way to improve the quality of instruction in scientific fields. The capacity of the medium to express exactitudes, make comparisons, and draw analogies makes this an admirable learning resource in the physical sciences, and many other areas as well.

☐ As early as about 1720, for example, a French mathematician by the name of Louis-Bertrand Castel proposed that the keys of a harpsichord might be associated with color transparencies to produce ''visible music,'' by relating the two major dimensions of movement in music—pitch and amplitude—to visible displays of movement and color. Today mathematicians are becoming interested in animation to the degree which makes it reasonable to predict that the animation stand will become the mathematician's blackboard; a method of making visual statements of mathematical principles which will expand the abilities of both teacher and student. An animation camera may become a commonplace component in the repertoire of instructional technology along with projectors, tape recorders, television systems, and computer terminals.

☐ The intriguing visual quality and control possible through this medium makes it not only an essential mode of presenting public information, but also a means of personal expression as well.

☐ It is no accident that a growing number of university students, teen-age movie makers, and adult amateurs—most of them working in 16mm or even 8mm formats—are beginning to make films in a medium where a single person can control most, if not all, of the creative process. It is easy to understand why young people are deeply interested in film as a form which may be their only way of expressing themselves in a world of increasing subtleties, ambiguities, and complexities which do not seem to lend themselves to verbal or other conventional forms of expression. The animation film, as a direct, concrete method of image-making with a high degree of individual control seems to have no counterpart in any other medium.

☐ Animation today is being used for a variety of purposes from the delivery of exacting screen images of reality to visions of exciting fantasies. Religion, social problems, folklore, and music are its province as well as science and entertainment. It is an excellent medium for satire, and perhaps a new Swift or Daumier may emerge from the ranks of young animator-artists.

☐ Of course, it is never all that easy. The techniques must be mastered sooner or later, along with the necessary wisdom, knowledge, intuition, and imagination to put ideas into anima-

tion form. This is the product of time, persistence, patience, and experience. The first step is to know when, and when not, to employ the art of animation at all. Somewhere in that delicately-shaded area, bounded on one side by live cinematography and on the other by slide, filmstrip, photograph, and conventional artwork, is the wonderful world of animation.

☐ The way to recognize, understand, and appreciate the nature of that special world is to look, again and again, at the work of Norman McLaren, Philip Stapp, John Hubley, Len Lye, Walt Disney, Stephen Bosustow, John Halas and Joy Batchelor, Saul Bass, Charles Eames, Robert Verral, Bruce Cornwell, and many other professionals in this country and abroad. Watch television commercials critically. Look at the work of young, experimental artists and animators, some of them still teen-agers or university film students whose work is shown at local, regional, or national film festivals. Learn all you can from the professional experience of the past. Then make animated films.

Robert W. Wagner, CHAIRMAN
Department of Photography & Cinema
The Ohio State University

ACKNOWLEDGMENTS

☐ I am pleased to acknowledge the cooperation freely given by many persons and organizations during the writing of this book.

☐ The National Film Board of Canada has made available many illustrations and much information; for this I wish to thank Norman McLaren, Jim Lysyshyn, and Gerald Graham.

☐ At the Oxberry-Berkey Technical Corporation I am grateful to John Oxberry, who gave his enthusiastic support and complete cooperation in making animation facilities and equipment freely available.

☐ At Hanna-Barbera Studios I wish to thank Bill Hanna for his long-distance assistance, and John Michaeli for his efforts to obtain illustrations to meet our specific needs.

☐ I owe a particular debt to the late Walt Disney, who was intensely interested in animation for education and was personally committed to its furtherance. Roy Disney, George Sherman, and their colleagues are thanked for extending the continuing cooperation of Walt Disney Productions.

☐ Herbert Kosower, Director of Animation at the University of Southern California, has my sincere appreciation for acting as representative of the International Tournee of Animation, for contributing illustrations, and for invaluable help in uncounted ways.

☐ I am indebted to Professor Donald Ely, Director of the Center for Instructional Communications at Syracuse University, who was quick to recognize the potentialities of animation for education and who contributed in many ways, not easily measured or described, during the writing of this book.

☐ Professor John Tyo, Director of Cinematography at Syracuse University, is thanked for his advice while I tested various chapters in my animation classes at Syracuse.

☐ Philip Stapp, now artist-in-residence at Ohio State University, deserves recognition for his leadership in animation for education, and for his contributions to this book.

☐ Eric Barnouw is acknowledged for taking time from his own important work at Columbia University to read the manuscript and write the Foreword.

☐ I wish to thank Robert W. Wagner, Chairman of the Department of Photography and Cinema at Ohio State University, for reading the manuscript, making valuable suggestions, and writing the Introduction.

☐ Mr. George Bouwmann, Director of Cinematography at Horace Mann High School, deserves thanks for offering the results of his pioneering work in animation at the secondary level, done in conjunction with students and teachers.

☐ At the Library of Congress, sincere appreciation is extended

ACKNOWLEDGMENTS

to John Kuiper and Paul Spehr, who placed staff and facilities at my disposal and who enabled me to view many old and rare examples of animated film.

☐ At the National Archives, Mayfield Bray and her associates are thanked for assisting in the search for suitable excerpts from the vast Ford Film Project.

☐ Dick Rauh, president of The Optical House, is thanked for having artwork photographed for this book, and for time spent advising me of the latest developments in animation photography.

☐ Milan Herzog and William Peltz, of Encyclopedia Britannica Films, receive my appreciation for meeting every request, reasonable and unreasonable.

☐ Allan Lane of Jiro Enterprises is acknowledged for his contributions, as are Lars Calonius of Pelican Films, Phil Arenson of Channel 15, San Diego, Lloyd Bruce Holman and Ernest Pintoff.

☐ At FilmFair Studios I offer my thanks to Dick Van Bentham, Director of Animation, who took time from his demanding schedule to obtain illustrations, and to Gus Jekel, president of FilmFair, for making them available.

☐ Among those who contributed animation done for the armed forces I wish to credit Norman Dulin, United States Navy, and Colonel James Warndorf, United States Air Force.

☐ Of those who read and criticized the technical aspects of the manuscript, I am especially indebted to John Lewis and Richard Rauh, who were incisive and constructive in their comments. In this regard, I wish to thank John Oxberry again for reading the manuscript with a sharp pencil in hand.

☐ At the New York Museum of Modern Art, Joseph Longo is acknowledged for ferreting out those rare illustrations from the museum archives.

☐ Others at colleges and universities whose aid I wish to acknowledge include professors Arthur Knight and Herbert Farmer at the University of Southern California, Robert Knutson, Director of the Cinema Library at USC, William Millard, Coordinator of Instructional Media in the School of Medicine at USC, Joseph Renteria, Chris Rager, and Vincent A. Molinare at San Diego State, David Shepard at Pennsylvania State University, William Harlow at the State University College of Forestry at Syracuse, William Mathews at the Jet Propulsion Laboratory of the California Polytechnic Institute, Jiri Trinka at the Film Institute, Prague, and Colin Young and Hugh Grauel at the University of California at Los Angeles.

☐ Many officials in corporations cooperated in obtaining illustrations and permissions, and those I wish to acknowledge include Milton Goodman and Harold Danziger of Columbia Pictures Corporation, Henry G. Saperstein of United Productions of America, Kenneth C. Knowlton of Bell Telephone Experimental Laboratories, Leo R. Dratfield of Contemporary Films, John Hubley of the Hubley Studio, Michael Myerberg of Myerberg Studios, Burton H. Hanft of Paramount Television Enterprises, Gordon Hubbard of Pacific Title and Art Studio, Martin Quigley, Jr., of the Quigley Publishing Co., and Louis de Rochemont of Louis de Rochemont Associates.

☐ Nina Lott Sosna deserves a lot of thanks for her many hours of cheerful assistance in the home stretch.

☐ Kathleen Connelly has my warm appreciation for her excellence, thoroughness, and skill in editing the manuscript and Joan Nagy for seeing it through to publication.

☐ I wish to thank my wife, Barbara, for those tentative sketches which became substantive illustrations, and for her inexhaustible patience.

ANIMATED FILM

chapter 1
BIRTH AND GROWTH

ANIMATION in film imparts the impression of life and movement to static images. And the story of the birth and growth of animated film recounts the attempts to create the pictorial illusion of life by means of differing media, growing technology, and artistic innovation.

☐ Over 300 centuries ago Neanderthal man drew pictures on his cave walls of the creatures he hunted and who hunted him. We can only speculate whether they were drawn for religious reasons, for self-expression, or for a vicarious fulfillment of success in the hunt. But we can see that very early in his aesthetic development the caveman artist became dissatisfied with drawing only static stick figures and stodgy smears of bistre and ochre. He wanted his pictures to come alive—to be *animated*.

☐ To create this impression of images in motion, he drew many lines to represent the movement of a single limb, or he drew *multiple* limbs on a single animal. At Altamira we see drawn a *multilegged* boar charging to attack an adversary who may have been the artist himself (Figure 1.1). Reindeer and horses leap across the vaulting caves of Lascaux and leave behind them the blurred contours of *multiple* hooves and an enduring record of the first attempts to make pictures move. Neanderthal man tried to capture the essence of images in

FIGURE 1.1   Running boar, Altimira.

motion, but could not, of course, succeed completely with the limited means afforded by cave painting.

☐ Later, Greek and Roman sculptors rendered gods and athletes in poses of transfixed action (Figure 1.2). The tale of the last battle between Achilles and Hector was told in a series of silhouettes painted around the rims of circular shields. The warriors spun their shields and watched a form of limited animation. During the Middle Ages, manuscripts were illustrated with sequences of drawings depicting important religious events—for example, the ascension of Christ into Heaven or the descent of Satan into Hell. But true animation was beyond the grasp of these early artists because they lacked the technology to present a sequence of progressive images quickly enough to deceive the eye into believing that a picture was moving.

☐ Motion pictures are made possible by a characteristic of the human eye known as *persistence of vision*. This phenomenon occurs because the retina retains the image of an object for a brief instant after the object has been removed. A series of still pictures presented in rapid sequence will blend together into a single continuous image. And if the still pictures depict the progressive phases of a single movement, the eye will perceive them as one continuous flow of motion.

☐ Persistence of vision was first noted in A.D. 130 by Ptolemy, the Egyptian scientist and philosopher. He watched sentries on night duty swing their fire-pots in wide arcs about their heads. When the pot swung slowly, the single flame of the pot appeared to be several separate splashes of flame; but when the pot was twirled quickly, the single flame seemed to fuse into a circle of flame. When Ptolemy saw the circle of flame, he correctly concluded that the fire-pot was moving too quickly for his eyes to distinguish the progressive stages of the arc. He could therefore perceive only one continuous movement. Centuries passed before this phenomenon found an application in motion pictures. The development of the art and technology which exploited the persistence of vision laid the basis for animated motion pictures.

DEVELOPMENT OF THE MOTION PICTURE

The first step toward the motion picture as we know it was the development of an image projector. In the seventeenth century a Jesuit priest, Athanasius Kircher, constructed a crude projector called a magic lantern. It combined a *camera obscura* with a mirror and lens and used candles or reflected sunlight as a light source. A series of slide pictures, mounted on a horizontal

FIGURE 1.2 Laocoon. Courtesy of Alinari.

feeding device, were projected on the wall of a darkened room. The image was poorly focused and quavered with every flicker of the candle, but the picture was on the wall (Figure 1.3).

☐ To introduce his invention, Kircher arranged a showing for his fellow priests. He drew a series of pictures on slides and included as the *pièce de resistance* a finely executed drawing of the devil. This was a time of great religious conflict, and Kircher got more of a reaction than he expected. With the projection of each succeeding slide, his audience grew more disturbed, and the presentation of the face of the devil threw the priests into an uproar. They accused Kircher of necromancy and collusion with the devil and complained to church authorities about his tinkering with the black arts.

☐ Alarmed by this turn of events, Kircher attempted to allay the fears of the religious by presenting a factual account of how the projector worked. In 1644 he published *Ars Magna Lucis et Umbrae* ("The Great Art of Light and Shadow"), which explained the phenomena of light, lenses, mirrors, reflection, and refraction and related these concepts to the nature of vision and the structure of eye. The book was a success; his

FIGURE 1.3 Kircher's Magic Lantern from *Magic Shadows*. Courtesy of Quigley Publishing Company, Inc.

magic lantern was accepted as a mechanical device, not as an instrument of the devil, and found immediate use as a medium of entertainment. Itinerant showmen began to carry magic lanterns throughout Europe and delighted audiences with slides portraying popular contemporary plays.

☐ The next phase in the development of motion pictures and animation was the invention of a projector which presented images in motion. Gaspar Schott, a pupil of Kircher and like him a Jesuit, wrote a treatise describing the variations that others had made upon the original magic lantern. He added an improvement to Kircher's device by mounting drawings on a wheel so they could be rotated and thus projected quickly (Figure 1.4).

☐ The first person to draw an "animated image," as we understand the term, was Pieter van Musschenbroek, a Dutch scientist. In 1736 he drew a series of slides depicting a windmill; the positions of the windmill's arms were progressively shifted until a full cycle was completed. By using an adaptation of Schott's rotary feed, he was able to project the slides quickly enough to utilize persistence of vision, thus creating the illusion that the arms of the windmill were turning.

☐ Few advances were made during the next hundred years. Then, at the beginning of the nineteenth century, a new utilization of persistence of vision appeared in the form of a toy called the thaumatrope. A thaumatrope is a disc with one picture drawn on the front and another on the back; a string tied on opposite sides is used to spin the disc. When the disc is spinning, the eye cannot distinguish between the two pictures, and the images appear to fuse. For example, if a mouse is drawn on one side of the disc and a trap on the other, the mouse appears to be in the trap when the toy is twirled. The popularity of the thaumatrope caught the attention of scientists and stimulated formal studies of persistence of vision.

☐ The advance toward motion pictures took a long step forward in 1824 when Peter Mark Roget published his classic study *Persistence of Vision with Regard to Moving Objects*. During his experiments Roget had spun a spoked wheel behind a shield which had vertical slots for viewing. These slots allowed the viewer to see only one spoke at a time as the wheel turned. Roget observed, however, that the multiple spokes of the wheel seemed to fuse into one blurred spoke and noted that this "single" spoke appeared to reverse direction from time to time.

☐ Roget stated four basic principles related to the phenomenon of persistence of vision which contributed to the

FIGURE 1.4 Improvements on Kircher's Magic Lantern from *Magic Shadows*. Courtesy of Quigley Publishing Company, Inc.

development of motion pictures. First, the viewer's vision must be restricted; this is analogous to the control exercised by the shutter of the motion picture projector, which permits the viewer to see only one still picture at a time. Second, the eye blurs many images into one image if they are presented in quick succession. Third, a certain minimum speed of presentation is required to produce this blurring effect. And fourth, a large quantity of light is essential to create a convincing continuous image. Roget's experiments with persistence of vision and Niepce's development of the first crude photograph in 1822 were the stimuli for experiments and inventions that would culminate in the new medium of motion pictures.

☐ A Belgian artist-scientist named Joseph Plateau was influenced by Roget's thesis on the persistence of vision. In 1829 he constructed a circular device, the phénakistiscope, on which sixteen pictures were mounted (Figure 1.5). Each drawing on Plateau's disc shared the same figure, but in a position which differed progressively from drawing to drawing; the entire series showed a complete movement. Viewing the pictures of the whirling disc through a slit to restrict his scope of vision, as suggested by Roget, Plateau experienced the illusion of seeing the figure move.

☐ A wide range of new entertainment devices, based on variations of Plateau's phénakistiscope, were designed during the nineteenth century. Most of them employed the slotted disc or the paddle wheel and presented the same cycle of action over and over.

☐ The viewer watched through a slit as dogs ran, horses jumped, or acrobats turned somersaults for as long as he cared to turn the handle. All these devices presented a series of progressively changing images which the eyes of the viewer fused into a continuous flow of motion. They were so popular that by 1898 no fewer than 109 "scopes" and "graphs" were being sold, ranging from *animatoscope* to *zoetrope*, including one labeled with unabashed crassness, *getthemoneyscope* (Figure 1.6).

☐ For those who could not afford a scope or a graph in their homes, the nineteenth-century counterpart of the seventeenth-century showman set up shop in little theaters. Emile Reynaud, for example, ran a parlor theater in Paris from 1892 until 1900 in which hand-drawn bands of pictures were synchronized with music. Now all that was needed for true motion pictures was a camera that could photograph successive images, long rolls of transparent flexible film, and a practical means of projecting the images quickly onto a screen. The camera was invented

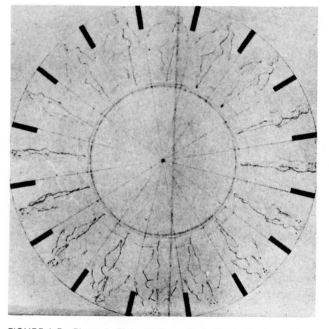

FIGURE 1.5 Plateau's Phénakisticope from *Magic Shadows*. Courtesy of Quigley Publishing Company, Inc.

FIGURE 1.6   Anschütz's Tachyscope from *Magic Shadows*. Courtesy of Quigley Publishing Company, Inc.

by the Edison laboratory, the film was developed by the East-man Company, and the first successful projection was achieved by the Lumière brothers in 1896.

☐   By the beginning of the twentieth century the development of motion picture techniques had diverged into two paths. The first employed actors, sets, and the mobile camera, and became live action cinema. The second, employing hand-drawn subjects and backgrounds and the static camera, became animation.

☐   The first animated film is generally believed to have been drawn by the American J. Stewart Blackton, who produced *Humorous Phases of Funny Faces* (1906) (Figure 1.7). Some historians, however, give the credit to Emile Cohl, the French-man who created *Phantasmagorie* (1908). But neither Blackton nor Cohl created the first animated film. On file in the Library of Congress is a paper print of an animated film produced by an unknown American artist in 1900 (Figure 1.8). This artist, employed by the Edison company, was photographed by live action photography as he sketched the face of a sad looking tramp on a large pad of paper. When he drew a cigar in the mouth of his cartoon face, the tramp grinned with pleasure and began to puff large clouds of smoke as the artist leaped back in mock astonishment. The smile and the billowing smoke were of course pure animation.

☐   In these early animated films, each drawing and its back-ground was completely recreated for every frame of film ex-posed, an extremely laborious and artistically inhibiting proce-dure. The problem was solved in 1914, when a transparent celluloid foil was invented by Earl Hurd. The action of each animated figure could now be rendered on a separate sheet of transparent acetate—a *cel*. The cels were then combined and photographed against the appropriate background. This innovation made possible the subsequent pictorial and cine-matic developments of animation. It now possessed the po-tential to evolve from a mere novelty into a new art form.

ENTERTAINMENT ANIMATION

Inspired by the work of Cohl and Blackton, Winsor McCay made an animated film of his comic strip character, *Little Nemo*, and released it as a theatrical short subject which proved a sensation. He followed it up with another film which was even more successful, *Gertie, the Trained Dinosaur*, and went on tour with it on the vaudeville circuit (Figure 1.9).

☐   The first cartoon films released in theaters were immensely popular. Audiences wanted more animated gags and stories, and a small but dynamic industry sprang up in New York City and Hollywood to meet this demand. The stories usually consisted of a series of gags in which a puny but ingenious character tried to cope with a bully. There were invariably chase sequences, in which the bully was flattened by a steamroller and emerged flat as a sheet of cardboard, or rose phoenixlike from the other catastrophes the wits of his little adversary had contrived for him.

☐ These early cartoon characters were based on geometric shapes because these shapes lent themselves to animation—a circle can be animated in any direction without difficulty. Felix the Cat and Flip the Frog were both variants on the circle. This practice of reducing the elements of an animated subject to its simplest graphic components has characterized the medium ever since.

☐ As Plateau's animation predated live action motion pictures, so an animated film with a sound track was produced before a comparable live action film was made. As early as 1920, Charles A. Hoxie of General Electric demonstrated sound on film in one of its laboratories. And between 1920 and 1922, research engineers of Western Electric made an animated sound film.

☐ From the beginning of entertainment animation, innovators like Pat Sullivan, Winsor McCay, and Max Fleischer endowed animals with human characteristics to tell their jokes and fables. Domestic animals proved to be the most popular subjects, probably because they are easy to stylize and have the greatest number of human associations. Felix the Cat and Oswald the Rabbit were the progenitors of Mickey Mouse, Bugs Bunny, and Huckleberry Hound.

☐ Walt Disney was the chief catalytic influence during a period in which the animated film was elevated from a crude type of entertainment to a true art form. With the première of *Steamboat Willie* in 1928, Disney Studios began a decade of artistic and technical innovations that brought to animation the elements of music and color and the charm of fables that poked fun at human foibles. During the thirties Disney's *Silly Symphony* series was released. Its world-wide popularity was rivaled only by the success of a single cartoon character, Mickey Mouse.

☐ Each new picture created new problems requiring new techniques. In response to these demands, the Disney technicians designed cameras, developed inks and paints, and made important contributions to sound and music recording.

FIGURE 1.7 *Humourous Phases of Funny Faces.*

FIGURE 1.8 *The Enchanted Drawing.*

Not the least of the Disney innovations was the *four-fingered hand* of Mickey Mouse, a simplification in animation technique which has been accepted by the public as an artistic convention.

☐ Disney's first feature-length animated picture was *Snow White and the Seven Dwarfs* (1937) (Figure 1.10). It was followed by many other feature-length productions—*Pinocchio, Bambi, Dumbo,* and *Alice in Wonderland,* to name only a few. With each new production the Disney Style gradually changed from its early form of zany exaggeration to one closely related to the actual movements of live models. Disney's greatest artistic success was perhaps *Fantasia* (Figure 1.11). In this production

FIGURE 1.9 *Gertie, the Trained Dinosaur* by Winsor McCay. Courtesy of the Museum of Modern Art, New York.

Beethoven's *Pastoral Symphony,* Tchaikovsky's *Nutcracker Suite,* Stravinsky's *Rite of Spring,* and Ponchielli's "Dance of the Hours" from *La Gioconda* were animated in exuberant flights of imagination. The Disney artists painted an enchanted realm of fauns and centaurs, seed pods and mushrooms, sea dragons and dinosaurs. For sheer beauty in an animated film, we may never again see the like of *Fantasia.*

☐ Artists in other nations were active in animation during this period, but their work took forms other than the cel technique which has tended to be generic when referring to "animated film." Creative work in animating cutouts, puppets, and objects was flourishing in Europe and other parts of the world. The development of sophisticated cel-animated films, however, was an American phenomenon, achieved largely under the inspired leadership of Walt Disney.

☐ The short film, *Gerald McBoing Boing,* produced by UPA (United Productions of America), heralded a change of pace in animation style for entertainment films during the post-World War II period (Figure 1.12). This new style, derived from abstract painting, was flat graphic, and linear, and carried caricature to new extremes. In contrast to the Disney style, which was closely related to the actual movements of real models, the UPA style created its own world, unrestricted by any natural laws. Design quality became paramount, and movement was suggested symbolically rather than presented literally. UPA simplified its animation almost to the point of abstraction. Its technique of limited animation became not only fashionable but the forerunner of things to come.

☐ With the advent of television, a radical change took place in the viewing habits of the American public, a change which had extreme repercussions in the entertainment industry. Instead of attending a neighborhood movie theater two or three times a week, the average American family bought a television set and were entertained at home. The decline in theater attendance severely injured the theatrical motion picture industry and has virtually put an end to the production of high-cost feature-length animated films. These films have been largely superceded by weekly television programs such as Disney's *Wonderful World of Color* which combine animation with live-action photography, and by serials produced by new giants of the industry like Hanna-Barbera Productions. Typical of these serials are *Huckleberry Hound* and *The Flintstones,* situation comedies which use the same characters every week in humorous skits for youngsters of all ages (Figure 1.13). Hanna-Barbera has developed a unique way of supplying the

FIGURE 1.10 *Snow White and the Seven Dwarfs.* Copyright Ⓒ Walt Disney Productions.

FIGURE 1.11 *Fantasia.* Copyright Ⓒ Walt Disney Productions.

vast quantity of films needed to meet the requirements of a television serial. Instead of doing full animation in the Disney manner, they confine the animation to a limb, a head, or even only an eye, and imply movement by various technical means.
☐ Animated television commercials and half-hour or hour animated programs, done either in the full techniques of Disney or in the modified techniques of Hanna-Barbera, will probably dictate the format of entertainment animation for many years to come. Every major studio has a feature-length manuscript in its top drawer that it hopes to produce for theatrical release someday. But for the time being it is television, not theatrical film, that dominates the entertainment world.

INSTRUCTIONAL ANIMATION

Animation for instructional purposes began in earnest with Thomas Edison in 1910. Edison regarded film as a revolutionary new teaching tool. He was so skeptical of its potential in entertainment that he would not spend the $150 then necessary to file a patent claim on his camera, a miscalculation that cost him millions of dollars. But his hopes for the medium as a teaching tool were unbounded: ''I believe that the motion picture is destined to revolutionize our educational system, and that in a few years it will supplant largely, if not entirely, the use of textbooks in our schools.''

FIGURE 1.12 *Gerald McBoing-Boing.* Courtesy of United Productions of America and Columbia Pictures Corporation, Copyright © 1950.

☐ Edison's first instructional film, *The Man Who Learned* (1910), dealt with the dangers of using unpasteurized milk. This was followed a few months later by *The Red Cross Seal* and thereafter by a full-blown instructional film production program which continued until 1917. Edison's films were essentially industrial training films, and he produced a series of technical films whose titles tell the story—*Science Education, Magnets, Mechanical Advantage, Electricity,* among others. His use of animation can be seen in an illustration from a film on the cream separator produced in 1912 (Figure 1.14).

☐ Henry Ford, a close friend and admirer of Edison, was impressed by Edison's films and used his own financial resources to embark upon a film production program that brought educational films to every theater in the country. The *Ford Educational Weekly* began in 1916 and was soon releasing from 400,000 to 500,000 feet of film to approximately 3,000 theaters each week. Around 1917 Ford produced an animated film which depicted the Bessemer steel process; this remarkably sophisticated film explained the complex technical process through animation without the aid of narration (Figure 1.15).

☐ The Ford film unit reduced the quantity of its production as educational films began to emerge from other sources, but the unit continued in existence until the death of Henry Ford in 1947. All the extant films were then stored in a basement room and forgotten until 1963, when someone wondered what was in ''that room.'' The films were discovered and were presented to the National Archives in Washington, D.C., where they await study by film scholars.

☐ The Ford and Edison films spurred a general demand for animated sequences in industrial and public relations films. In 1917, Bray Studios of New York opened a technical animated film department, a venture which proved so lucrative that animated film studios soon sprang up in major industrial centers, including Detroit, Chicago, Cleveland, and Pittsburgh.

☐ The use of animated instructional film grew rapidly. Two major Corporations—Eastman Kodak and Western Electric—stimulated the use of film in the classroom by producing educational films and making them available to schools. Between 1927 and 1942 the *Eastman Teaching Films* unit produced several hundred educational films on a wide array of subjects which were distributed to elementary and secondary schools all over the world. Careful research was done on every subject, and in more than one third of the films produced, difficult or abstract concepts were clarified by animation.

FIGURE 1.13 Fred Flintstone, Yogi Bear, and Associates. © Hanna-Barbara Productions, Inc., 1969.

FIGURE 1.14 *The Cream Separator.*

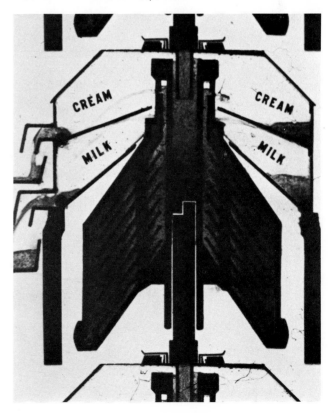

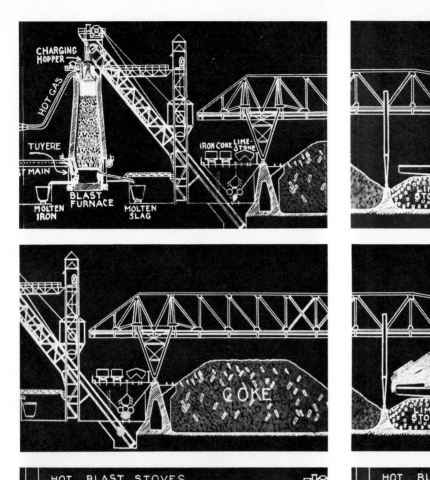
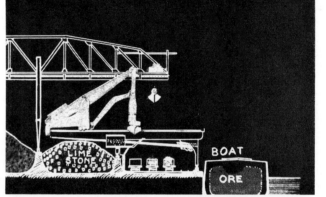
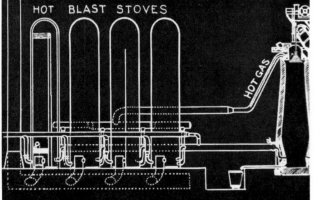
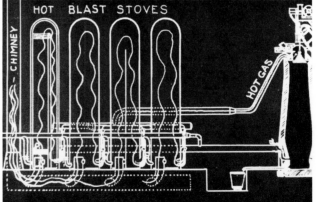

FIGURE 1.15 *The Bessemer Process.*

☐ In 1932 a division of Western Electric Co., ERPI (Electric Research Products, Inc.), began to produce educational films in conjunction with advisors from major American universities. ERPI's most noteworthy series dealt with the physical and biological sciences. Animation was used throughout this series, and the sequences made for Heart and Circulation, done in collaboration with the University of Chicago, contain classics of instructional film animation.

☐ A major difference in film technique exists between entertainment and instructional films. An entertainment film is most often either entirely live action or entirely animation; an instructional film, however, is likely to be live action in concept, but contains animated sequences to clarify concepts which cannot be otherwise explained. The instructional film that is entirely animated is exceptional. Research has shown that animated sequences are used in a third of all live-action instructional films, a proportion that has remained constant from Edison's films to today's productions.

☐ World War II gave added impetus to the development and utilization of instructional film techniques. The Armed Forces found themselves desperately short of competent instructors to train recruits, and turned to motion pictures to do the teaching job. After 1941 the Army Pictorial Service (Signal Corps) expanded its nucleus of a few persons into a major production unit which produced great numbers of technical films. It developed the cartoon character, Private Snafu, who was to serve as the arch-fool of the Armed Forces. The Air Force also established an animated film unit, and a Navy production unit produced animated sequences for the Navy, Marine Corps, and Coast Guard. Special issues of the *Movie Weekly*, distributed to hospitalized veterans, used animation to explain probable postwar trends and job opportunities. The multiple uses to which animation had been put during the war vastly expanded its postwar potential for instructional use.

☐ From World War II to the present the Armed Forces have continued their extensive use of animation. The rapid development of scientific and aerospace technology has prompted Air Force film-makers, in particular, to make increasing use of its flexibility (Figure 1.16). They find animation the best technique for explaining engineering problems, theories, the workings of an enclosed mechanism, or a proposed trip to another planet.

☐ The successful experiment in mass teaching by motion pictures during World War II gave a powerful thrust to the postwar utilization of films in the classroom. So great was the demand for sound film projectors that until 1949 supply could

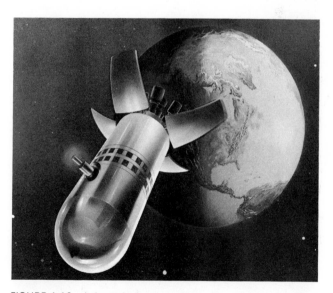

FIGURE 1.16 Animated treatment of aerospace technology. Courtesy of the U.S. Air Force.

not catch up with demand. Research groups became interested in the aspects of film techniques which might affect the learning process, and Pennsylvania State University undertook a series of tests to evaluate the teaching effectiveness of such cinematic elements as the point of view of the camera, color film versus black and white, production quality, and animation. One university professor made an intensive study of the production characteristics of the most frequently used teaching films listed in the Educational Film Library Association's report, and discovered that almost one third of the films contained some form of animation.

☐ A new trend emerged in the production of animated films by American universities. Animation in university-produced films, in terms of total footage produced, increased 360 percent from 1959 to 1961 (Figures 1.17 and 1.18). In addition, animation has gradually become accepted as an art form

FIGURE 1.17 *A Child's Introduction to the Cosmos* by Hal Barwood. Courtesy of the University of Southern California.

worthy of academic study and credit. Animation courses are being offered in an increasing number of colleges and universities, ranging from an occasional seminar or one semester offering to the three semester curriculum of the University of Southern California.

☐ High schools and junior colleges are also beginning to use animation for in-school production and course work. Horace Mann High School in New York, for example, has an extensive program of in-school animation production to meet the needs of its teachers. The animation is not being done by professional artists but by the teachers and students themselves.

☐ The greater part of today's animation is being produced outside the limelight of the entertainment industry. Wherever motion pictures are produced for sales, training, or instructional purposes, animation in some form is usually present. Many of the major production and service industries in the United States have in-plant film facilities, with either a staff animator or a contract to have their animation done for them. Important agencies of the United States Government produce films containing animation, and many state and municipal governments have comparable production units or are in the process of organizing them. Banks, aircraft factories, and other businesses having specialized needs are installing small animation stands in increasing numbers. New motion picture centers to produce instructional materials are springing up in the underdeveloped countries of the world. In short, wherever abstract ideas need to be communicated in the clearest possible way, we find the use of animation.

INTERNATIONAL ANIMATION

Ambitious, creative animated films are being produced in many other film making nations of the world. These films vary greatly according to their sponsorship and purposes. Sometimes the work is done by a government for political or educational goals, sometimes as a commercial venture for sales or entertainment purposes, and occasionally by individuals or small groups who dig into their own pockets for the privilege of expressing their dreams and ideas in animation.

☐ In Canada animated films are largely the product of the National Film Board of Canada, a government agency founded in 1940 by John Grierson to interpret Canada to Canadians and to other nations. Most of the Film Board's productions are made to meet the instructional and public relations needs of the nation in the form of documentary, dramatic, and animated

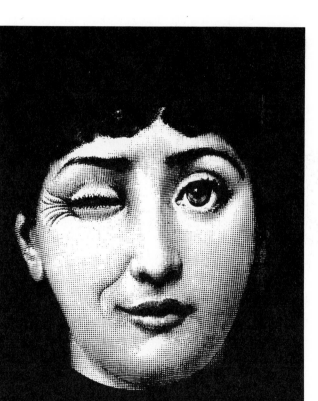

FIGURE 1.18 *The Face* by Herbert Kosower. Courtesy of International Tournée of Animation.

films (Figure 1.19). A great deal of freedom is given to Canadian animators to choose the means by which they achieve their assigned ends. Their animation techniques are not standardized, as in most of the major studios in the United States, but range from simple outline drawings on paper to complex cel renderings, from paper cutouts to free-standing puppets.

☐   Norman McLaren, a leading experimental animator, has enjoyed a unique position at the Film Board of Canada. He can largely follow his fancy in what he chooses to do in animation and his fancy has opened up many new realms in experimental film. McLaren's concepts of abstract and expressionistic design in motion have influenced animators the world over (Figure 1.20). An indefatigable experimenter, he has invented his own tools and techniques and has departed from conventional animation methods to the extent of painting picture and sound directly on raw film stock—eliminating both camera photography and sound recording. McLaren has experimented with counterpoint in sound and picture, with synthetic sound effects and music, with intermittent and impressionistic animation, and with destroying the single frame concept by painting abstract animation lengthwise through the film. His short animated abstractions have surprised, delighted, and outraged audiences everywhere in the world.

☐   In Britain animation has tended to be organized in a manner analogous to the medieval artisans' guilds. The animators cluster together in small units, with the young learning from the old by practical experience at the animation tables. Formerly they produced most of their animated films under the sponsorship of official bodies, governmental departments, and international authorities. In recent years, however, with the diminution of government support, animators have begun to produce sales and training films for industry and advertisements

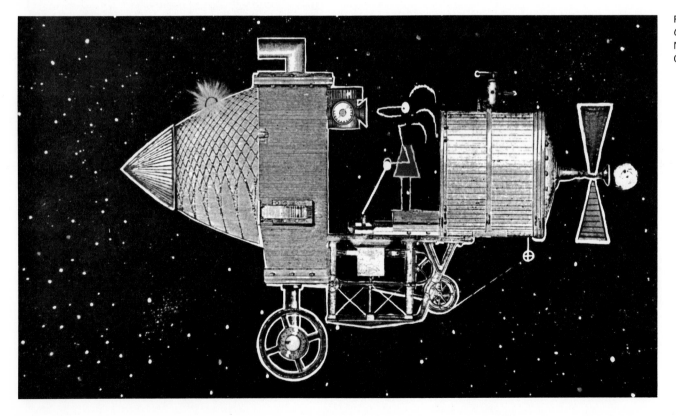

FIGURE 1.19 *Christmas Cracker.* Courtesy of the National Film Board of Canada.

for commercial television. British animation cannot be discussed without reference to John Halas and Joy Batchelor. Together they led the film unit that produced the first major British puppet animation production, the first experiment in stereoscopic animation, and the first British feature-length animated film, *Animal Farm* (Figure 1.21).

□   On the European continent animation developed from ancient art forms. Consequently, Europeans have often worked in genres that are relatively undeveloped elsewhere. Europe has a tradition of puppetry which goes back to the Middle Ages and is still quite strong in Eastern Europe. Puppet animation emerged from this tradition in 1934 when Ptushko made *The New Gulliver*. At the same time Starevich of France and George Pal of Holland began to produce similar films. In the post-World War II period, puppet films were produced primarily in the motion pictures studios of Poland and Czechoslovakia. Among the more talented artists in this field are Jiri Trnka (Figure 1.22), Hermina Tyrlova, and Karel Zeman of Czechoslovakia, who base their work on themes of social satire, classics of drama, or fairy tales having morality-play overtones. Puppet animators in other parts of the world, lacking subsidies or a popular tradition among the people, have generally turned away from puppetry to work on those forms of animation which receive commercial support or public patronage.

□   A number of continental Europeans work in esoteric genres which they have raised to the level of art forms. In 1926, Lotte Reinegger of Germany produced her first film of animated cutouts, *Prince Achmed*, and followed it up in 1928 with *The Adventures of Dr. Doolittle*. Her animated figures are cut from black paper with the delicacy of filigree work. The figures are assembled with fine joints and photographed in silhouette, with subtle and charming effect. She has been followed in this type of animation by Berthold Bartosch in France and Norman McLaren in Canada.

□   A unique genre called ''pinhead shadow animation'' was created during the same period by Alex Alexeiff. Rows of pins pressed in a board are raised and lowered, with strong cross-lighting, and the changes of shadows are rendered by stop-motion photography.

□   In the Communist nations, animated films are regarded as one of the national art forms and are fostered in state-subsidized studios. The purposes served by Communist animators are varied, but most of their work is directed toward ideological goals. Moreover, film styles are affected by ideological considerations; the Marxist-Communist view of art (Socialist

FIGURE 1.20   *La Poulette Grise.* Courtesy of the National Film Board of Canada.

FIGURE 1.21   *Animal Farm.* Courtesy of Louis deRochemont Associates, Inc.

Realism) holds that all subjects should be rendered in realistic forms so that the works of art may be understood and appreciated by the greatest number of persons.

☐ The first of the Communist animated film studios was established in 1936, when the Soviet government created in Moscow an organization called *Soyuzmultfilm*. It assembled graphic artists who were interested in producing animated films and provided them with the best available facilities. *Soyezmultfilm* became the prototype for similar studios now found in Poland, Communist China, Hungary, Rumania, Yugoslavia, and Czechoslovakia. The governments of these countries encourage the production of films containing political and social satire. There are also scientific, instructional, and educational films, fables, fantasies, fairy tales, and musical comedies. A good deal of freedom is permitted in re-creating popular folklore. Socialist Realism, however, dominates the interpretations of these subjects, and there is little of the aesthetic experimentation derived from abstract art which is typical of recent trends in the West. Nonrepresentational styles are either unknown or undeveloped or unencouraged. Only the work of the *Zagreb* studio of Yugoslavia seems to reflect the design orientation and brittle graphic approach now typical of Western Europe and North America (Figure 1.23).

☐ In Japan artists began to experiment with animation during the Thirties and Forties; but because their country was then involved in a protracted war, Japanese animators were from the beginning involved in propaganda work. In Germany there had been a tradition of experimentation in animated films stemming from the avant garde art movement of the Twenties, which was uninfluenced by the government; but with the first shot fired over the Polish border in 1939, animated film production was diverted, as in Japan, to the ends of war and propaganda. Only after World War II was there a resurgence of independent creative work in either Japan or Germany.

☐ Animation is now used everywhere and fulfills important functions in films for business, industry, television, education, and entertainment. In addition, there are increasing numbers of artists who come to animation from painting to add the dimension of movement to their work and to explore and experiment with new relationships of line, form, and color. But the richest opportunities for animators may lie in the sciences—

FIGURE 1.22 *Old Czech Legends.* Courtesy of Jiri Trinka.

where animation can give tangible form to concepts now existing only at the theoretical level. This will require a new breed of animators with advanced technological and scientific education to enable them to work effectively with their new colleagues in the sciences. But the trend is clear and the opportunities are there for those who can measure up to the challenge.

FIGURE 1.23 *Discoverer* by Boris Kolan, Zagreb, Yugoslavia. Courtesy of International Tournée of Animation.

chapter 2
CONCEPTS AND LANGUAGE

MOTION pictures are the culmination of the quest for representation of movement which began with the multilegged boar drawn on the cave walls of Altamira. As we have seen, the history of the motion picture is that of the growth and development of a technology that made the pictorial illusion of movement possible. The motion picture is a new art form of the twentieth century, and animation is its artistic and technological child. This chapter defines the concepts and terms which constitute the language of film, and, more particularly, of animated film.

☐ Every motion picture may be defined in three ways—physically, optically, and conceptually. Physically, a motion picture is a flexible length of cellulose triacetate, perforated along one or both edges, and bearing a light-sensitive coating which enables photographic images to be produced in black and white or color. Optically, it is a series of still photographs on films which, when projected on a screen in rapid enough succession, create for the viewer the illusion of a continuous image. Conceptually, a motion picture is an orchestration of pictorial concepts, sounds, and movements. The language of film derives from these physical, optical, and conceptual characteristics.

SILENT AND SOUND SPEEDS

The convincing illusion of motion is dependent upon a minimum speed in projection of images. The two usual film projection speeds for motion pictures are the silent and sound speeds of 16 and 24 fps (frames per second). The silent speed of 16 fps was the original speed of the theatrical motion picture, and gave the movies its early nickname, the "flickers." The 16 fps speed created the illusion of a continuous flow of motion, but when the optical sound track was introduced, 16 fps proved too slow for accurate reproduction of voices and music. Warner Brothers experimented with various projection speeds for *The Jazz Singer*, the first feature film with an optical sound track, and found 24 fps the most suitable. When the film had its premiere in 1927 and was a resounding success, the film world accepted as standard a sound film speed of 24 fps.

☐ Adequate silent films can still be made at 16 fps; but once a film is photographed at silent speed it can never be used at sound speed or dubbed with sound without appearing ridiculously fast when projected on the screen. Therefore, the sound speed of 24 fps is the only one we will consider in planning animation.

LIVE-ACTION FILM COMPARED WITH ANIMATION

Movement is cinema's breath of life in both live-action films and animation, but there are many differences between the cinematic effects of each form because of the differences in the means by which the images of each are conceived and achieved. In live-action films camera techniques are extremely flexible. Photography is planned and executed in a broad general way, with the camera capable of being turned in any direction and moved to almost any position—on land, in the air, and beneath the surface of the sea—to achieve a desired effect. A subject performing a given dramatic action is often photographed several times, from different angles and distances and with different lenses and lighting. The resulting footage is then assembled into a motion picture. The action is generally photographed in continuous runs of the camera with exposure of hundreds or even thousands of frames in a single run.

☐ In animated films, on the other hand, camera movements are severely restricted. The animation camera is mounted vertically on a stand, looking down at the flat subject, and can only advance toward or move away from the subject. It remains fixed at a right angle to the subject and cannot be turned in any other direction. Moves of the subject before the camera are plotted almost microscopically and implemented by small shifts of minutely calibrated controls. In most instances, the visual portion of an animated film is photographed at one time, in one location, and exactly in the sequence in which it will appear on the screen. Except for the addition of a sound track, and perhaps the execution of certain optical effects achievable only in a film laboratory, the film is far along to completion when it has been photographed in the animation camera.

☐ Single-frame exposure is a distinctive characteristic of animation cinematography. In contrast to live-action cinematography, most animation work involves the manipulation of inanimate subjects which are moved a short distance at a time between each exposure. All cameras designed for animation cinematography therefore have both single frame and continuous exposure controls. A live-action camera having these features may be adapted for animation cinematography if it also has a flexible shutter control with appropriate calibration. Live-action cameras are not always acceptable for animation work, however, because they often lack the precision in film registration found in animation cameras.

☐ Film makers have evolved a set of production terms which are a unique language. But these terms acquire a different shade of meaning in animation from their meaning in live-action motion pictures. The following concepts and terms are presented only in the context of animation.

SCENE AND SEQUENCE

A *scene* is the exposed film which lies between the beginning and the end of one continuous roll of the camera, unbroken by any change to another visual. A *sequence* is a complete dramatic action within the film. A film sequence is composed of a series of scenes.

CUT

A *cut* is an instantaneous change from one scene to another; it is used in film when there is a continuous flow of action within a sequence (Figures 2.1a and 2.1b). For example, a sequence of two persons talking would consist of cuts back and forth to the face of each person as he spoke or reacted to the speech of the other.

FADE-IN AND FADE-OUT

The *fade-in* is the gradual appearance of a scene from a darkened screen (Figures 2.2a and 2.2b). Its first and universal use is as the introduction of a motion picture. The length of a fade-in can be as brief as a quarter-second (6 frames) for a fast-moving television commercial, or as long as a minute (1,440) frames) if the intention is to build a brooding mood for the opening scene. A *fade-out* is the gradual disappearance of a scene to a darkened screen (Figure 2.3). It is used as the finale to a single scene, to a sequence of scenes, or to the film itself. Fade-in and fade-out are the rising and falling curtains of motion pictures.

☐ Another function of fades is to separate major sequences of action within a film. Then its order of use is reversed; it becomes fade-out, fade-in (Figure 2.4). The first sequence is ended by a fade-out to black, and the second is begun by a fade-in. Here fades make a decisive break between different parts of the film—one complete sequence is ended and a new one is begun. A fade-out, fade-in denotes a long lapse of time or a major change of location, or both. Again, the longer the effect is sustained, the heavier the emotional overtones become.

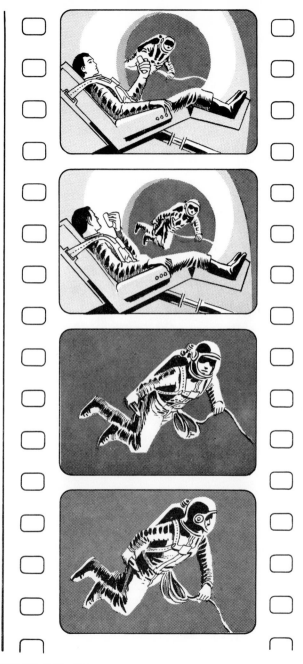

FIGURE 2.1a Cut.

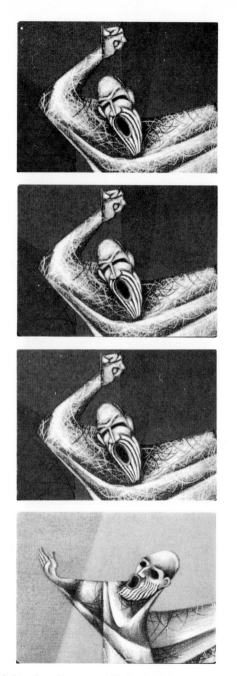

FIGURE 2.1b Cut. Courtesy of Phillip Stapp and the International Film Foundation.

FIGURE 2.2a Fade-in.

FIGURE 2.2b Fade-in. Courtesy of Phillip Stapp and the International Film Foundation.

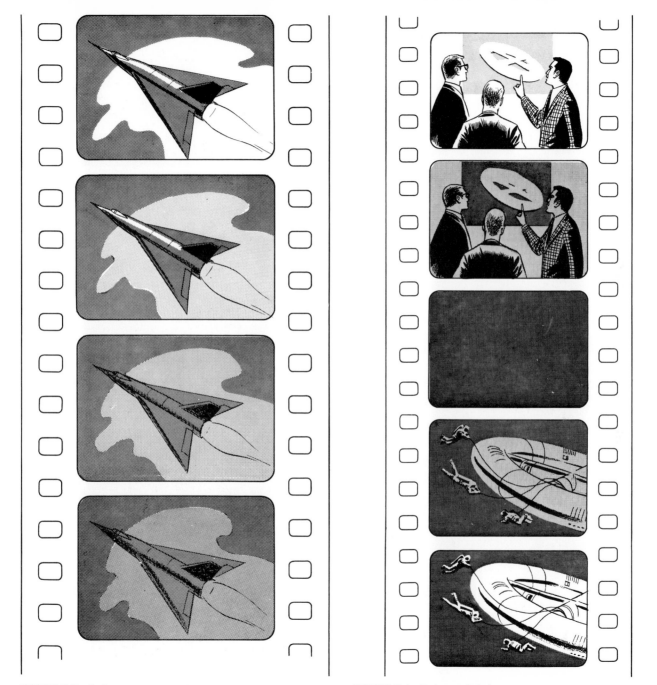

FIGURE 2.3 Fade-out.

FIGURE 2.4 Fade-out, fade-in.

FIGURE 2.5a   Dissolve.

FIGURE 2.5b   Dissolve. Courtesy of Phillip Stapp and the International Film Foundation.

DISSOLVE

A *dissolve* consists of a fade-in superimposed over a fade-out within the same length of film (Figures 2.5a and 2.5b). The scene which is first on the screen gradually yields and disappears as a second scene simultaneously replaces it. A dissolve is a transitional device used to connote a minor change of location or a short lapse of time. Long dissolves are often used between similar or related still pictures to create the illusion of continuous growth or movement. As in the use of the fade, the length of the dissolve is determined by its intended effect.

DOUBLE EXPOSURE

A *double exposure* is a strip of film which is exposed twice in the camera in order to combine separate images which cannot be photographed during a single run of exposures (Figure 2.6). A dissolve is often executed in the camera by double exposure. In this type of double exposure both images are seen on the screen at the same time, one appearing as a translucent phantom before the other. The double-exposure technique is also used to create the illusion of a ghost and to produce stream-of-consciousness effects.

□ Double-exposure techniques are frequently used to combine white or colored titles with animation or with a background which cannot be photographed at the same time. In this instance, however, the two images are not combined translucently; the titles of one exposure are so strongly lighted as to burn in through the images of the other exposure, and leave only clear film within the area of the titles (Figure 2.7). Double exposure for the effect of translucency and double exposure for burning in titles require different techniques of exposure control, which are described in detail in Chapter 12.

SUPERIMPOSITION

Superimposition, like double exposure, refers to combining two or more separate images on one strip of film (Figure 2.8). Unlike double exposure, however, the effects are not translucent. Superimposition means that separate pictorial elements are so photographed, in multiple runs through the camera, to give the effect that one image is opaquely placed before the other, as a foreground is placed before a background. While the term is sometimes loosely used as a synonym for double exposure, it refers specifically to combining separately photographed images by means of multiple exposures.

FIGURE 2.6   Double exposure.

FIGURE 2.7   Double exposure: burning in titles.

FIGURE 2.8 Schematic of superimposition.

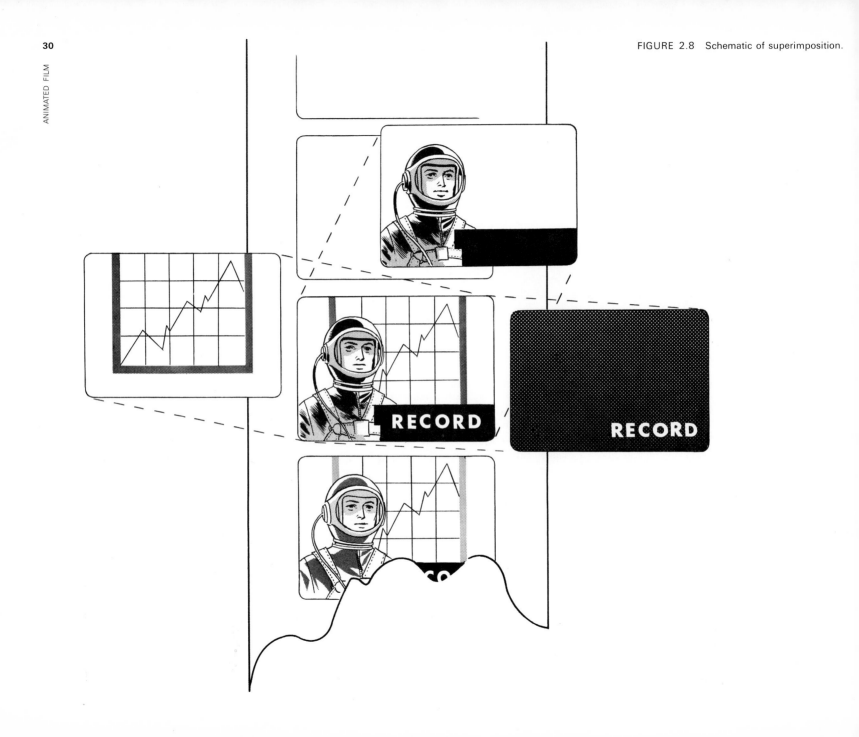

☐ In a live television broadcast superimposition has a somewhat different meaning. If a baseball game is being televised, for example, a commercial often is superimposed in white letters over the action in order to avoid interrupting it.

POP-ON

A *pop-on* is an instantaneous appearance of a new image within a scene already on the screen (Figure 2.9). This effect is common in television, sales, and instructional films in which titles and labels, arrows, or similar ''directive symbols'' suddenly pop on wherever desired.

WIPES

A *wipe* is an optical effect whereby the scene on the screen is apparently physically displaced by the following scene, with a distinct edge between the outgoing and incoming scenes (Figure 2.10). The edge between the two scenes may be soft or hard. It may be a straight line or a complex shape such as a star, clock, or barn-door wipe (Figure 2.11). Wipes in an immense variety of shapes and movements are executed by film laboratories specializing in such work.

☐ Wipes were commonly used in theatrical films as a transitional device between sequences, until it become evident that the novelty of the wipe distracted the audience from the dramatic action. Consequently, wipes were generally replaced by dissolves. But the attention-catching characteristics of the wipe make it a valuable technique for dramatizing products in sales films and television commercials. In instructional films, wipes are sometimes used to show cause-and-effect relationships or to depict two separate processes occurring at the same time.

FLIP

The *flip* is an effect in which a still scene begins to revolve on its center axis in acute perspective, and a new scene or a new title is introduced with each half revolution (Figure 2.12). The flip is an attention getter, used frequently in television commercials for presenting products and product names and occasionally in live-action dramatic films to present titles and credits.

FIGURE 2.9 Pop-on.

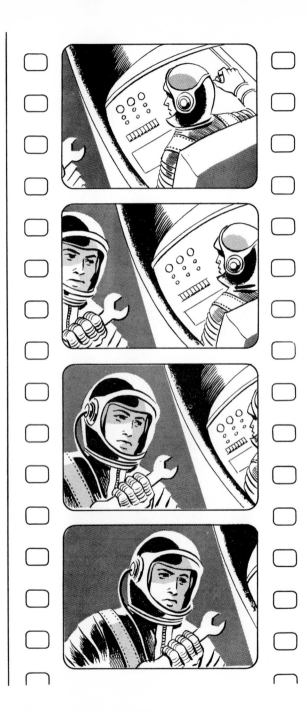

FIGURE 2.11   Star wipe.

FIGURE 2.10   Wipe.

SPIN

The *spin* consists of rotating a scene or title around its own center point (Figure 2.13). The spin, like the flip, is used to hold the gaze of the viewer until the rotating scene slows down and stops—revealing, for example, the name of a product or sponsor.

ZOOMS

A *zoom-in* is a continuous approach by the camera to a subject; that is, the area being photographed is gradually reduced. A zoom-in is used to draw attention to a part of the artwork which has special meaning or to enable the viewer to examine a detail while remaining aware of its relationship to the surrounding context (Figure 2.14).

☐ A *zoom-out,* the reverse of the zoom-in, is a progressive retreat from the subject by the camera (Figure 2.15). It begins with a detail of a picture; as the camera recedes from the subject, the area being photographed gradually enlarges to reveal the relationship of the detail to the whole.

☐ The speed of a zoom is usually determined by its purpose. If the subject is to be studied carefully, a slow zoom-in is desirable. If the whole context of the scene is established, and the intention is only to single out a significant detail within it, the zoom-in can be as fast as eight frames. A zoom-out, on the other hand, is usually done slowly to maintain viewer orientation.

PAN

A *pan* is a horizontal scan of the subject by the camera (Figures 2.16a and 2.16b). In animation, however, the camera cannot scan in this manner; it can only advance toward the subject or draw away from it. But the illusion of a pan can be created by moving the subject under the camera while it is being photographed.

☐ The direction of a pan is described in terms of points of the compass. Right and left are called *East* and *West,* and up and down, *North* and *South.* Similarly, a diagonal pan would be described as, for example, North–East to South–West.

FIGURE 2.12 Flip. Courtesy of The Optical House.

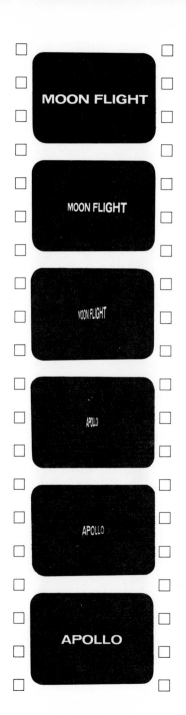

FIGURE 2.13 Spin.

FIGURE 2.14 Zoom-in.

☐ A pan is most often made to show a relationship between two persons or objects that cannot be included within one frame at the same time, or to scan material that is to be studied in detail. The purpose of the pan determines how long it should take. If the purpose is simply to transfer the viewer's gaze from one subject to another it can be fairly fast, two or three seconds. A *swish pan,* used in cartoons to give the effect of speed, can be as short as a few frames. But if the viewer is to scrutinize the material carefully, the pan may be ten to fifteen seconds or longer depending upon the importance and complexity of the content.

☐ Sometimes a pan appears to move across the screen in short staccato jumps. This effect is called *strobing.* Strobing occurs when persistence of vision fails to bridge the gaps between the still pictures which are presenting the progressive movements of the subject. This may occur when the subject has excessive value contrast or, more frequently, when there are strong directional lines perpendicular to the direction of the pan.

CLOSE-UP

A *close-up* is a photograph of a detail within a larger picture on the animation stand. It is defined by a size reference called field size which is discussed under *Field Guide* (Figure 2.17).

STANDARD ASPECT RATIO

A motion picture consists of a sequence of still photographs. The proportion of each photographed or exposed frame of film is approximately a 3 by 4 rectangle, and is called the *standard aspect ratio.* In the two film widths most widely used by professional film producers, 16mm and 35mm, this proportional ratio is more precisely stated as 2.94 by 4.10 for 16mm film, and .631 by .868 for 35mm. In animation planning, this ratio is translated to proportions of 36 by 50.

FIELD GUIDE

The *field guide* is unique to animation (Figure 2.18). It is the stage upon which all the moves in animation are planned. A

FIGURE 2.15 Zoom-out.

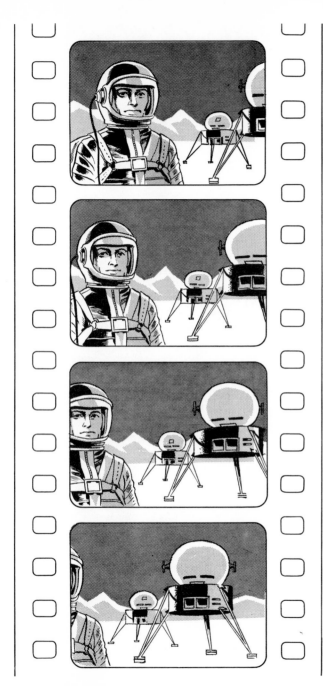

FIGURE 2.16a   Pan.

FIGURE 2.16b   Pan. Courtesy of Phillip Stapp and the International Film Foundation.

field guide is a chart on clear acetate representing the entire area which may be photographed on the animation stand. Every subdivision within this field area can be used as a point of reference in planning the photography of the animation. Three holes are punched at the top of the field guide to correspond to three pegs, or peg bars, on the animation stand. The relationship between the punched holes and the subdivided areas of the field guide is the same as that of peg bars and photography area on the animation stand. This enables the animator to plant his artwork on a drawing disc with peg bars, with confidence that there will be no discrepancies between the plotted moves and their execution on the animation stand.

☐ The field guide is a rectangle whose width and length are in the standard aspect ratio for animation, 36 by 50, with all the rectangular divisions within the field area having the same proportions. There are twelve field sizes on the field guide, ranging from the 12 field, which is the total area of the field guide, down to the 1 field in the center. Each field size is indicated by number at each of its four corners.

☐ Field size is determined by the distance of the camera from the subject; the closer the camera approaches to the artwork, the smaller is the size of the area which can be photographed, and the smaller will be the corresponding field size. An 11 field represents a greater proximity of the camera to the subject than a 12 field, a 10 field indicates a greater proximity than an 11 field, and so on down to the 1 field. The 12-field maximum indicated on the field guide does not actually represent the maximum possible area of photography. There are many animation stands on which the camera can go high enough to photograph an area 24 fields or even 32 fields in extent. The 12-field size is, however, the practical working size for most forms of animation, and most animation artwork is planned and photographed within the field guide's 12-field maximum.

☐ The field guide is divided by two perpendicular lines into four equal parts; these lines are designated according to the points of the compass, North–South (N–S) and East–West (E–W). The intersection of the N–S and E–W lines at 0–0 is the point of reference to which all animation moves and positions are related. Each step away from the 0–0 center toward any given compass point is called a *field step*. Moves are described according to the number of field steps taken and the direction moved. Two steps North from 0–0 is called 2 North or 2N. In the opposite direction, two steps South of 0–0 is 2S. The same principle applies to the E–W line, which is also

FIGURE 2.17   Close-up.

FIGURE 2.18   Field guide.

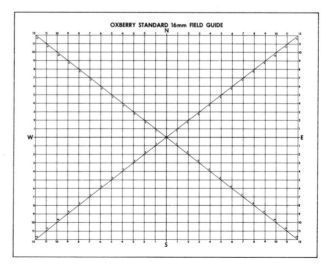

calibrated from 0–0. Six field steps West of 0–0 is 6W; four field steps East is 4E, and so on.

☐   To describe a point on the field guide, we determine two dimensions. That is, we count the number of field steps from the given position to the N–S line, then count the number of steps to the E–W line. For example, suppose we mark a point arbitrarily on the field guide. We find that it is three field steps north of the E–W line; the first dimension of its position is thus 3N. Next, we see that the point lies six field steps west of the N–S line; the second dimension is 6W. The location of this point on the field is therefore written (3N–6W).

☐   Notice that this field position, (3N–6W), is indicated in parenthesis. This is because field size is usually stated with field position of the center, and the parenthesis serves to separate the two figures and prevent confusion. For example, if an area the size of a 4 field were being photographed with its center at (3N–6W), it would be stated as 4 (3N–6W).

☐   The importance of the field guide to the animator cannot be overemphasized. It is the basis of the planning and execution of every move which is made in the course of photographing an animated film. We shall now proceed to the animation stand and see how the basic concepts and effects defined in this chapter are implemented.

chapter 3
THE ANIMATION STAND

EVERY animator has a two-pronged task—to *plan* his film and to *photograph* it. Planning animation involves a detailed frame-by-frame outline which pinpoints every move and effect. But in order to plan accurately, the film maker must be completely aware of the capabilities of the animation stand, the apparatus that makes animated film possible. In Chapter 2 we defined the language of animated film. We will now put that language to use in examining the animation stand and the effects each of its parts is designed to execute.

INTRODUCTION

The animation stand is designed to provide a precise yet flexible relation between the camera and the artwork it is photographing. To achieve this, two engineering principles are employed. First, because the slightest misalignment of the camera is greatly magnified on film, the movements of most animation cameras are restricted to *vertical* moves up or down the column. Second, the compound tabletop which carries the artwork is restricted to *horizontal* N–S, E–W, or diagonal moves under the camera. The movements of the camera and the tabletop are coordinated with minutely calibrated controls.
□   Two types of animation stand are commonly used in the film industry—the single- and twin-column vertical stands. They are alike in their essential functions, but differ in size, film utilization, flexibility, potential for creating special effects, and capacity to photograph large artwork. The single-column Filmaker animation stand is typical of the smaller unit and is designed to satisfy the requirements of the average industrial and educational film producer (Figure 3.1). Its camera is precise enough to photograph standard effects; for more sophisticated work, however, we must turn to the large, two-column animation stand which is designed to meet the exacting demands of the television and theatrical motion picture industry (Figure 3.2).
□   The major components of the animation stand are: (1) the control panel; (2) the camera; (3) the column; (4) the compound; and (5) the lighting units.

THE CONTROL PANEL

The control panel regulates the exposure of the film and the movement of the film through the camera (Figure 3.3). The on-off switch activates the power of a stop-motion motor, which in turn drives the camera. The forward-reverse switch regulates the direction in which the film runs through the camera. The single-exposure button is used to expose one frame of film at a time, while the continuous-exposure switch allows multiple-frame exposures in the camera. The shutter control varies the degree of shutter opening in making fades and dissolves, and the numerical scale offers a range of fade and dissolve lengths.

THE ANIMATION CAMERA

Although conventional live-action cameras are sometimes adapted for animation, optimum quality requires an animation camera designed and constructed specifically for animation and stop-motion photography (Figure 3.4). An animation camera should have these capabilities: (1) single-frame and continuous-exposure control; (2) forward and reverse movement of film; (3) an intermittent movement (shuttle) and registration system which moves and holds each frame of film in precisely the same position for each exposure; (4) a variable opening shutter with calibrated scales; (5) a reflex or rackover viewfinder which permits viewing of the artwork through the camera lens without exposing the film; and (6) a camera lens suitable for the film format used, with manual or automatic focusing control.

☐ *Exposure control and movement of film.* The animation camera is driven by a stop-motion motor, which turns a single drive shaft to the camera and moves the film one frame with

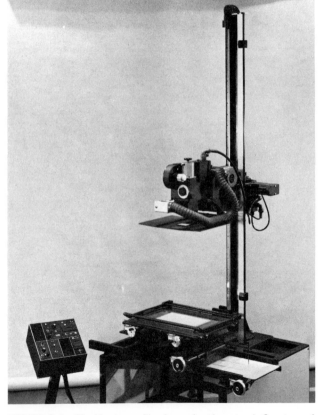

FIGURE 3.1 Single-column filmaker animation stand. Courtesy of Oxberry-Berkey Technical.

FIGURE 3.2 Two-column animation stand. Courtesy of Oxberry-Berkey Technical.

each revolution of the shaft. The motor functions for single frame or continuous exposure in either a forward or reverse direction, and should have a minimum of backlash or whip in the drive system to preclude frame-to-frame exposure variations. A stop-motion motor usually offers five exposure speeds: 30 rpm (revolutions per minute) with 1-second exposure; 60 rpm with ½-second exposure; 120 rpm with ¼-second exposure; 180 rpm with 1/6-second exposure; and 240 rpm with ⅛-second exposure. These standardized speeds permit the use of slow or fast film stock, allow for variations in lighting, and simplify exposure calculations. Every frame of film must be accounted for in animation; therefore the frame of film in position for exposure at any given moment is indicated by a cumulative frame counter mounted beside the camera.

☐ *Shuttle and registration system.* The internal mechanism of an animation camera has special features necessary for animation photography (Figure 3.5). In order to hold each frame of film in precisely the same position for each exposure, a pair of fixed registration pins is inset beside the film gate. The intermittent movement, or shuttle, which transports the film, mounts each frame on two registration pins. One pin fits both the length and width of the film perforation exactly; the other fits the length, but is shorter than the film width to provide for expansion and contraction of film stock and for variations in perforation.

☐ To execute multiple exposures and other special effects accurately, it is vitally important that the shuttle and the registration pins be manufactured with the utmost precision. The shuttle and pin system described above is the ''I'' system, which was developed by the Bell and Howell Company and which is used as the basis for the most precise camera mechanisms.

☐ In another, newer registration system, the film is guided to a correct exposure position through a fence channel corresponding to the path taken by film in a projector. The film is advanced by one carrier pin and held in place by one locating pin. The basic test of a registration system is its ability to hold the film precisely in the same position for each exposure. Whatever system is used, the pressure plate of the shuttle should have a removable cut-out in order to facilitate special projection work, which is discussed below.

☐ Film magazines on both 16mm and 35mm professional cameras are removable to facilitate darkroom loading and changing film while work is in progress. Some adapted conventional cameras have only 100′ capacity magazines, but this

FIGURE 3.3 Control panel. Courtesy of Oxberry-Berkey Technical.

can prove a nuisance when photographing longer sequences. A magazine with a minimum capacity of 200′ should be a standard fixture. Two-inch plastic cores are used to hold the film in the supply and takeup compartments. The supply core and takeup core are mounted on compartment shafts driven by two semitorque motors, which can feed the film in either direction to permit dissolves and other multiple-run effects. The motors are not truly torque because they do not compensate for changes in tension on the film; therefore, when there is a large roll of film accumulating on the takeup core the cameraman may have to adjust the tension somewhat in order to avoid buckles and to prevent damage to the film sprocket holes. The film should end up in a snug roll on the takeup core, emulsion side out, and ready for processing.

☐ The film is fed off the supply core with its emulsion side *in,* as it comes from the supplier, and is rewound on the takeup spool after being exposed with its emulsion side *out,* so that it may be quickly ascertained in the darkroom whether a given film has been exposed. This can be done by feeling or licking the film; the emulsion side when moistened is stickier than the base side.

☐ *Variable opening shutter.* The variable opening shutter is the primary means of creating fades and dissolves with the animation camera. A camera shutter is a disc with a sector removed, usually to yield an aperture of 170°. It rotates once for each frame of film exposed (Figure 3.6). On stop-motion motors the stop occurs when the solid shutter is obstructing the light path, with the film held suspended in mid-transport between frames. A variable opening shutter consists of two such discs rotating on the same axis, so aligned as to be capable of progressively reducing the shutter opening from 170° to 0°. When the shutter opening is closed down in progressive phases the amount of light reaching the emulsion for each succeeding frame of film is reduced. Images are progressively darkened until the shutter is completely closed, and a fade-out results.

☐ A fade-in is an application of the same principle in reverse. The shutter opening is set at 0° and progressively increased

FIGURE 3.4   Animation camera. Courtesy of Oxberry-Berkey Technical.

FIGURE 3.5   Internal mechanism. Courtesy of Oxberry-Berkey Technical.

for each successive frame of film until the sector opening reaches its maximum of 170°. If, however, the shutter is opened or closed in equal degree increments, the developed film will show a barely perceptible change at the beginning of the fade and an abrupt change at its end. The increment intervals must be worked out to provide a visually smooth transition, and the intervals decided upon stated in the form of a fade scale (Figure 3.7). Progressive fade scales are a standard fixture of the animation camera; adapted live action cameras generally must have them specially installed. Moving the indicator one increment down the fade scale for each exposure produces a smooth fade-in. Moving the indicator one increment up the fade scale for each exposure produces a smooth fade-out.

☐ A dissolve has been described as a fade-in fused with a fade-out and this is roughly how it is executed with the animation camera. The same length of film is exposed twice—once with a fade-out of the outgoing scene, and once with a fade-in of the incoming scene. For example, if a 24-frame dissolve is being used as a transition from one scene to another, the shutter closes one increment on the fade scale for each of 24 exposures of the outgoing scene until the fade-out is complete. Then, the directional switch is thrown to ''reverse'' and the film is backed up in the camera for 24 frames with the shutter closed, until the point is reached where the fade-out began. The directional switch is flicked over to ''forward,'' and the incoming scene is placed under the camera. It is photographed with a 24-frame fade-in, and the dissolve is complete.

☐ Fades can be executed either manually or by means of an automatic shutter control operated from the console. To operate an automatic fade control, a dial selector is first set to the desired length of a fade, with the directional switch turned to ''in'' or ''out.'' When the continuous exposure switch is turned on, the automatic shutter control changes the shutter, opening the correct amount for each exposure for the entire length of the fade. For example: When the dial selector is set at 72 and the directional switch set at ''in,'' and the continuous exposure switch is turned on, the automatic shutter control will change the shutter opening the correct amount for each exposure to create a fade-in over 72 frames of film. Dissolves are photographed with an automatic shutter control in the same manner as with a manual camera; the same length of film is exposed twice—once with a fade-out on the outgoing scene and once with a fade-in on the incoming scene.

☐ *Viewfinder.* In many aspects of animation photography it

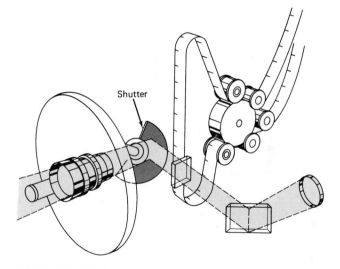

FIGURE 3.6 Shutter.

is important to see the artwork through the camera lens in order to focus the lens, compose the scene properly, and check on the accuracy of complex moves. Good viewfinders have a monocular eyepiece with individual eye focus adjustment. Useful markings may be etched in the ground-glass reticle, such as camera and projection apertures drawn in the proportions of the standard aspect ratio, dotted television cut-off lines, and horizontal and vertical center lines (Figure 3.8).

☐ Two types of viewfinders are commonly used on animation cameras. The first of these is the reflex viewfinder, which employs a beam-splitter or a mirror between the camera lens and the film to permit the film maker to view the exact area being photographed (Figure 3.9).

☐ The second type is the rackover viewfinder (Figure 3.10). To use this viewfinder the main body of the camera is moved to one side on a precision track. Then the viewfinder is brought into alignment with the film aperture, and fixed in position by registration pins to assure direct alignment with the central viewing axis through the lens of the camera. By looking at the ground glass of the viewfinder, we can see the artwork exactly as it will appear on the screen. After the scene is composed and the lens focused, the viewfinder is racked over to one side and the camera body is returned to its former position for actual photography. Rackover viewfinders may be operated manually or automatically from the control panel.

☐ The viewfinding system should be fitted with film registration pins and a projection lamp so that frames of a film clip or a reticle etched on the ground glass may be projected onto the photography area for alignment. For greater precision, the cutout in the film gate of the camera may be used. Projecting images down through the taking shuttle onto the photography area is vitally important in making mattes and in planning animation which is to be combined with live-action photography, techniques described in detail in Chapter 12.

☐ *Lenses*. The lens is the eye of the camera and determines to a great extent the reproduction quality of the photographed image. It should be as free as possible from such defects as distortion, curvature of field, and spherical and chromatic aberrations. The lenses used on animation cameras are usually of the same focal length as those commonly used in conventional live action cinematography—1 inch for 16mm film, and 2 inch for 35mm film. Specialized forms of animation in which depth of field is important, such as multiplane animation, require special lenses and adapting devices.

FIGURE 3.7 Fade scale. Courtesy of Oxberry-Berkey Technical.

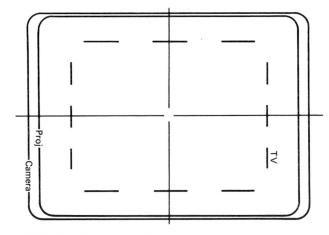

FIGURE 3.8   Markings on the reticle.

FIGURE 3.9   Reflex viewfinder. Courtesy of Oxberry-Berkey Technical.

FIGURE 3.10   Rackover viewfinder. Courtesy of Oxberry-Berkey Technical.

☐ A lens may be focused manually by turning the focusing ring while looking through the viewfinder. Focusing a lens changes not only the focus but also the apparent position of the subject being photographed. A high-quality lens yields proportional linear reduction size ratios if precisely set in a rigid lens mount. However, if the optical scale of the lens is even slightly out of alignment with the axis of the lens mount, rotating the lens gives the effect of a shifting film plane. Therefore, the lens mount should be constructed with the seated lens on a precise vertical axis, and it should be possible to focus the lens by the focusing ring alone without turning the lens.

☐ In addition to being focused manually, many animation cameras can be focused automatically at almost any height by means of a mechanical linkage device attached to the column of the animation stand; this is discussed below in the section dealing with the column.

☐ A number of auxiliary optical devices may be attached to the camera for creating special effects—including flip and rotator lenses, soft-focus wipe mattes, in- and out-of-focus devices, and multiple lenses for multiple-image effects, to name only a few.

THE COLUMN: FIELD SIZES AND ZOOMS

The camera unit is mounted on a mobile carriage which rides on one or two vertical steel columns, the number and height of the columns depending upon the purpose and function of

FIGURE 3.11 Positions of camera carriage. Courtesy of Oxberry-Berkey Technical.

the animation stand. These columns are attached to the rear of the compound tabletop. The camera carriage rides up and down the columns to place the camera in the correct position for various field positions and to implement zooms (Figure 3.11). On most modern animation stands the carriage is moved on the column by a motor controlled from the console, but hand cranks still are used for final precise positioning.

☐ Field size varies with the distance of the camera from the surface of the animation table. The closer the camera approaches to the surface the smaller will be the field size photographed. The farther the camera withdraws from the photography surface the larger will be the field size photographed. The range of 1 to 12 on the field guide is a practical working size for a film maker, but its extremes do not correspond exactly to the capabilities of the animation stand. Although many cameras can rise to photograph a 20-field area or larger without any adapting devices, most cannot approach closer than a 3 field without a special adapting ring for the lens.

☐ The precise point at which the camera will photograph each field size depends upon what lens is being used. It is best determined by projecting the viewfinder reticule through the lens onto a field guide placed on the compound. The exact point at which the camera will photograph each field size is marked on a scale mounted parallel to the column of the animation stand (Figure 3.12).

☐ Each point marked is referred to as a ''field position level.'' It is prudent to run a film test to make sure that the camera is actually photographing the field size area indicated before marking the field position level on the column.

☐ Mounted on the camera carriage is a mechanical counter—a ''zoom counter''—which measures movements up and down the column in hundredths of an inch (Figure 3.13). This zoom counter may be set to measure upwards from any point on the column. The numbers on the zoom counter corresponding to minimum and maximum field sizes and to each field position level should be noted for convenient reference. In this way, the camera can be run to any given field position level by looking at the numbers of the zoom counter and stopping the camera carriage when the number corresponding to the given field appears. Once the field position levels have been determined and film-tested, the camera can be positioned quickly and easily to photograph any desired field size.

☐ As we have seen, a zoom-in is created by lowering the camera toward the subject, gradually reducing the field size being photographed between each exposure. Conversely, a

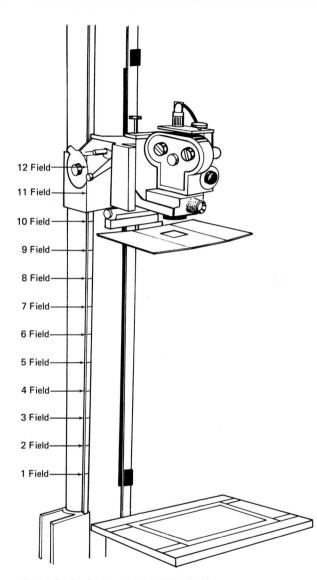

12 Field
11 Field
10 Field
9 Field
8 Field
7 Field
6 Field
5 Field
4 Field
3 Field
2 Field
1 Field

FIGURE 3.12   Scale of field position levels.

FIGURE 3.13   Zoom counter. Courtesy of Oxberry-Berkey Technical.

FIGURE 3.14   Follow-focus cam. Courtesy of Oxberry-Berkey Technical.

zoom-out is created by moving the camera away from the subject, gradually increasing the field size. A zoom consists of a series of small moves up or down the column, with an exposure taken at each step.

☐   The lens must be refocused for each exposure following a move of the camera. For example, a 48-frame zoom from a 12 field to a 4 field requires that the lens be refocused 48 times—once after each move. In theory, the lens can be refocused manually each time while looking through a viewfinder at the subject, but this is apt to lead to a rough motion when the film is viewed. Fortunately, an automatic follow-focus mechanism is available which may be mounted on the stand to keep the lens in focus. The cam system is probably the most common follow-focus device. A cam is a metal bar mounted vertically at the rear of the column; a feeler arm linked to the camera lens rides the cam as the camera carriage moves up and down the column, and constantly refocuses the lens according to the height of the camera above the tabletop (Figure 3.14).

THE ANIMATION COMPOUND

The animation compound carries the subject being photographed (Figure 3.15). Horizontal and rotary movements of the subject are achieved by moving a compound or its peg tracks before the camera between each exposure of film. Although some compounds are motorized and may be operated from the console to execute pans and rotary movements, most have only manual controls.

☐   The major components of the animation compound are: (1) the photography area or tabletop and its registration pegs; (2) the platen; (3) the controls for N–S, E–W movements of the compound and traveling pegbars; (4) the pantograph unit; and (5) the rotary unit. Auxiliary devices are available for creating further effects.

☐   *Photography area and registration pegs*. The photography area of the compound is in the center of the table, aligned directly under the central axis of the camera lens. On the lower sides of this photography area there are three registration pegs which correspond to the three holes punched in the field guide and in the artwork. The proportions of the three pegs may vary, but all compounds have a round peg in the center and oblong pegs on the ends (Figure 3.16). Any artwork punched with the proper holes and planned with the field guide will fit over these registration pegs and be photographed as planned.

All the equipment for a given stand, including the field guide, must be made to a single registration peg standard. The importance of the field guide–registration peg relationship cannot be overemphasized. It is the master reference system of animation and the basis for all planning. Although the registration pegs may be moved or removed when photographing oversize artwork or three-dimensional objects, the subject being photographed must still be aligned to the established standard of the peg registration system in order to be recorded accurately on film.

A cut is executed on the animation stand by replacing the artwork photographed in the last frame of the outgoing scene by the new artwork to be photographed in the first frame of the incoming scene. The effect on the screen is an instantaneous change of scene. To execute a pop-on, a cel containing artwork or titles is superimposed between exposures on the scene being photographed. The effect on the screen is an instantaneous pop-on of the new artwork over the same scene.

Platen. Most forms of animation artwork need to be pressed together in order to eliminate shadows from the side-lights (Figure 3.15). A platen system containing water white glass is used to hold cels and cutouts in a flat position to be photographed. There are two types of platen, manual and automatic. The manual platen has a ratchet enabling it to stay up in either of two stationary positions. The automatic platen is operated with a footpedal and has only the open and closed positions. Platens are most often made for 12-field and 18-field work but are also available for Cinemascope and other wide-screen proportions. When photographing three-dimensional objects, it may be necessary to move the platen out of the way. A floating platen rollaway unit may be fastened to the stand for this purpose.

N–S, E–W controls. Pans are usually executed by moving the compound tabletop bearing the artwork between each exposure of film. The compound is attached to two lead screws, one controlling N–S movement, the other controlling E–W movement. Each of these lead screws is manipulated by a rotary hand crank which is interlocked with a cumulative counter system calibrated to measure the compound's movements at 100 increments to an inch (see N–S and E–W con-

FIGURE 3.15 Animation compound.

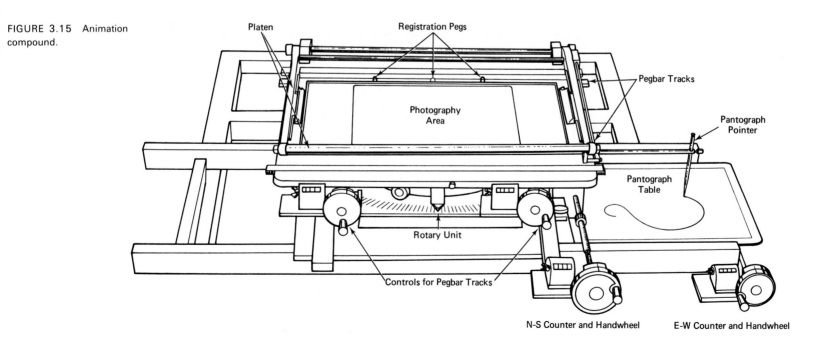

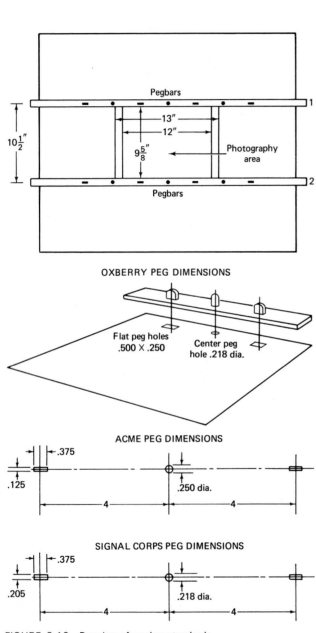

OXBERRY PEG DIMENSIONS

ACME PEG DIMENSIONS

SIGNAL CORPS PEG DIMENSIONS

FIGURE 3.16 Drawing of pegbar standards.

trols in Figure 3.16). There are two counters; one indicates N–S movements, the other E–W movements. By using the N–S and E–W manual controls together, it is possible to execute diagonal and curved pans. A few animation stands have motorized compound controls which enable the camera-man to implement pans and zooms operated from the console panel, but most compounds are manually controlled.

☐ We have noted that the standard aspect ratio for animation is 36 to 50 and that all the field size subdivisions within the field guide also exhibit this 36 to 50 proportion. In other words, in planning a pan, the moves are divided into 36 incre-ments for each field step North or South of 0–0, and 50 increments for each field step East or West of 0–0.

☐ To distinguish between north and south of 0–0 on the N–S counters, each field step north of 0–0 cumulatively *adds* 36 increments to 00000, and each field step south of 0–0 cumulatively *subtracts* 36 increments from 00000 (as if it were 100000). For example, a pan north from 0–0 to 1N would add 36 increments to 00000 and appear as 00036 on the N–S counter; a pan from 0–0 to 1S would subtract 36 incre-ments from 00000 and read as 99964.

☐ The same principle of cumulatively adding and subtracting in relation to 0–0 applies to the E–W controls, but each E–W field step is divided into 50, rather than 36, increments. Thus, a pan east from 0–0 to 1E would add 50 increments to 00000 and read as 00050 on the E–W counter. A pan west from 0–0 to 1W would subtract 50 increments from 00000 and read as 99950. Moves in any direction may be made in increments comprising only a fraction of a field step, but the principle of adding and subtracting increments with relation to 0–0 applies at all times.

☐ A diagonal or curved pan can be created by moving both the N–S and E–W controls. For instance, a diagonal pan from 0–0 to the (1N–1E) position is made by turning the N–S control north and the E–W control east, between each expo-sure, until the compound has shifted the center of its photog-raphy area to the 1N–1E position.

☐ Pans may also be implemented by using the top and bottom registration pegs, which are mounted in two movable E–W tracks called "traveling pegbars" (Figure 3.17). These are in turn embedded in the tabletop. Each traveling pegbar can be moved independently east or west, and each has a separate control and counter system which is calibrated at 100 incre-ments to the inch. As we face the animation compound, the left control moves the nearest track and the right control moves the farthest track. Again, movements in either direction from dead center add to or subtract from 00000. Moving the traveling pegbars does *not* move the compound.

☐ The traveling pegbars enable us to mount a background from one side and cels from the other, so that each will be able to move independently of the other. These independent functions of the two tracks are utilized in the following ways: to create the illusion that a subject is moving across a static background; to create the illusion that a subject is moving across a changing background; and to allow multiple E–W movements in conjunction with the E–W compound controls.

☐ A word of caution—each traveling pegbar can be moved in its track a distance of a little over three standard cel widths from one extreme to the other. When the pegbar units are extended beyond this point, they go beyond their propelling screw and stop; but the counter continues to add increments. When the pegbar unit is then returned to its controlling thread, the counter reading will be incorrect and fail to read 00000 when the pegbar is returned to dead center.

☐ A compound move is a zoom-in or a zoom-out combined with a pan in any direction on the compound (Figure 3.18). Each of the controls—the zoom control, the N–S control, and the E–W control—is manipulated between each exposure of film. The final effect on the screen is that of a sweeping movement in and across the master scene to a detail within it.

☐ *Pantograph.* To the right of the animation compound, behind the E–W control, is a flat metal surface with a field guide mounted on it and a steel pointer suspended over it. This unit is called the pantograph. (Figure 3.19.) The pantograph field guide corresponds exactly to the photography area on the compound tabletop. The pantograph needle marks the point on the pantograph field guide that corresponds to the center of the area being photographed on the tabletop at any given moment. Whenever the compound moves during the execution of a pan, the pantograph needle also moves and indicates the new center of the field being photographed. Every move made with the N–S or E–W controls and counters is accompanied by an equivalent move of the pantograph pointer over its field guide.

☐ The primary function of the pantograph is to facilitate the execution of curved and free-form pans. To do this a pantograph chart is drawn, based on the field guide and the artwork over which the pan is to move; this chart is mounted over the pantograph field guide. Then, the N–S and E–W controls are manipulated to align the pantograph needle with the succes-

TRAVELING PEGBAR CONTROLS

FIGURE 3.17   Traveling pegbars. Courtesy of Oxberry-Berkey Technical.

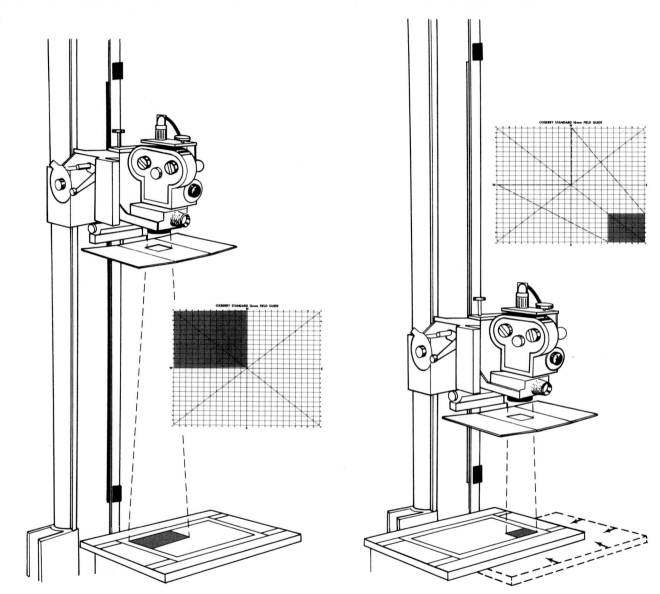

FIGURE 3.18   Compound move.

sive field positions marked on the pantograph chart. In this manner, a pan can be made without using the counter system of the controls. This facilitates making subtle curved and complex moves which would be difficult to execute without a motorized compound.

☐ A second purpose of the pantograph is to enable the film maker to position the center of the photography area anywhere on the field guide without having to refer constantly to the N–W and E–W counter numbers. For example, if the E–W control is turned west until the pantograph needle points to 4W on the field guide, the E–W counter will read 99800. If the N–S control is turned north until the needle points at 6N on the field guide, the N–S counter will read 00216, and so on.

☐ Because of the angle at which the pantograph needle is viewed it is sometimes difficult to align its point with the increments of a pantograph chart. This is particularly true when the increment steps of the chart are small. An alternative which has proved very efficient is a transparent plastic sheet with intersecting N–S and E–W lines scribed on its under surface. The plastic sheet moves over the pantograph chart, in lieu of the steel pointer, and because the viewer can lean directly over it and examine it closely, he is able to make precise alignments. It also speeds the operation of moving to a given point on the chart. When the N–S hairline coincides with the point of the chart the E–W cranking is stopped, and similarly with the E–W hairline and the N–S cranking. Thus alignment is made with no hunting or backtracking. Making pantograph charts is discussed at length in Chapter 4.

☐ The relation between the compound and the pantograph field guide may be either "inverted" or "corrected," depending upon whether an adapted live action camera or a specially designed animation camera is being used. An "inverted" relationship means that either the photography area or the photograph field guide is right side up while the other is upside down. A "corrected" relationship means that both the photography area and the pantograph field guide are right side up. Because so many animators implement their pans with pantograph charts, they generally prefer to have the pantograph field guide right side up regardless of the orientation of the photography. An inverted relationship can sometimes be changed to corrected without modifying the camera simply by reversing the normal film direction within the camera, that is, by loading the raw film stock on what is normally the takeup reel, and taking it up on the supply reel.

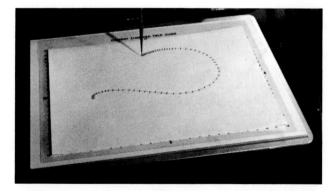

FIGURE 3.19 Pantograph. Courtesy of Oxberry-Berkey Technical.

FIGURE 3.20   Rotary unit. Courtesy of Oxberry-Berkey Technical.

FIGURE 3.21   Floating pegbars. Courtesy of Oxberry-Berkey Technical.

☐ *Rotary unit.* The animation compound may be mounted on a rotary unit which enables the film maker to turn the table to any angle, or in a complete circle (Figure 3.20). This unit is used primarily for creating spin effects and diagonal pans. The rotary unit is calibrated with a total of 360 increments for a full circle, enabling us to plan precisely how fast to make a spin or what angle to use for a given diagonal pan. Once the proper angle has been found, the pan is implemented by the traveling pegbars. Some units have a counter attached for position reference.

☐ *Auxiliary compound devices.* The so-called "floating pegbars" consist of registration pegs, mounted on a strip of metal which is aligned by being clamped to the upright columns of the animation stand, with a mechanism permitting the same N–S and E–W movements found in the conventional controls (Figure 3.21). Like the conventional controls, the movements are made with hand cranks whose controls are calibrated at 100 increments to the inch. Floating pegbars in effect provide an additional set of N–S and E–W controls with which to create multimovement effects.

☐ A flip title can be photographed directly on the animation stand by means of a special adapting device placed directly over the insert of the photography area, which is then lighted from underneath (Figure 3.22). The flip box holds a Kodalith film negative title as it is progressively turned and photographed, according to the calibrations on its side.

LIGHTING

The manner of lighting a compound depends upon what is being photographed. For the flat artwork of conventional animation, diffuse and even lighting is desirable in order to reduce textures and surface differences and to permit only the lines, shades, and colors of the artwork to be photographically visible. The ideal light source would be a broad concentric ring of light surrounding the artwork. This, however, is impractical. The stand is lighted in practice by two large light sources, one on each side of the compound (Figure 3.23). A pair of 300 watt tungsten lamps calibrated at a color temperature of 3200° Kelvin is often used, as are tungsten-halogen quartz lamps with reflectors. Photoflood bulbs can be used if a Color Tran® converter is available to change the color temperature of the emitted light to conform to the color temperature specifications of the film. Spun glass scrims and barn doors on the light fixtures are desirable in order to obtain maximum diffusion and light control.

☐ For black and white photography two banks of fluorescent tubes are adequate if used with voltage-regulated direct current. Pulsed- or strobe-type lamps are sometimes employed, but they are impractical for fades or dissolves because their uneven light emissions become evident when the shutter is nearly closed, and show up on the film as "flickers." The photography area of the compound must be lighted evenly and carefully, with a sufficiently high power for the kind of film being used. In order to determine correct exposure, we must use a light meter. There are two types of light meters—incident and reflectant. In animation the incident meter is preferable.

☐ A different type of lighting is required when three-dimensional objects are being photographed on the compound tabletop. Crisp highlights, textured surfaces, and well-defined shadows are important in creating the sense of tangible reality when photographing an object. For this purpose, the reverse of diffuse and even lighting is preferable. Instead, the live action ratio of 4:1, key light to fill light, is used (Figure 3.24). The 4:1 ratio is best determined with an incident light meter and confirmed with a light-test exposed at half-stop intervals.

☐ *Underneath lighting.* Pencil tests, color transparencies, kodalith negative titles, and certain special effects require that the subject be lighted from beneath in order to be properly photographed. Provision is made for this in most animation compounds by having a removable 9" × 12" insert in the photography area which can be replaced by a panel of translucent glass (Figure 3.25). Beneath the glass insert there is a bank of either photoflood or fluorescent light bulbs. Although light meters perform poorly in testing underneath lighting, a rough estimate may be obtained from a reflectant meter pointed at a transparency mounted on the light source. To obtain exact exposure, run an exposure test at half-stop intervals.

ADAPTED CONVENTIONAL CAMERAS

There is sometimes a temptation to adapt a conventional motion picture camera having a single frame exposure control to animation purposes. But most conventional cameras, particularly 16mm cameras, are unsuitable for several reasons.

☐ First, smooth dissolves can seldom be done on adapted conventional cameras. The adapted camera lacks the registration pins necessary to hold each frame of film in exactly the same place during both film runs of the dissolve; it has only pull-down claws to move the film. Because the film is not being held in precisely the same place during the second run, the resulting dissolves may have overlapping frame lines at the top

FIGURE 3.22   Flip box. Courtesy of Oxberry-Berkey Technical.

FIGURE 3.23   Conventional light positions.

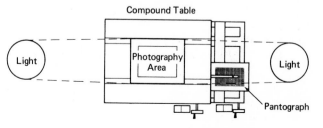

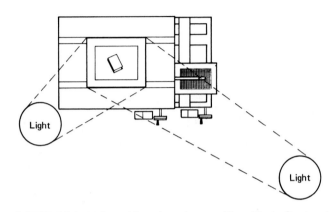

FIGURE 3.24 Light position when photographing objects. Courtesy of Oxberry-Berkey Technical.

FIGURE 3.25 Underneath lighting. Courtesy of Oxberry-Berkey Technical.

and the bottom that will show when projected on a screen. Second, there is so much play in the structure of a conventional shutter that, even with an extended shutter control and a fade scale, fades and dissolves tend to look irregular. Third, many adaptable cameras are spring-wound. This means that tension on the drive will vary with the degree of pressure remaining in the spring and affect the exposure of the film as it grows slack. The results of using conventional cameras in animation are often disappointing; use animation cameras designed for the purpose.

MULTIPLANE CAMERA

Portraying depth is a problem in cel animation because the animated subject and its background are in direct contact under the platen when being photographed. The Disney studio resolved this depth problem some years ago by creating the multiplane camera, by means of which the subject and its backgrounds were actually mounted at different distances under the camera, with each plane lighted and panned at a separate speed from the others (Figure 3.26). For example, the subject, its middleground, and its background are mounted under separate platens, one beneath the other. Then, by panning the subject fastest, the middleground slower, and the background slowest, a convincing impression of depth was created. The Disney studio commonly uses as many as five or six planes at a time to create a vivid sense of depth in its films.

TROUBLESHOOTING

Reflections. To prevent the shiny metallic surfaces of the camera or its components from being reflected off the surface of the platen and photographed, a black cardboard shadowguard is affixed horizontally to the camera carriage (Figure 3.27). The shadowguard has a circular hole cut in the center through which the lens of the camera peers. When the camera approaches the surface of the animation table during a zoom-in, the shadowguard may, however, tend to cut off the light. It is therefore provided with hinged flaps on each side, tied with strings which run up to the ceiling; when the camera approaches the surface of the table, the strings hold back the flaps and permit the light to continue falling on the subject.
□ Sometimes reflections appear in the finished film despite a correctly mounted shadowguard. This spoilage is almost always caused by human error. Failure to pull the arm back

from the fade scale or the lens when exposing the film is a primary cause of reflections—the white image on the film is probably a shirt cuff or a forearm.

☐ If an error of the operator was not the cause of the problem, then the source of the reflection may be traced in the following way. Lay a mirror down on the surface of the animation table and lower the camera to the field position level at which the reflections were picked up. Then stop down the lens aperature and increase the amount of light falling on the mirror. Finally, either view the mirror through the lens of the camera or expose some film to determine, from the images revealed by the mirror, what is causing the unwanted reflections.

☐ *Newton rings.* One problem arising from the use of multicel levels under a platen is the appearance of a circular shape known as a "Newton ring." This is most often caused by a high area of paint on which the platen bears down heavily and causes contact between two adjacent cels. This area should be treated with the faintest dusting of face powder, which is then carefully wiped off. Just enough powder will remain to create the desired separation, but not enough to be photographed.

☐ *Dust.* Motes of dust which adhere to the platen will be reproduced on film in the form of specks. Keep the glass clean with a few drops of vinegar or ammonia dissolved in water. Do not use a commercial window cleaner as these often contain substances which refract the spectrum; and the window cleaner, once applied, is difficult to remove.

☐ Sometimes it is not possible to keep an animation room airtight and dustproof and we find that dust motes are attracted to the platen and cels by static electricity. One way to cope with this problem is to use polaroid filters over the camera lens and light source. Polaroid filters transmit only the subject's image and do not photograph intervening dust.

☐ The polaroid filter for the camera is sandwiched between two plates of glass and mounted over the lens. The polaroid filters for the light sources are much larger and must be mounted "right side" up. If the directional mounting is not indicated on the filter itself, the correct orientation of each filter can be ascertained as follows. Look at any glossy subject at a 30° angle; then hold up the polaroid filters and rotate them

FIGURE 3.26 Multiplane camera.

FIGURE 3.27   Shadowguard. Courtesy of Oxberry-Berkey Technical.

until the shine or glare of the subject disappears and only a sharp image remains. The filter is now correctly oriented and must be mounted in this way before the light source, at a distance from the bulb sufficient to prevent burning. The filter for the camera must be turned at right angles to the filters for the light source to achieve the polaroid effect. Run an exposure test with film to determine optimum exposure.

☐ *Film scratches.* Scratches on a film ruin it for commercial use and impair its value for in-plant functions. A long scratch in the film emulsion suggests that the film has been damaged somewhere in its passages from the supply magazine through the mechanism of the camera to the takeup magazine. We can determine where the injury is occurring in the following way. First, take a length of color film, which has a very soft emulsion surface, and examine it carefully to make sure that there are no marks on it; then thread it through the normal path in the camera. Run three or four feet through the camera to pass film which may have been marked in threading. Take a grease pencil and mark a line across the width of the film at the eight points—the top and bottom of the film gate, the four sprockets, and the two magazine entry points. Cut the film at the supply and takeup slots and carefully remove it. By noting at which of the grease pencil lines the scratch begins, we can tell where the damage is being done and take remedial action. Light leaks in the camera can be traced in the same way, using needle scratches to mark the film. By cutting and unthreading in the dark and then developing the film, we can determine where the light leak occurred.

☐ *Static Electricity.* If the lines appearing on the emulsion are in the form of short angular squiggles, they were probably caused by static electricity induced when the raw stock was unrolled too quickly in the darkroom. Be sure to unroll your film slowly. Any atmospheric condition of low humidity and low temperature tends to induce static electricity. One more caution with regard to handling film. If you are in the middle of photographing a length of animation and must, for some reason, leave the film in the camera for a couple of hours, take the time to run the film back to the beginning. If you leave it at a frame midway through the reel, the film may take a ''set,'' peel back from the aperture, and ruin the next frame you try to expose. By noting the number at which the last exposure was taken, it is an easy matter to return to the correct frame for further work.

☐ *Cleaning lenses.* In the course of normal use, film particles and dust from inside the camera mechanism drop through the aperture and lie on the inside of the lens. These particles will of course appear on any film exposed through the lens. Be sure to clean the lens before beginning to photograph animation. Clean it with lens tissue, not cotton. Cotton has an abrasive quality and may injure the coating of the lens. Be particularly careful to remove fingerprints, as these contain a corrosive acid.

☐ *Cel punches.* For those planning to do extensive work with cel animation, it is an economy measure to own a cel punch and purchase the cels unpunched. Certain precautions should be taken in the use of a cel punch machine. Do not punch more than six cels at one time, or the equivalent of eight sheets of 16-pound bond paper. The male and female dies have a tight fit and an attempt to punch more than this number may result in misshaping the holes, with an attendant loss of accuracy in registration. Moreover, persistent abuse of this kind eventually causes malformation of the dies. The male and female punch dies should be lubricated every six months. This is done by slipping a sheet of flat dental wax into the punching position, and punching a slug of wax into each of the female dies.

chapter 4
PAN AND ZOOM: PLANNING AND EXECUTION

N Chapters 2 and 3 we studied the language of animation and the capabilities of the animation stand. We know *what* a pan and a zoom are; now we will learn the *how*—how these moves are actually planned and executed. The field guide, the pantograph chart, and the zoom chart are the most important tools in planning and executing animation moves; in this chapter we will see how each of these is used in practice.

PLOTTING PANS NUMERICALLY

A pan is executed on the animation stand by exposing one frame of film between each movement of the animation compound. As we know, the compound is moved by turning the N–S and E–W controls. Each movement is measured in increments, which are shown on the N–S and E–W counters. Remember that each field step north or south of 0–0 is 36 increments and that each field step east or west of 0–0 is 50 increments. The number of increments which the N–S or E–W control is turned between each film exposure is determined, in principle, by dividing the number of increments of the pan by the number of frames of film to be exposed. That is, the distance of the pan is divided by the time alloted to it. For example, in a pan from 1N to 1S, 72 (2 × 36) increments are traversed on the N–S counter. If this pan is made in one second, 24 frames will be exposed. By dividing the number of increments by the number of frames to be exposed (72 ÷ 24 = 3), we find that we must move the N–S counter 3 increments between each exposure in order to complete the pan in one second.

☐   In practice, however, a pan photographed in equal increments is visually disagreeable; the pan begins with a jerk and crawls woodenly across the screen until it ends abruptly. A smooth pan requires that the move begin with small increments which lengthen until a constant increment is reached. The pan continues at the constant increment until it is near the end of the move; the increment is then reduced until the pan terminates.

☐   The progressive acceleration at the beginning of the move and progressive deceleration at the end of the move are known as "ease-in" and "ease-out." This principle (ease-in–constant speed–ease-out) is applied to all but the shortest pans. The number of ease-in and ease-out frames to use with a given move is dependent on the duration of the pan; in general, the ease frames should comprise at least one-eighth of the total number of frames exposed.

FIELD MASKS

A valuable tool in planning pans and other moves over artwork is a series of field masks. A field mask is a sheet of black construction paper with a rectangular hole in the center whose dimensions correspond exactly to a field size on the field guide. A set of 12 field masks with holes ranging from a 1 field to a 12 field should be on hand throughout the planning phase of animation.

□   Field masks serve four basic purposes in planning. The first

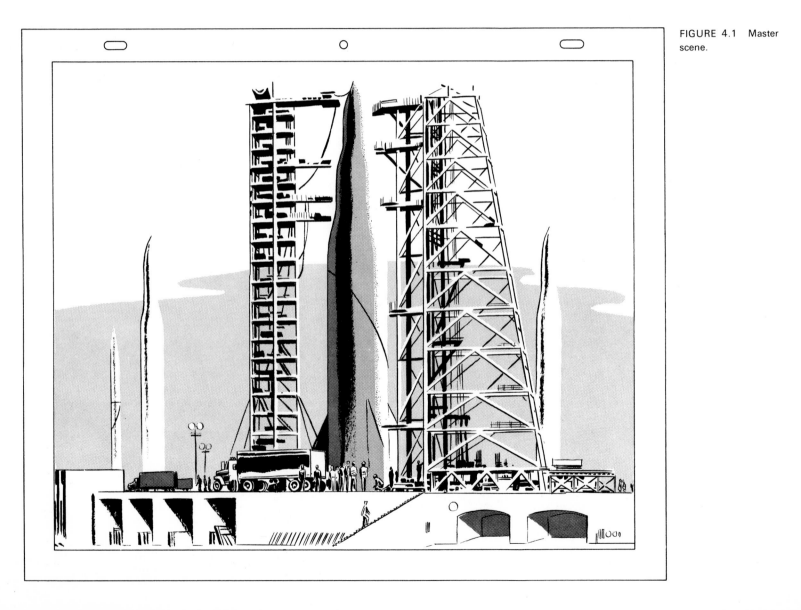

FIGURE 4.1   Master scene.

function is to crop that portion of a picture which will best communicate your ideas at a given point in the film; this is composing for *content*. The second function is to determine the best field size to use for the *aesthetic balance* of the content within the rectangle. The third function is to pinpoint the *location* of the composition on the field guide. The fourth function of the mask is to determine the beginning and end *positions* of all pans to be made on the animation table, as well as to see how the picture will look as the camera scans it during the move.

PLANNING AND EXECUTING A PAN

Let us follow a pan, including ease-in and ease-out, from conception through execution on the animation stand. The master scene shows a missile standing on its launching pad with a gantry at its side and maintenance workers at its base (Figure 4.1). We are going to pan south from the service car at the nose cone to the crew working at the base of the gantry. The illustration is mounted on punched animation paper, and its center is aligned with 0–0 on the field guide.

☐ The first step is to try out field masks of different field sizes to see which gives the best composition of content and aes-

thetic balance at the beginning and the end of the N–S pan. Cropping with an 8-field mask is a poor choice; the composition includes an immense expanse of sky at the beginning of the pan and a garbled mess of buildings, trucks, and people at the end of the pan (Figure 4.2). A 4-field mask is also a poor selection—so much has been eliminated that it is impossible to tell what is being done (Figure 4.3). A 6-field is about right; the mask crops the subject well to communicate what is going on at both ends of the move and the subject is attractively composed at the beginning and end points of the pan (Figure 4.4).

☐ The field guide is now placed on the pegbar over the picture of the missile. We examine the beginning and terminal points of the pan through the 6-field mask, in each case using the center marks on its sides to determine where the center of the composition falls on the field guide. The field guide shows that the starting point of the pan is two field steps north of 0–0 or 2N; the terminal point of the pan is 5 field steps south of 0–0 or 5S. There are seven field steps from 2N to 5S. Since each field step north or south is 36 increments the total distance in increments is found by multiplication:

36 (increments per field position)
×7 (number of field steps)
252 (number of increments to be covered)

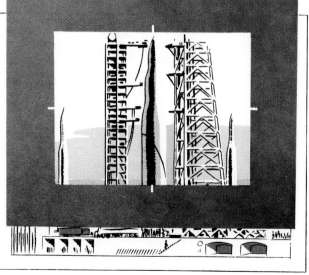

FIGURE 4.2 Master scene cropped with 8-field mask.

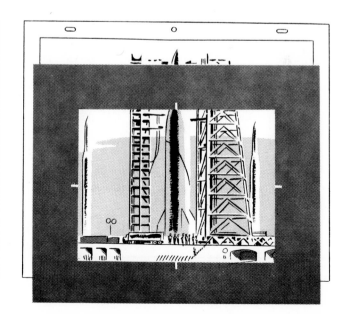

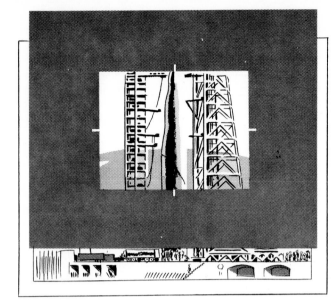

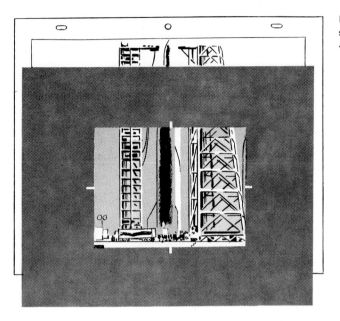

FIGURE 4.3   Master scene cropped with 4-field mask.

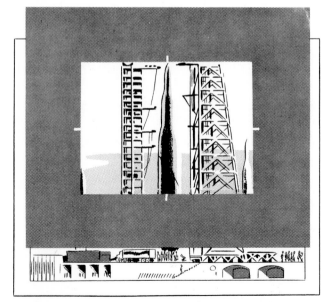

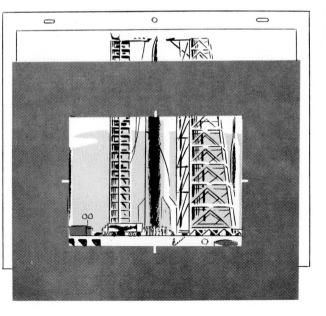

FIGURE 4.4   Master scene cropped with 6-field mask.

The distance on the field guide may also be measured with a decimal ruler; then the total distance to be covered is determined in terms of counter calibrations (100 increments per inch).

☐ The next decision is a choice of time. How long should we take to go from 6(2N–0) to 6(5S–0)? The pan is being made to establish a relation between the work on the nose cone and the crew at the base of the gantry. Since we want to show a point-to-point relationship and are not specifically concerned with the content in between, the move can be done quickly. If it were a short distance, we could do it in one second. But since this pan should appear to cover a long distance, two seconds is a better choice. Remember that a second equals 24 frames; therefore a 2-second pan takes 48 frames.

☐ We now have to determine how many increments must be moved between each exposure in order to pan a distance of 252 increments in 48 frames. This increment is found by dividing the distance to be traveled by the time chosen to travel this distance—252 increments ÷ 48 frames = 5¼ increments to be moved between exposures.

☐ We have seen that it is visually unattractive to make a move in equal increment steps. An ease-in and ease-out are required. But the ease-in, ease-out technique shortens the actual distance of the planned move. We must compensate for this reduction by adding increments through a method known as "overage." We select a constant-speed increment *larger* than 5¼ in order to get the overage or surplus which will compensate for the eases. Trying an increment of 6, we determine the total number of increments by multiplying the increment size by the time of the move:

$$48 \text{ (number of frames to be exposed)}$$
$$\times 6 \text{ (test increment)}$$
$$288 \text{ (total without eases)}$$

The pan from 2N to 5S consists of 252 increments; the difference of 36 increments between 252 and 288 is the overage.

☐ This 36-increment overage is used for the eases. The number is divided in half—18 increments are used for the ease-in and 18 increments for the ease-out. We are thus able to make our eases and simultaneously eliminate the excess increments. The first small step of the ease-in is 1 increment. Since we are not moving a 6-increment step, we have elim-

inated 5 excess increments. The second step of the ease-in is 2 increments. Since we again are not moving 6 increments, we have eliminated 4 excess increments. This pattern continues for the entire ease-in.

Ease Steps	Increments Dropped From Overage
1	5
2	4
3	3
4	2
5	1
Total	15

☐ We have eliminated 15 increments from the overage. But an 18-increment overage was allotted to the ease-in; there are still an excess of 3 increments. These extra increments are eliminated by sandwiching a 3-increment step into the center of the ease-in.

Ease Steps	Increments Dropped From Overage
1	5
2	4
3	3
3	3
4	2
5	1
Total	18

☐ The ease-out increments are identical to those of the ease-in, but are executed in reverse order. We have now planned the entire pan: the ease-in increments are 1-2-3-3-4-5; the increment repeated throughout the center of the pan is 6; and the ease-out increments are 5-4-3-3-2-1. The result is the desired pan of 252 increments in 48 frames.

☐ Execution of this pan on the animation stand is our next step. The control panel switch is turned on to activate the

FIGURE 4.5   N–S control.

FIGURE 4.6   Pantograph indicating 2N position.

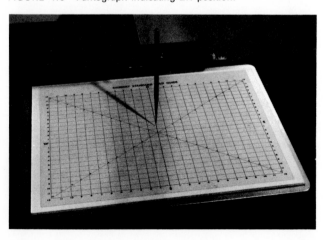

animation stand motor. Then the illustration is placed on the pegbars of the animation table, and the platen is lowered to hold it in place. The camera is now lowered to the 6-field position level. If the camera is *not* set at the correct field position level on the column, it may photograph outside the edge of the picture at the beginning and at the end of the pan.

☐   The 2N position is 00072 on the N–S counter; the N–S control is turned north until this figure appears on the N–S counter (Figure 4.5). Notice that the pantograph needle points to the exact center of the 2N position on the field guide (Figure 4.6). An exposure is made before making the first move of the pan and serves as its beginning.

☐   We then turn the N–S control south 1 increment to 00071 for the first move of the ease-in and expose the first of our 48 frames. For the second step of the ease-in, we turn the N–S counter south 2 increments to 00069 and expose the second frame. This process is continued until the ease-in is complete. The pan then continues south in steps of 6 increments on the N–S counter until 42 of the 48 frames have been exposed; the procedure of the ease-in is then reversed for the ease-out. The N–S counter is moved 5 increments and an exposure is made, then 4 increments for another exposure, then 3 increments for another, and so on, until the pan is terminated. If the pan has been executed correctly, the N–S counter will read 99820, and the pantograph needle will point at 5S. We have completed a pan of 252 increments from 2N to 5S in two seconds, as planned.

☐   An east or west pan is plotted using the same basic principle as a north or south pan. The only difference is that the number of increments per field step is 50 instead of 36, a distinction which can be ignored if a ruler is used to measure the distances. The same sequence of decisions is made in composing with the field masks, determining the beginning and end positions with the field guide, and computing the increment distance with overage for the eases. And the procedure at the animation stand is, of course, the same.

☐   It is sometimes necessary to use fractions of an increment. A ½-increment step can be executed by stopping the N–W or E–W counters midway between numbers. The surest way to implement smaller fractional moves is to make a scale to tape around the rotary wheel of the control hand cranks (Figure 4.7). Wrap a strip of masking tape around the rotary hand crank to find its exact circumference. Since one revolution of the hand crank causes a move of 10 increments, its circumference will represent 10 increments on our scale. Remove the tape and divide its length into the desired fractions of an increment. Remount it on the circumference of the rotary hand crank. Fractional moves are made turning the hand crank in relation to the fractions marked on the tape.

☐ If it proves difficult to work out a numerical pan with even numbers, there are a few ways around the problem. First, an increment or two difference in the beginning and end positions of a pan does not make a noticeable difference in the composition. Second, a frame or two of film can be added to or subtracted from the constant portion of the pan without conspicuously affecting the timing. Third, a frame can be added to the middle portion of an ease-in and an ease-out.

☐ Pans can begin at any area in the artwork that is contained within the maximum field size and can move to any other area subject only to the limitation that the composition falls within the photography area. The diagram shows a west to east pan from 2(10N–10W) to 2(10N–10E), as well as an east to west pan from 4(8S–8E) to 4(8S–8W) (Figure 4.8). Each pan is computed in field steps of 50 increments or measured with a decimal ruler. Also shown is a north to south pan from 5(6N–4E) to 5(6S–4E) (Figure 4.9). This pan is computed in field steps of 36 increments or measured with a ruler. The smaller the field size, the greater is the latitude of movement in either direction. Small field sizes permit what appear on the screen to be wide sweeping moves; larger field sizes permit little more than shifts of composition.

☐ Only a few of the moves made in animation are purely N–S or E–W. Most pans are diagonal; the majority begin at points other than 0–0 and may terminate at any point of the field guide that encompasses the field size. A diagonal move is made by determining its E–W and N–S components separately on the field guide, and executing them together on the E–W and N–S counters between each exposure.

☐ For example, let us implement a 72-frame pan from (1S–3W) to (4N–7E) (Figure 4.10). To plot this diagonal move numerically, we compute its N–S and E–W component moves separately. We first compute a pan from 1S to 4N in 72 frames, using the technique of overage to determine our eases. We then compute a pan from 3W to 7E in 72 frames, again using the technique of overage to determine our eases. These computations result in a 72-frame ease-in–constant speed –ease-out for the N–S control and for the E–W control. By executing the two separate pans in conjunction, we achieve a diagonal pan.

FIGURE 4.7   Scale taped on rotary wheel.

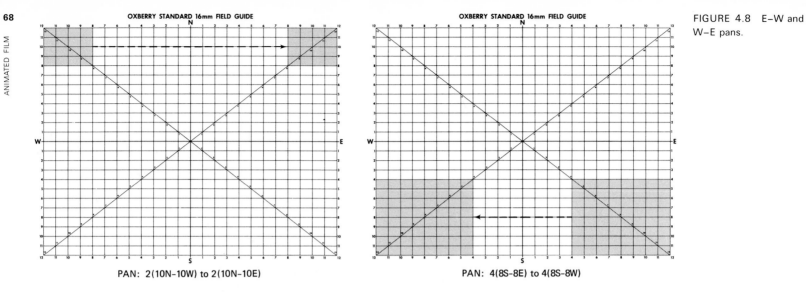

OXBERRY STANDARD 16mm FIELD GUIDE

PAN: 2(10N–10W) to 2(10N–10E)

OXBERRY STANDARD 16mm FIELD GUIDE

PAN: 4(8S–8E) to 4(8S–8W)

FIGURE 4.8 E–W and W–E pans.

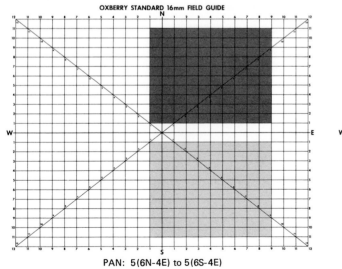

OXBERRY STANDARD 16mm FIELD GUIDE

PAN: 5(6N–4E) to 5(6S–4E)

OXBERRY STANDARD 16mm FIELD GUIDE

PAN: (1S–3W) to (4N–7E)

FIGURE 4.9 N–S pan.

FIGURE 4.10 Diagonal pan.

☐ At the animation stand the N–S control is turned south until the counter reads 99964 and the pantograph needle points at (1S–0). Then the E–W control is turned west until the counter reads 99850 and the pantograph needle points at (1S–3W). This is the beginning of our diagonal pan and a frame is exposed. Using the increment steps which we have computed, we turn the N–S control north and the E–W control west for the first step of the ease-in—and expose a frame.

☐ This procedure of moving both the N–S and E–W controls for the required increment steps between each exposure is repeated for a total of 72 exposures. The pan then terminates at (4N–7E). The compound has moved in a diagonal direction under the camera, and a diagonal pan over the artwork has been photographed.

☐ A straight line diagonal pan is sometimes executed by using the rotary unit to move the whole compound diagonally. There is then only one control for which to compute an ease-in—constant speed—ease-out. Diagonal pans can also be achieved automatically on a motorized compound.

PANTOGRAPH PLANNING

Pans may also be planned by making a pantograph chart, which delineates the path and distance of the move, and are implemented without using the counter system of the N–S, E–W controls. The chart is mounted on the field guide of the pantograph table, and the pantograph needle is aligned with the chart for each exposure of the move (Figure 4.11). Making a pantograph chart is a simple task. The distance the pantograph needle will move is measured on the field guide, and a line of the same length is drawn on a separate sheet of paper. This sheet of paper is the chart. If the move is to be made in equal steps, the distance is divided by the number of exposures to be made, and the divisions are marked on the chart. The chart is then taped onto the pantograph table.

☐ If, however, an ease-in, ease-out is desired, the method of making the pantograph chart is different. As before, the actual distance the pantograph needle will travel is measured on the field guide, and a line of the same length is drawn on a separate sheet of paper. A semicircle is then scribed from one end of the line to the other (Figure 4.12). The semicircle is divided with calipers into segments of equal length, one for each move in the pan. Then each point marked on the semicircle is projected to the original measured distance, the points at which the projections intersect the original line are the points

FIGURE 4.11 Pantograph chart.

FIGURE 4.12 Scribing a straight-line pantograph chart.

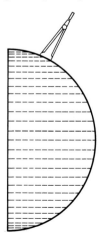

of alignment for the pantograph needle. The chart is cut out and mounted on the field guide of the pantograph table. The move is now made without referring to the N–S and E–W counters.

☐ Another way of plotting a straight-line pan with a pantograph chart is by means of the plastic crossline pointer, described earlier as an alternative to the standard steel pantograph pointer. This type of pantograph chart requires the use of graph paper and charting tape to plot the pan including ease-in and ease-out. The pantograph chart shown, portraying a pan from (2N–3W) to (4N–4E) in 72 frames, is intended for use with a crossline pantograph pointer (Figure 4.13). The straight-line "motion track" reveals the actual path and true distance the crossline pantograph point travels in executing the pan. Below the motion track is the "speed curve," which is used to plot the ease-in–constant speed–ease-out. The horizontal distance of the speed curve duplicates the true E–W distance of the motion track. The time (72 frames) is represented by 72 increments on the vertical axis of the graph paper. A diagonal straight line drawn from lower left to upper right graphically portrays the relationship between the E–W distance of the pan (horizontal distance) and the time duration of the move (72 frames), if no provision is made for an ease-in and ease-out. The eases are plotted by arbitrarily changing the angle of the straight-line center section, and then using a curved line of charting tape at each end to reconnect the diagonal line with the terminal points of the pan. The curved line–straight line–curved line cutting across the graph paper provide us with an ease-in–constant speed–ease-out for the pan.

☐ At the animation stand, the pantograph chart with its motion track and speed curve is mounted over the field guide of the pantograph unit. When the table counters are set at (0–0), the vertical and horizontal axes of the graph paper are aligned with the N–S and E–W crosslines of the plastic pantograph pointer. The pan is begun by manipulating the control until the crosslines of the plastic pointer are directly over (2N–3W), the starting position of the pan. (This is the hold position of the artwork under the camera before the move.) The N–S line of the plastic pointer is aligned with the beginning of both the motion path and the speed curve.

☐ Each move of the pan is made by cranking the crossline pointer horizontally until the N–S line of the plastic pointer intersects the graph line of the speed control curve. Once the distance move is made horizontally, the crosslines of the pointer are moved vertically until they intersect the motion path, and

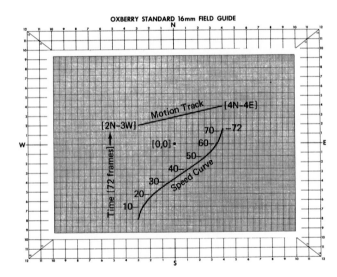

FIGURE 4.13 Lewis pantograph chart.

the exposure is made. The angle of the speed curve determines the distance of the move on the motion track. This procedure is repeated 72 times until the pan terminates at (4N–4E).

☐ The use of a speed curve in conjunction with a motion track on graph paper may be applied to any straight-line or gently curved pan. For a 45° diagonal pan either N–S or E–W component would serve equally well to control the speed of the movement through the ease-in–constant speed–ease-out of the speed curve. If the pan is dominantly N–S, the speed curve should control the N–S component. Similarly, if the pan is dominantly E–W, the speed curve should control the E–W component.

☐ A pantograph chart is also helpful in planning an irregular move over the artwork, a move that takes the camera casually here and there, slowing down at one place and speeding up at another, hesitating here and sweeping there. Irregular moves are extremely difficult to compute on the N–S and E–W counters, but are easily done with a pantograph chart. An overlay of transparent paper is placed on the artwork, and the path of the move is planned with the desired field mask. The center of this path is indicated with a single line which the pantograph needle will follow. Then the line is divided, according to the effects desired, to indicate the points at which each frame is to be exposed. When mounting an overlay on the pantograph table be sure the alignment is correct, or the camera will not photograph the correct area. The point of the pantograph needle must be aligned precisely with the exposure marks on the pantograph chart.

ZOOM

A zoom-in is a reduction from a larger to a smaller field size; a zoom-out is an expansion from a smaller to a larger field size. These effects result, of course, from moving the camera closer to the artwork in order to examine a detail within it, or from moving the camera away from the artwork to show the relationship of a detail to a greater whole.

☐ Like a pan, a zoom is planned by using field masks. But here there is a difference—with zooms we are working with more than one field size. Instead of framing only one composition, we need to frame two field sizes—one for the beginning and one for the end of the zoom. The same principles of composing for content and aesthetic balance as were used in planning pans apply to each end of the zoom.

☐ The illustration shows the structure of the atomic particles in hydrogen (Figure 4.14). The purpose of the zoom-in is to show the nucleus in detail. The zoom begins at 12(0–0) and ends at 6(0–0), a 6-field zoom. The diagram is cropped at the beginning of the zoom-in with a 12-field mask and at the end with a 6-field mask (Figure 4.15). Since the structure of hydrogen would be established on the screen for some time before a zoom-in, a fairly rapid zoom of 2 seconds (48 frames) would be acceptable.

☐ This zoom is plotted using the basic principle common to every move in animation—distance is divided by time in order to determine how far to move between each exposure. The distance of the zoom is how far the camera has to travel up or down the column between the field positions at the beginning and end of the move. This distance between field position levels varies with the focal length of the lens of the camera. This means that the distance between the field position levels of each animation stand must be measured and noted. On the Oxberry Filmaker, for example; this zoom from 12(0–0) to 6(0–0) measures 16 inches on the column scale.

☐ The zoom-in to the hydrogen atom is therefore plotted by dividing 48 frames into the measured distance of 16 inches or by dividing 48 frames into the total number of increments traversed as indicated by the zoom counter. The result would be equally divided steps between each exposure of the move. But if the camera moves down the column in equally divided steps, the zoom appears to start abruptly, move woodenly, and end with a jerk. To cushion the shock of beginning and ending the zoom, it is important to ease-in and ease-out of the move. By starting with a very small increment step and increasing its length with each step, a satisfactory ease-in can be made. Eases for zooms may also be computed by the coverage technique already described for pans.

☐ There are two ways to plot a zoom—by using the increments of the zoom counter or making a zoom chart. A zoom chart is made in the following way. The actual distance the camera travels on the column for the zoom is marked on a sheet of stiff paper or cardboard (Figure 4.16). A semicircle is scribed from end to end. This semicircle is measured with calipers for the number of exposures in the zoom. Each point on the semicircle is projected back to the original true distance. The points at which the projected lines intersect the original measured line will serve as the increment steps of the zoom chart. When the intersections have been emphasized with marks in ink, the zoom chart is ready to be cut out and taped to the field position scale.

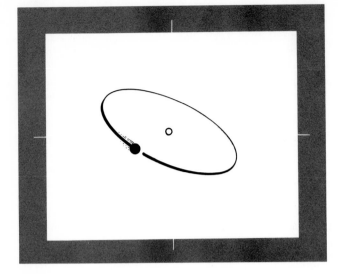

FIGURE 4.14   Master scene of hydrogen atom.

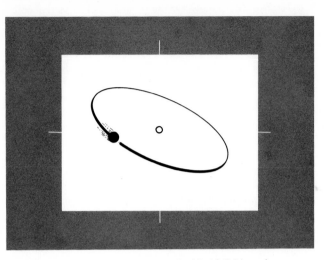

FIGURE 4.15   Master scene cropped with 12-field mask.

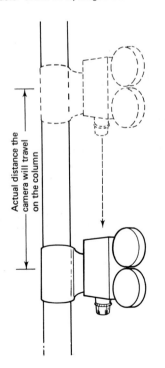

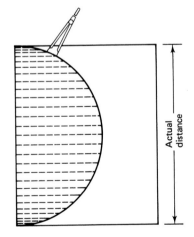

FIGURE 4.16   Making a zoom chart.

☐ The illustration shows a 24-frame, 6-field zoom chart mounted on the field position scale of the animation stand (Figure 4.17). It is taped to the scale with its top aligned at the 12-field position level, and its bottom aligned at the 6-field position level. Notice how small the increment steps are at the top, how they grow progressively larger toward the center, and how they decrease in size toward the bottom. For this 24-frame zoom, the camera indicator is aligned for one exposure at each mark on the zoom chart as the camera moves from the 12-field position down to the 6-field position. When the finished film is projected on a screen, the zoom begins almost imperceptibly, gains speed as the move reaches the center, and then slows down and ends as gently as it began. Planning an individual zoom chart is time-consuming. The animator should make a set of zoom charts and hang them on the wall in the animation camera room, ready for use when needed.

☐ This set is made as follows: Make eight zoom charts, for zooms of 12, 24, 36, 48, 60, 72, 84, and 96 frames—but make them all the same length. This gives a time range of zooms from ½ second through 4 seconds at ½-second intervals. Then enlarge (or reduce) each chart photostatically to the length of a 1-field zoom, a 2-field zoom, a 3-field zoom, and so on. Charts can also be made for fractional field position levels as well—for instance, for a 1½- or 2½-field zoom. These photostatic reproductions should be dry mounted on cardboard, cut into strips, labeled according to the length of the zooms, and hung on the wall of the animation camera room. This set of zoom charts gives a comprehensive time range to meet almost every zoom distance. Obviously, zoom charts must be made for a specific animation stand, taking into account the height of the column and the lens of the camera.

COMPOUND MOVE

A compound move is a combination of a zoom and a pan. It is used to emphasize details and to shift the balance of composition for better aesthetic effect. Despite its apparent complexity the compound move is simple to plan, plot, and execute. In planning, extend the time of the move a bit to compensate for the dual character of the sweep; too quick a compound move is disturbing to see. In plotting, compute the two components (zoom and pan) separately. At the animation stand, make each move on the zoom chart, the N–S counter, and the E–W counter between every exposure of a frame of film. A compound

FIGURE 4.17 Zoom chart mounted on the column.

move, like a diagonal move, is no more than the sum of its parts. Before proceeding to show how to plan, plot, and execute a complete sequence of film, it would be worthwhile to summarize the various techniques of planning and executing moves.

PLANNING AND PLOTTING

1. Decide how large the field sizes will be at the beginning and the end of each move by framing the areas with field masks.

2. Locate the center point of each composition on the field guide.

3. Decide how long the move should take, qualified by the following factors:

    a. Purpose of the move—
    Point to point move to establish a relationship.
    Detailed scanning of content.

    b. Emotional impact of the move—
    Fast move for dramatic impact.
    Middle speed for neutral or negligible emotional quality.
    Slow speed for heavy overtones.

4. Translate the chosen time into the total number of exposures at 24 frames per second.

5. Compute moves for the animation table with the field guide. Count the number of field steps the move is to traverse or measure the distance with a decimal ruler. Multiply this number by 36 or 50, depending on the direction of the move, to find the total distance in increments. Divide the total distance with overage for ease-in and east-out by the time desired, expressed at 24 fps, to find how many increments to move on the N–S and E–W counters between each exposure.

6. Compute zooms on the same principle. Divide the distance that the camera has to travel on the column by the time desired for the move, expressed in frames, to find the distance to move the camera between exposures. Plan your ease-in, ease-out on a zoom chart, or with the increments of the zoom counter.

EXECUTING THE MOVES

1. Load the magazine and thread the camera.

2. Check the illumination with a light meter and confirm the correct f/stop.

3. Turn on the control panel activating switch.

4. Set the camera at the correct field position level on the column.

5. Focus the lens, if there is no follow-focus device.

6. Set the fade control for whatever length is desired.

7. Set the N–W and E–W counters to the hold position of the first scene.

8. Check the pantograph to be sure the needle is pointed at the correct location on the field guide.

9. Expose the first frame of film with the single-exposure button or with the continuous-exposure switch if there are to be repeated exposures.

10. Reset the camera at its new field position level, if there is to be a new one, and refocus the lens.

11. Move the N–S and E–W controls the desired number of increments between exposures.

12. Expose the film. Repeat steps 10, 11, and 12 until the move is completed. Then, for more precise confirmation—

13. Compare the numbers registered on the N–S and E–W counters at the termination of the move to the corresponding numbers on the calibration chart.

14. Glance at the position of the pantograph needle to confirm that it is pointed at the desired position on the field guide.

chapter 5
THE FILMOGRAPH

FILMOGRAPH is an animation technique in which still photographs or artwork are infused with the spirit of life and the illusion of motion by means of optical effects, zooms and pans over the pictures. Filmographs have been made which almost defy detection as not being fully animated films or live-action motion pictures. They can be made by anyone who has access to the still pictures he needs and who knows how to plan and execute moves on the animation stand. Filmograph is the least expensive form of animation and is widely used in the educational and industrial fields.

☐ The first step in filmograph production is to select the pictures to be used in the film and to arrange them in the order they are to appear on the screen. Any photographs used in filmographs should be free of graininess or blemishes; the slightest defect is photographed and greatly magnified when projected on the screen. As a rule, the photographs should have a low to medium contrast level, be printed dark enough to make texture and highlights show clearly, and have a glossy finish unless texture is being used as an aesthetic factor.

☐ Each picture should be mounted on the animation paper at the 0–0 position of the field guide so that all moves may be plotted from that point. Put a thin spread of one-coat rubber cement on the animation paper (*not* on the photograph). Rubber cement should not be applied to the picture because it may soak through and leave stains on the front, ruining it for filmograph purposes. When the rubber cement has dried, mount the photograph on the paper. This is done by placing the field guide on the peg bars, putting the semi-transparent animation paper over them, and then aligning the picture with the field guide lines which are visible through the paper.

☐ In planning and plotting the filmograph, the composition and treatment of each picture is worked out and recorded before proceeding to the next, usually in the following steps:

1. The picture is composed with a mask; that is, a field guide is superimposed over the picture (mounted at 0–0), and the correct field size is chosen. The picture should extend a half field beyond the edge of the selected field size. This "bleed" precludes the possibility of photographing outside the edge of the picture.

2. The optical transition to the picture, or between pictures, is selected and its length determined by the desired effects.

3. The zooms and pans within each picture are composed, planned, and computed.

4. As each decision is made, it is recorded on a sheet of paper, which is used as a filmograph exposure guide when photographing on the animation stand.

FIGURE 5.1a Master scene.

FILMOGRAPH PRODUCTION

The best way to learn how to apply animation techniques to filmograph is to follow a production, step-by-step, from planning through plotting to execution. The subject of the sample filmograph sequence presented here is the life cycle of the frog. The film opens with a female frog laying eggs in the shallows of a pond. One egg is singled out and is followed through each stage of its development until maturity, when it is then compared with its mother.

☐ Six pictures are selected to tell the story: (1) Our master scene—the frog and her eggs in their natural environment; (2) the single, translucent egg; (3) the legless tadpole; (4) the tadpole with hind legs; (5) the tadpole with both front and hind legs; (6) the new adult, seated beside its parent for comparison in size and characteristics.

☐ All the pictures are not the same size; they need not be. A 3″ × 4″ picture photographed at a 4 field fills the screen as completely as an 8″ × 10″ one photographed at a 10 field. Size differences between the original visuals are undetectable when the finished film is projected on the screen. The animation stand is so flexible that pictures of a hundred different sizes can be used in the same film without the disparities being evident to the audience.

☐ These six static pictures will be transmuted into a motion picture lasting more than a minute by using zooms, pans, and optical effects to infuse them with life. We shall first give a summary of the film, then a detailed explanation of the techniques used in making it.

☐ A fade-in to the master scene of the pond is followed by a quick zoom singling out the mother frog. A brief pause is followed by a pan to the eggs she has laid, another brief pause, and a pan to the reed on which the eggs are anchored. A fast dissolve to select a single egg is followed by slow dissolves to each major stage of development until the adult stage is reached; each stage is accompanied by an apparent steady growth in size. The sequence ends when the camera recedes from the new frog in a compound move and permits the viewer to compare the young adult with its parent. The film is terminated by a fade-out. The complete life cycle of the frog is presented in motion, using only six still pictures and without saying a word.

☐ The first illustration measures 8″ × 9½″, and so it must be photographed at no larger than a 9 field. Since it is the first visual in the film, it is introduced by a fade-in, the rising curtain of motion pictures (Figure 5.1a). This is a short film, and a fast fade-in of 18 frames is acceptable. The picture is mounted dead center on the field and its N–S and E–W calibration reading is 0–0. This information is recorded for later reference at the animation stand as follows—

(1) *Figure 1:* Fade-in 9(0–0) in 18 frames.

Notice that this one-line statement includes all the information necessary to execute the first move at the animation stand.

☐   This master scene itself should be held on the screen for a few seconds to orient the audience to the context of the film. There is no change of visuals, so this information is indented and written as follows:

(*a*) *Hold:* Master scene 9(0–0) for 96 frames.

☐   Once the scene is established it should be pointed out visually that the subject of the film is the frog and the eggs she has laid. A zoom from a 9-field master scene to a 3-field closeup of the frog would single her out (Figure 5.1b). As the zoom serves the purpose here of initiating a cycle of events whose context is already established, it can be a fairly fast zoom of 32 frames. This would be stated as follows, with a reminder to make a zoom chart before photographing the filmograph:

(*b*) *Zoom:* 9(0–0) to 3(0–0) in 32 frames (chart).

☐   Whenever a fast, disorienting move has been made, a pause is desirable to let the viewer get his bearings. This pause is also recorded:

(*c*) *Hold:* Closeup, frog 3(0–0) for 72 frames.

☐   The next point to make is that the frog has just laid her eggs in the water; this is demonstrated by panning from the frog down to her eggs. A pan is first planned aesthetically, and then plotted arithmetically. The terminal point of the pan is first composed with a 3-field mask around a cluster of eggs. Then we superimpose the field guide over the illustration and the composing mask, and find that the center of the composition is located at 3(4S–0) (Figure 5.1c). As this move traverses an area which contains no important information, it is best to make as fast a move as can be executed smoothly; a 2-second pan of 48 frames would do.

☐   The next step is to plot the move on the field guide so that when the pan is made on the animation stand the camera photographs a smooth transition from 3(0–0) to 3(4S–0) in 48 frames. We must determine how many increments to move the N–S counter between each of 48 exposures.

FIGURE 5.1b   Zoom-in.

FIGURE 5.1c   Planning beginning of pan.

☐ There are 36 increments for each field step south on the N–S counter of the animation stand; we are moving 4 field steps south. The 4 field steps are multiplied by the 36 increments of each step to find the total number to be traversed— 4 × 36 = 144 increments. The number of increments to be traversed (144) is divided by the time allotted for the pan (48 frames) to find the number of increments to be moved between exposures. Thus, 144 ÷ 48 = 3 increments.

☐ Every pan should consist of an ease-in, constant speed, and ease-out. To provide for eases, we use the technique of overage and choose 3½ as the constant-speed increment. Multiply this constant-speed increment by the number of frames to be exposed (3½ × 48 = 168) and obtain 168 increments. The number of increments from 3(0–0) to 3(4S–0) is 144; the overage is therefore 24 increments (168 − 144 = 24). Use 12 increments of the overage for the ease-in and 12 for the ease-out. As we have seen, the ease-in begins with small increments and continues with progressively larger ones.

Ease Steps	Increments Dropped From Overage
½	3
1	2½
1½	2
2	1½
2½	1
3	½
Total 10½	Total 10½

We have eliminated 10½ increments of the 12 increments allotted to the ease-in. To drop another 1½ increments, we add an extra 2-increment step to the ease.

Ease Steps	Increments Dropped From Overage
½	3
1	2½
1½	2
2	1½
2	1½
2½	1
3	½
Total 12½	Total 12

The ease-out is executed in the same increments, but in reverse. Our pan has now been plotted with an ease-in (7 frames; 12½ increments), constant speed (34 frames × 3½ constant speed increment = 119 increments), and ease-out (7 frames; 12½ increments). As we originally planned, the pan is executed in 48 frames (7 + 34 + 7 = 48) and covers 144 increments (12½ + 119 + 12½ = 144).

☐ This information is added to the filmograph exposure guide:

(d) *Pan:* frog to eggs, 3(0–0) to 3(4S–0); ½, 1, 1½, 2, 2, 2½—steps of 3½—2½, 2, 2, 1½, ½ in 48 frames.

This scene is held briefly to orient the viewer—

(e) *Hold:* Eggs 3(4S–0) for 36 frames.

☐ To show the thousands of eggs laid by a single frog, we pan slowly over them to the reed on which they are anchored. As before, we compose an attractive arrangement of subject matter at the terminal point of the pan and superimpose the field guide to see how far east the center of the new composition lies. It falls at a point that is approximately ¼ field step beyond 7 east on the field guide (Figure 5.1d). This introduces a common problem—the best compositions do not always fall neatly at the intersections of the field guide for easy computation. In this instance, by using a ruler and computing 100 increments to the inch, we find that the pan is 368 increments long.

☐ This pan is different from the previous one in that it traverses an area whose content is important. The purpose of making the pan is to draw attention to the large quantities of eggs the frog has laid and the move should be slow enough so the viewer can study the clusters. A pan of from 5 to 8 seconds would be adequate to do the communication job here. Let us strike an average between the two extremes, and plot a pan of 6½ seconds (156 exposures). Again, we divide distance by time to get the average increment—368 increments ÷ 156 frames = 2 56/156 increments.

☐ To get rid of this unwieldy increment step size and obtain additional increments for a suitable ease-in and ease-out, we select a larger increment step size of 2½. The total number of increments is then 390 (2½ × 156 = 390). Using the overage technique we obtain an ease of ¼, ½, ¾, 1, 1¼, 1½, 1¾, and 2. To execute this ease, we mount a length of masking tape indicating ¼ increments on the E–W control (see p. 67). As this move is still part of Figure 1 it is stated—

(f) Pan: Eggs to reed, 3(4S–0) to 3(4S–7¼E); ¼, ½, ¾, 1, 1¼, 1½, 1¾, 2—steps of 2½—2, 1¾, 1½, 1¼, 1, ¾, ½, ¼ in 156 frames.

Again there should be a pause for study and reorientation; 72 frames would be good, and the hold is stated—

(g) Hold: Reed 3(4S–7¼E) for 72 frames.

☐ All the relevant information in Figure 1 has now been presented. The eggs in the cluster at the base of the reed are too small for one to be singled out for development, so we proceed to a single egg (Figure 5.2). The field guide is superimposed over the picture to determine at what field size the egg is most likely to be accepted as an egg, keeping in mind that there will be subsequent stages of growth. The field sizes for all the stages of maturation are selected on the basis of the size change, or lack of size change, from one visual to the next. A 10-field at 0–0 seems good.

☐ The single egg will therefore be photographed at 10(0–0) on the N–S and E–W counters. Since our last position on Figure 1 was at 3(4S–7¼E), we must decide how to make a visually acceptable transition from a 3 field to a 10 field and from 4S–7¼E to 0–0. This problem is best solved by a dissolve. Since a dissolve is a fade-in superimposed on a fade-out, the cluster of eggs fades out while the single egg fades in. The audience will accept this dissolve as the selection of a single egg from the cluster. A dissolve of 18 frames would do here, since we want to pass on to the next stage of development as quickly as possible. After an 18-frame fade-out of Figure 1 has been photographed, the film is rewound back to the beginning of the fade, and an 18-frame fade-in of Figure 2 is photographed. (For a detailed discussion of dissolves, see Chapter 3.)

☐ This dissolve to Figure 2, with a subsequent pause on the single egg, is stated—

(2) *Figure 2:* Dissolve 3(4S–7¼E) to 10(0–0) in 18 frames.

(a) Hold: Frog egg 10(0–0) for 72 frames.

☐ Figures 3 through 6 represent the successive stages of the frog's growth. The problem here is to create the illusion of progressive development as the egg transmutes into a tadpole, then grows hind and front legs, and finally matures into an adult. We must create the illusions of both maturation and

FIGURE 5.1d Planning end of pan.

FIGURE 5.2 Egg.

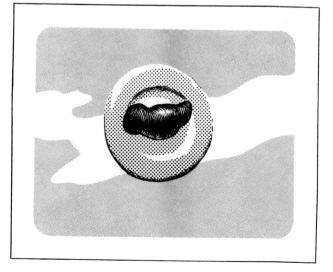

FIGURE 5.3   Tadpole.

FIGURE 5.4   Tadpole with hind legs.

growth in size to communicate a valid picture of the process.

☐   The effect of maturation is created by using long dissolves between each stage of development. Dissolves of 48 frames or longer make the transitions appear gentle and gradual, and the frog will seem to pulsate with life. Each stage of development dissolves to the next one, with a pause of 3 or 4 seconds at each stage. The subjects should be aligned one above the other when being mounted to facilitate transitions at the 0–0 position.

☐   The second illusion—that the egg is apparently growing in size as it matures—is created by moving the camera a field size closer with each stage. Even though the egg and the tadpole are the same size in the original pictures, by photographing the egg at a 10 field, the tadpole at a 9 field, the hind legs at an 8 field, and so on, the illusion is created on the screen that the frog is undergoing vast increases in size as it matures. This sequence is indicated on the exposure record:

(3) *Figure 3:* Dissolve 10(0–0) to 9(0–0) in 48 frames.
   (a) *Hold:* Tadpole 9(0–0) for 72 frames.

(4) *Figure 4:* Dissolve 9(0–0) to 8(0–0) in 48 frames.
   (a) *Hold:* Tadpole with hind legs 8(0–0) for 72 frames.

(5) *Figure 5:* Dissolve 8(0–0) to 7(0–0) in 48 frames.
   (a) *Hold:* Tadpole with four legs 7(0–0) for 72 frames.

(6) *Figure 6:* Dissolve 7(0–0) to 6(0–0) in 48 frames.
   (a) *Hold:* New adult 6(0–0) for 72 frames.

☐   This method of creating the illusion of growth and change through long dissolves and progressive changes in field size is a useful technique. It is an inexpensive and effective way of creating the illusions of movement and growth with a minimum of artwork.

☐   Figure 5.6 shows the newly mature adult in a closeup at 6(0–0). Off-screen and to the left is the parent frog: As our final move in this sequence, we want to show that, while the youngster is an adult in form, it is not yet as large as its parent. In order to make this comparison of size, we must zoom-out and pan diagonally northwest to encompass both frogs (Figure 5.7).

☐   First we must find the best field size and composition for the terminal point of the move. A 10-field mask centered at 2N–3W frames the two frogs well, but the field mask extends beyond the field guide by a full field step. Fortunately, there is an inch of ''bleed,'' which permits us to proceed with the move at a 10 field.

☐ The next choice is one of time—how long should a compound move from 6(0–0) to 10(2N–3W) take when the aim is to compare the sizes of two creatures. As the purpose is to go from one point to another without necessarily transmitting information, the move is made as quickly as possible without losing the orientation of the viewer. Three seconds, or 72 exposures, would be good.

☐ We shall plot a zoom and diagonal move from 6(0–0) to 10(2N–3W) in 72 frames. As explained earlier, each of the components of a compound move is computed separately, but both are executed simultaneously. The zoom of 72 frames can be made by the zoom chart method or, if a zoom counter is on the column, by dividing the total number of increments used in moving the camera four field sizes by 72 frames and allowing for eases.

☐ The diagonal move is created by plotting a N–S pan from 0 to 2N in 72 frames and by plotting a E–W pan from 0 to 3W in 72 frames. The two moves are executed together between each exposure.

☐ The N–S component of the compound move is computed as before. The number of increments in each N–S field step, 36, is multiplied by the number of field steps taken, 2, to find the total number of increments traversed, which is 72. In this instance, because of the shortness of the pan and the length of the zoom, eases are not necessary. We need only divide 72 increments by 72 frames to find the increment moved between each exposure—72 increments ÷ 72 frames = 1 increment. The E–W pan is plotted using the same method. The number of increments (150) is divided by the number of frames (72)—150 ÷ 72 = 2 6/72 increments to be moved between exposures. The answer (2 6/72) is an impractical figure to work with. The problem may be dealt with by overage, but an alternative technique is to add or subtract a couple of frames to the divisor and thereby even the numbers. Here we add 3 frames, which gives us a 2-increment step between exposures (150 ÷ 75 = 2). The additional 3 frames represent only ⅛ second of screen time and will therefore make a scarcely noticeable difference when the film is projected on the screen. To make the E–W pan coincide with the zoom and the N–S pan (which are both 72 frames long), we start it two frames earlier and end it one frame later. The information for this move, a terminal pause of four seconds, and an 18-frame fade-out are added to the exposure record.

FIGURE 5.5   Tadpole with four legs.

FIGURE 5.6   New adult.

(b) *Compound move:* 6(0–0) to 10(2N–3W) in 75 frames. Execute together:

1. *Pan:* (0–0) to (0–3W); steps of 2 in 75 frames.
2. *Pan:* (0–0) to (2N–0); steps of 1 in 72 frames (begin two frames after 1 begins and end one frame before 1 ends).
3. *Zoom:* 6 field to 10 field in 72 frames (begin two frames after 1 begins and end one frame before 1 ends).

(c) *Hold:* Two frogs, 10(2N–3W) for 96 frames.

(d) *Fade-out:* Two frogs, 10(2N–3W) in 18 frames.

☐ The animation moves and optical effects have now been worked out and recorded sequentially; the exposure guide should look like the chart below with a cumulative frame count stated to the right.

☐ A glance at the exposure guide reveals that it has all the information necessary to photograph the filmograph on the animation stand. It contains—

1. the sequence of the pictures and their field sizes, and the transitional optical effects used between them
2. the number of exposures to take of each visual and optical effect

Filmograph Exposure Guide	Cumulative Count	Filmograph Exposure Guide	Cumulative Count
(1) *Figure 1:* Fade-in 9(0–0) in 18 frames.	18	(a) *Hold:* Tadpole with hind legs, 8(0–0) for 72 frames.	860
(a) *Hold:* Master scene, 9(0–0) for 96 frames.	114	(5) *Figure 5:* Dissolve 8(0–0) to 7(0–0) in 48 frames.	908
(b) *Zoom:* 9(0–0) to 3(0–0) in 32 frames (chart).	146	(a) *Hold:* Tadpole with four legs, 7(0–0) for 72 frames.	980
(c) *Hold:* Closeup of frog, 3(0–0) for 72 frames.	218	(6) *Figure 6:* Dissolve 7(0–0) to 6(0–0) in 48 frames.	1028
(d) *Pan:* Frog to eggs, 3(0–0) to 3(4S–0); ½, 1, 1½, 2, 2, 2½— steps of 3½—2½, 2, 2, 1½, 1, ½ in 48 frames.	266	(a) *Hold:* New adult, 6(0–0) for 72 frames.	1100
(e) *Hold:* Eggs, 3(4S–0) for 36 frames.	302	(b) *Compound move:* 6(0–0) to 10(2N–3W) in 75 frames. Execute together:	
(f) *Pan:* Eggs to reed, 3(4S–0) to 3(4S–7¼E); ¼, ½, ¾, 1, 1¼, 1½, 1¾, 2—steps of 2½—2, 1¾, 1½, 1¼, 1, ¾, ½, ¼ in 156 frames.	458	1. *Pan:* (0–0) to (0–3W); steps of 2 in 75 frames.	
(g) *Hold:* Reed, 3(4S–7¼E) for 72 frames.	530	2. *Pan:* (0–0) to (2N–0); steps of 1 in 72 frames (begin 2 frames after 1 begins and end 1 frame before 1 ends).	
(2) *Figure 2:* Dissolve 3(4S–7¼E) to 10(0–0) in 18 frames.	548	3. *Zoom:* 6 field to 10 field in 72 frames (begin 2 frames after 1 begins and end 1 frame before 1 ends.	1175
(a) *Hold:* Frog egg, 10(0–0) for 72 frames.	620	(c) *Hold:* two frogs, 10(2N–3W) for 96 frames.	1271
(3) *Figure 3:* Dissolve 10(0–0) to 9(0–0) in 48 frames.	668	(d) *Fade-out:* two frogs, 10(2N–3W) in 18 frames.	1289
(a) *Hold:* Tadpole, 9(0–0) for 72 frames.	740		
(4) *Figure 4:* Dissolve 9(0–0) to 8(0–0) in 48 frames.	788		

3. the size of the increment steps to move the N–S and E–W counters for pans and the zoom chart indications
4. cumulative counter numbers

Once the zoom charts are constructed (see p. 72), the filmograph is ready to be photographed on the animation stand.

PHOTOGRAPHING THE FILMOGRAPH

The first step in preparation for photography is to determine the light level with a light meter, to confirm that the light falls evenly over the photography area and to establish the correct f/stop for the ASA exposure index of the type of film being used.

☐ The first illustration is placed under the platen. As indicated by the exposure guide, the camera is set at the 9-field level of the column, and the N–S and E–W counters are set at 0–0. The sequence begins with a fade-in of 18 frames; at the beginning of the fade-in, the shutter is closed; it is progressively opened for each of 18 exposures. At the end of the fade-in, the shutter is completely open. Move (1a) calls for a hold on the master scene of 4 seconds, and so the continuous run switch is turned on for 96 exposures.

☐ Move (1b) is a 32-frame zoom from a 9 field to a 3 field at 0–0; a zoom chart, providing smooth ease-in and ease-out is made and taped to the column of the stand. The top is aligned with the 9-field position bar and the bottom with the 3-field position bar. The camera level indicator is set at the first mark on the zoom chart, and a frame is exposed. Then the camera level indicator is lowered to the next mark of the zoom chart and another frame is exposed. This procedure of a 1-increment move and 1-frame exposure continues for each frame of the 32-frame zoom. The follow-focus cam of the complete animation stand eliminates the need for manual refocusing of the camera between exposures. If, however, an adapted conventional camera is used, the camera lens must be refocused by hand for every frame. Unless this is done precisely, the focus will fluctuate throughout the zoom. A focusing disc is sometimes fastened to the rotary ring of the lens with the edge of the disc calibrated for field position levels.

☐ After the termination of the zoom, move (1c) is a 3-second closeup of the frog, and the continuous run switch is turned on for 72 frames. Move (1d) is a pan from the frog down to the eggs at 4 South in 48 frames. For the first ease-in step (½ increment), the N–S counter is turned from 00000 to

FIGURE 5.7 Compound move (zoom-out and pan).

99999½, and one frame is exposed. For the second ease-in step (1 increment), the N–S counter is turned to 99998½, and one frame is exposed. This procedure is continued for the entire pan. The photographer consults the exposure guide and moves the N–S counter the indicated number of increments between each exposure. At the end of the 48-exposure, 144-increment pan, the N–S counter will read 99856 (00000 − 00144 = 99856). Move (1e) is a hold on the eggs at 3(4S–0) for 36 frames. The continuous run switch is therefore turned on for 36 frames.

☐ Move (1f) is a pan over the eggs to the reed. This is the move for which tape, marked in ¼ increments, has been attached to the circumferance of the E–W control. For the first ease step, we turn the E–W control east ¼ increment, and expose a frame. For the second ease step, we turn it ½ increment and expose a second frame. Then we turn it ¾ increment and expose a third frame, and so on, until the ease-in is complete. Then the E–W counter is moved 2½ increments east between each exposure for 140 frames. The 8-frame ease-out is executed in the same increment sizes as the ease-in. At the end of 156 exposures the E–W counter reads 00368. Move (1g) is a 72-frame hold, and so the continuous run switch is turned on for 72 frames.

☐ The exposure guide now indicates an 18-frame dissolve from Figure 1 at 3(4S–7¼E) to Figure 2 at 10(0–0). To accomplish this dissolve, the shutter is gradually closed for each of 18 exposures of Figure 1. The film is backed up in the camera with the shutter closed for 18 frames (the point where the fade-out began). Figure 1 is removed from the platen and replaced by Figure 2. The exposure guide calls for a 10 field at 0–0 position, so the camera level is raised to the 10 field position, and the N–S and E–W counters are cranked back until each reads 00000. The shutter is gradually opened for each of 18 exposures of Figure 2, until the 18-frame dissolve is completed at 10(0–0) and the shutter is wide open. Move (2a) is a 72-frame hold and so the continuous exposure switch is turned on for 72 frames.

☐ Step (3) on the exposure guide calls for a dissolve from Figure 2 at 10(0–0) to Figure 3 at 9(0–0). The dissolve is done as before: The shutter is gradually stopped down for each of 48 exposures until it is closed; the film is then backed up in the camera, with the shutter closed, for 48 frames, until it reaches the point where the fade-out began. Figure 2 is removed from the platen and replaced by Figure 3. The camera level is lowered until the side indicator points to the 9-field level. Now the shutter is opened gradually for each of 48

frames, and the dissolve is complete. A hold of 72 frames is called for by move (3a), and the continuous run switch is turned on for 72 exposures.

☐ This procedure is repeated for Figures 4, 5, and 6. Each illustration is dissolved to the following one by fading out in 48 frames on the first illustration, backing up the film for 48 frames with the shutter closed, then fading in on the following illustration in 48 frames. Each succeeding illustration is photographed one field size closer so that, in conjunction with the dissolves, it appears that the frog has grown through a complete life cycle, with each stage of development held for 72 frames.

☐ After holding on the young adult frog for 72 frames (6a), we make a compound zoom-pan from 6(0–0) to 10(2N–3W) in 75 frames to compare the young adult to its mother. Each dimension of this move is computed separately, and the exposure guide indicates:

(b) Compound move: 6(0–0) to 10(2N–3W) in 75 frames. Execute together:
1. Pan: (0–0) to (0–3W); steps of 2 in 75 frames.
2. Pan: (0–0) to (2N–0); steps of 1 in 72 frames (begin 2 frames after 1 begins and end 1 frame before 1 ends).
3. Zoom: 6 field to 10 field in 72 frames (begin 2 frames after 1 begins and end 1 frame before 1 ends).

☐ It is wise to adopt a definite sequence for the three moves made between each exposure to be sure none is omitted. A 72-frame zoom chart is taped to the column, aligned with the 10 field at the top and the 6 field at the bottom. The moves for the first ten exposures are—

	Zoom Chart	E–W Counter	N–S Counter	
(1)	———	99998	———	expose a frame
(2)	———	99996	———	expose a frame
(3)	1 increment	99994	00001	expose a frame
(4)	1 increment	99992	00002	expose a frame
(5)	1 increment	99990	00003	expose a frame
(6)	1 increment	99988	00004	expose a frame
(7)	1 increment	99986	00005	expose a frame
(8)	1 increment	99984	00006	expose a frame
(9)	1 increment	99982	00007	expose a frame
(10)	1 increment	99980	00008	expose a frame

If these moves are executed correctly, a smooth compound move from 6(0–0) to 10(2N–3W) will result. At this point, the exposure guide calls for a hold of 72 frames, so the continuous run switch is turned on for that number of exposures. An 18-frame fade-out completes the filmograph.

□ The filmograph *Life Cycle of the Frog* includes most of the basic moves and fundamental problems faced in creating and implementing a filmograph.

□ The animation techniques which are employed to treat these six static pictures will give them the dimension of motion and the spirit of life. These techniques can be applied to such diverse fields as television commercials and industrial films or to any area where it is desired to bring still visuals to life as motion pictures.

chapter 6
SCRIPT, STORYBOARD, AND FILM STYLE

AN instructional film is as valuable as its content, and its content in turn is as effective as the script and storyboard. The script is a written statement of the film's content, and the storyboard is its pictorial expression. They represent the first phase of film planning. Factual errors, weaknesses in continuity, and areas of muddled thinking should be discovered here—not during production or after the film is finished.

WHY USE ANIMATION?

Before starting an animated film, we should ask ourselves, "Why use animation? Why not use live-action cinematography?" The techniques of animation are exacting. If it is possible to express the idea of the film as effectively and more easily by other means, it certainly makes sense to do so. But the phrase "if it is possible to express the idea" points to the primary reason for using animation—through animation, concepts can be put into pictorial form which cannot be presented adequately by any other technique.

☐ Animation makes it possible to depict processes which cannot be completely visualized by live-action cinematography —for example, the internal functioning of the human body. The functions of interrelated parts and critical areas can be pointed out, slowed down, speeded up, and lifted out of context for closer examination. And every dimension of line, form, value, color, and movement offered by motion pictures is at the disposal of the animator to present these processes clearly.

☐ Through animation we can simplify processes and ideas. The important details of a problem or presentation can often be singled out and logically isolated only by animation. A good example is the problem of explaining the human nervous system. How could it be interpreted simply except through some form of animation?

☐ Through animation it is possible to show not only how things work, but also what they mean. Although ideas are intangible, they influence people's behavior. Prejudice, tolerance, and freedom have been given persuasive form in such films as *Boundary Lines, Can We Immunize Against Prejudice?,* and *Quest for Freedom.* And the effectiveness of arousing a fighting spirit by embodying the forces of good and evil in animated form was dramatically shown in Disney's *Victory Through Airpower.*

☐ By animation it is possible to make visual generalizations from specific examples and thereby to project future expectations. The true significance of a scientific or industrial experiment having limited immediate use but incalculable possibilities can be presented through animation. This potential for generalization applies also to sales films and to television commercials.

☐ And finally through animation we can provide visual cues to point out what is important and to eliminate or subordinate what is unimportant. The degree of control and selectivity inherent in its techniques is perhaps the greatest determining factor in a decision of whether or not to use animation. In live-action cinematography we are limited to what we can stage before the camera. In animation we are limited only by our imagination and our ability to give an idea vital and communicative form.

☐ Animation techniques, therefore, should be considered for the following purposes:

1. to depict processes which cannot be visualized through live action cinematography
2. to simplify complex processes and structures
3. to give pictorial form to abstract ideas
4. to make visual generalizations and project future possibilities from specific examples
5. to provide visual cues for the purpose of clarification

☐ There are six distinct phases in planning instructional animation: task analysis, synopsis, research, treatment, script, and storyboard. Omission of any of these steps may compromise the teaching effectiveness of the finished film.

TASK ANALYSIS

The first step in producing a film that communicates well is a correct analysis of the teaching task. What do you want the viewers to know or to do as a consequence of seeing the film? What are the behavioral objectives?

☐ Define clearly the objectives of the film. Know in detail what knowledge the viewer should derive from the film. Then relate this statement to the information and skills the viewers already have and state the conceptual approach in a synopsis.

SYNOPSIS

A synopsis is a one-page outline stating the essential concept of a projected film; several synopses are often developed for each film (Figure 6.1). The purpose of the synopsis is to explore various solutions to a communication problem and to discover whether the film maker and his sponsor are discussing the same film. Each synopsis should be composed of the following elements:

1. *Target audience:* For whom is the film intended? What special characteristics does the audience have that should be taken into account when writing the script?

2. *Purpose:* What does the film maker want the target audience to do or to understand as a result of having seen this film?

3. *Subject:* What is the subject of the film and how does it relate to implementing the educational purpose of the film? (There may be a dozen different subjects suitable for any given purpose.)

4. *Core idea:* What does the film maker (or sponsor) have to say of significance about the subject?

5. *Plot:* How will the film maker present the content of the subject? That is, in what sequence will the basic information be organized?

6. *Identification:* How will the target audience be persuaded to identify with the core idea of the film and respond to it? What will be included that is relevant to the life space of the target audience? ("Life space" refers to the immediate environment of an individual—his job, home, and family.)

7. *Cinematic form:* If the animation is part of a larger live-action film, why must this sequence in it be animated?

RESEARCH

The next step is research into the subject for clear, accurate, and objective information. The importance of thorough research cannot be exaggerated. The smallest error is intolerable in an educational film; inaccurate information has no place in the classroom. If the animation is finished and found to be inaccurate, the entire production may have to be discarded.

☐ In some instances, especially if the subject is technical or scientific, the instructional film maker works closely with experts on the subject from planning through production, to completion of the animation. But more often the instructional film maker must accept the responsibility for doing necessary research. And the research must be accurate.

☐ To ensure that your information is accurate, seek out the most authoritative sources. Visit museums and laboratories to see the subject at first hand. Go to the major libraries in universities and large cities for basic reference works in every field. Consult experts or technicians, who can point out key reference

FIGURE 6.1 Synopsis: *Tree Improvement and Genetics.* Courtesy of the State University College of Forestry at Syracuse, New York.

TARGET AUDIENCE:	Male senior high school students who are scientifically oriented and already have a strong academic background in biology, zoology, chemistry, and mathematics, who plan to attend college and have the intellectual potential for eventually doing graduate work—and who are about to make a decision regarding a career in one of the natural sciences.
PURPOSE:	To interest qualified students in pursuing forest genetics as a lifetime profession, and to per-. suade them to enroll as undergraduates with a major in forestry.
SUBJECT:	The pollination techniques used to improve the quality of the white pine on different forest plantations around the world.
CORE IDEA:	Forest genetics is a dynamic, expanding area of natural science which will challenge a young mind and make use of all the new ideas brought to it—a field of increasing importance in a world of diminishing natural resources and burgeoning population.
PLOT:	The film will present a complete life cycle in the reproduction of the white pine, from pollination through maturity, with emphasis upon the role and the techniques of the forest geneticist in shaping the physical and genetic characteristics of the trees. The film will open with a study of the differences between the growth rate and quality of trees allowed to pollinate indiscriminately and those grown by careful genetic selection and control. The techniques shown will include selection of superior trees, grafting in greenhouses, manufacture of pollen bags and their use in protecting white pine seedlings, the laboratory study of genetic processes and the statistical computation of genetic statistical data. The latter two processes will be animated.
IDENTIFICATION:	Students of senior high school and freshman college are portrayed, in the live-action portion, as assisting forest geneticists in all the activities dicated in the plot, with emphasis upon the intellectually stimulating and physically vigorous character of the work of the forest geneticist.
CINEMATIC FORM:	Primarily a live-action film, in color, with sequences in *animation* used to present genetic and statistical phenomena. Animation must be used because the processes of meiotic cell division and chromosome reduction are too diffuse and subtle to be presented clearly by any known photomicrography process. The concepts of selective breeding and crosspollination cannot be adequately shown by live-action photography because of the difficulty of staging the process and controlling it for photography. And the concepts of ''heritability,'' ''genetic differential,'' and ''genetic gain'' are concepts having no counterpart in reality which can be visualized by means other than animation.

books pertaining to the subject at hand. In the case of sales films or television commercials, dig deeply into the characteristics of the product and delve thoroughly through the life space conditions of the target audience.

☐ The kind of information to search for is *visual* information that will make the processes to be animated self-explanatory. Although narration can be used to clarify content, do not plan to carry key information in the commentary. The eye remembers, the ear forgets; at least 90 percent of the film's content should be visual.

☐ Assemble more information about the subject than can be included in the film. There may come a point in the presentation of the subject when the original interpretation proves unworkable or less effective than anticipated. Then alternative approaches may be suggested by research material originally thought to be superfluous.

☐ Work from authoritative written sources, rather than taking the word of professionals in matters of factual accuracy. It is surprising how often even experts make minor errors. Because the instructional film maker bears the responsibility for what finally reaches the screen, he is not supposed to be human—he is supposed to be right. It is prudent to keep a record of all the sources of information used in the animation.

☐ Use the expert primarily as the means of locating authoritative sources of information. Any man qualified in his field can direct the film maker to the books and periodicals that contain the bedrock facts necessary to an instructional, sales, or industrial film. If you encounter technological jargon, use the expert again for a translation of the information into everyday English.

☐ Try to understand the content clearly. When dealing with scientific and technological concepts, this may be very difficult, but it is important that a film maker have a working knowledge of his subject matter.

TREATMENT

Once the research material has been compiled, the next phase of production is to organize the selected information into a logical sequence and embody it in a "treatment" (Figure 6.2). A treatment is a two- or three-page prose description of the projected film. It should indicate where the film will begin, what will constitute the main body of the film, and how it will conclude. It is an expansion of the "plot" dimension of the synopsis, and it gives a fairly detailed summary of content organization.

☐ A treatment should indicate what information has been selected from the mass of researched material for inclusion in the animation. If the subject is densely factual, limit the technical content and indicate in the treatment what those limits are. Identify the specific content points that are appropriate for animation. If a great deal of commentary is needed to explain what cannot be shown on the screen, revise the approach or reconsider the use of media other than animation.

SCRIPT

The script is the final written presentation of the subject before the film is actually produced. Its format is that of a split page; references to visual elements are on the left and references to sound on the right (Figure 6.3). The split page enables the film maker to establish a working relationship between visual content and aural elements of narration, music, and sound effects.

☐ *Instructional films.* Scholars, universities, and research groups have conducted tests to determine the optimum formulation of content for an effective instructional film. Some of their conclusions are directly applicable to script writing for animation.

☐ The objectives of an instructional film should be specific, limited in number, and determined by the capabilities of the target audience. The viewer should be told at the beginning of the film what he is expected to learn from it. In addition, each new sequence or major segment of the film should be introduced by telling the viewer what he can expect to learn from it.

☐ Similarly, as each major portion of knowledge within the film is completed, briefly summarize it, relating it to what the viewer is expected to learn. The more unfamiliar the concept is to the target audience, the more carefully it must be summarized at the conclusion of each major sequence. At the conclusion of the film present a summary of the major points and indicate what the viewer should have learned from the film.

☐ The content should be presented no faster than the target audience can absorb it. This may seem obvious, but many instructional films are paced at the rate of theatrical entertainment films, which is far too fast. The rate of development of a film should be deliberately decreased when the target audience brings little pertinent background to the film. For example, a film depicting women's monthly ovulation in relation

FIGURE 6.2 Treatment of animation: *Tree Improvement and Genetics.* Courtesy of the State University College of Forestry at Syracuse, New York.

When a student leans over to look through the microscope, in the last scene of the live action portion, we dissolve to the first of eight stages of meiotic division in the development of the mature pollen grain. The animation depicts the following phases: achesporial, zygonema, pachynema, diakenesis, late anaphase I, anaphase II, quartet of grains within the walls of MMC, and the mature pollen grain, all the while progressively changing the shape and color of the cell according to the stage of microsporogenesis.

The second sequence of animation depicts the process of pollination. Pollen grains are shown drifting from a selected pine having one set of characteristics to another pine having a second set of characteristics. A detail presents a branch bearing female flowers in the path of the drifting pollen. An extreme closeup of a female flower reveals in schematic animation what takes place during the union of a male gamete with an egg.

The next sequence shows, with pop-ons, the protean tree forms that can issue from these two trees through the random reduction and recombining of their chromosomes.

Then, the possible effects of a single color gene pair are shown in three sample seedlings. The presence of A-1, A-1 in one seedling causes it to be dark green. The presence of A-1, A-2 (recessive) still permits the second seedling to be a true green color. But in the third seedling, when only A-2, A-2 are present, the color of the pine has a strong yellow cast.

The statistical methods of determining genetic gain are presented. The tallest tree is compared to the even aged population in which it is growing. The numerical difference, the "selection differential," is used to determine inheritance patterns and the potential genetic control. The degree of genetic control is termed "heritability." These concepts are given symbolic form and their mathematical and biological relationships depicted by scratchoff techniques in achieving an accurate estimate of the possible degree of "genetic gain."

The animation sequences end and we dissolve to live action.

ANIMATED FILM

(11) C.U. Mature pollen grain, with chromosome development complete and nucleus defined.

DISSOLVE TO:

(12) E.S. Two distinctively contoured pines are set off from the forest. The pollen drift pattern from one to the other is animated.

(13) M.S. A white pine branch bearing female flowers.

ZOOM IN: Slowly, to a detail of one female flower being fertilized.

DISSOLVE TO:

(14) A diagrammatic design: The two parent trees at the top are stylized to emphasize their salient physical characteristics. POP-ON the symbolic variety of tree shapes and characteristics that the issue can have.

DISSOLVE TO:

(15) Three seedlings in grey silhouette grow side by side. As a gene designation appears, the selected pine assumes the appropriate color . . . A-1, A-1 comes down to stop before the left seedling, and it becomes dark green.

NARRATOR: (with finality) . . . And these divisions finally form the male gametes, or pollen grains.

NARRATOR: (after a pause) During pollination, the male chromosomes are carried in the pollen grains to—

the female flowers.

MUSIC: (pastoral and low)

MUSIC UNDER:

NARRATOR: At fertilization, the union of a male nucleus with a female nucleus produces the first cell of a new tree embryo.

MUSIC: (Continues quietly through animation of the fertilization process.)

MUSIC OUT:

NARRATOR: From the two parent trees—

a variety of new tree types are formed through the random reduction and recombining of chromosomes.

NARRATOR: Traits of interest in forest genetics are sometimes governed by a single gene pair—one gene being received on a chromosome from each parent. . .The dominant color gene A-1, A-1 causes the pine seedling on the left to be dark green.

FIGURE 6.3 Script of animation: *Tree Improvement and Genetics.* Courtesy of the State University College of Forestry at Syracuse, New York.

to birth control should present its content far more slowly for an audience of women with a grade school education than for an audience of women with a high school education. The latter audience brings a background of biological knowledge to the film which the former most probably does not have.

☐ The rate of development should also decrease when new words or new visual concepts are introduced. When a film on human anatomy presents the shinbone for the first time, the picture of the bone and the label ''tibia'' should remain on the screen long enough for the viewer to identify the new word with the new object. The greater the number of new items the viewer is expected to learn from a single film, the longer the final items in the sequence should be held on the screen.

☐ Finally, the rate of development should slow to a snail's pace if the viewer is expected to learn a manual skill from watching the film. If the skill is one to be practiced as the film progresses, it may be necessary to plan for gaps allowing the viewer to execute each step of the skill as the film progresses.

☐ There is one aspect of teaching a skill that should be considered in writing a script—learning to perform a skill usually means making some mistakes. Film research indicates that it is desirable to show what can go wrong while learning a skill and how to correct the errors. Plan to show the viewer how to perform the skill correctly. Then demonstrate what can go wrong and how to correct possible errors. Finally, repeat the correct way of executing the skill.

☐ Repetition is important to the retention of learning. New concepts and skills are retained only temporarily unless they are reinforced by repetition. This repetition can often be provided by the summaries and conclusion. In films teaching skills, the repetition should be provided by showing the right way to execute the skill more than once. Repetition may also be provided by film loops and cartridge films.

☐ In summary, remember the following points when writing a script for an instructional film:

1. Limit the number of objectives to those which the target audience can comfortably absorb in a single sitting. One film cannot do everything and be everything.

2. Begin by telling the viewer what he is expected to learn from the film. Tell him what to look for in each major segment of the film.

3. Summarize the content at the conclusion of each major portion of the film. At the conclusion of the film summarize the high points and indicate what the viewer is expected to know or to do.

4. The rate of development should be slower than a theatrical film, and should be correlated with the age, intelligence, film literacy, and level of formal education of the target audience. The rate of development should *decrease* with the presentation of—

new and unfamiliar ideas
content or ideas inherently difficult to understand
new words to be identified with new objects
a skill to be learned from the film

5. When writing a film to teach performance skills, show what errors can be expected as well as how to correct them; then repeat again the correct way of performing the skill.

6. Repeat the knowledge or skill to be learned several times.

STORYBOARD

The storyboard establishes the film's style, continuity, and visual approach (Figure 6.4). Each major change of scene, sequence, or concept in a film should be indicated with a storyboard sketch. Every movement—zooms, pans, turns, and so on—should be indicated by movement lines within the sketch. Sometimes, as in the case of a pan over a long background, more than one sketch may have to be made to show the beginning and the end of a move. A space is usually provided below each sketch for narration, music, and sound effects. It is important to present both picture and sound simultaneously because a visual may often be keyed to a single word.

☐ On a storyboard, a zoom-in is indicated by framing the terminal point of the zoom and drawing arrows toward it from the panel's corners (Figure 6.5). A zoom-out is indicated by reversing the direction of the arrows (Figure 6.6). A long background pan may be indicated by two adjacent sketches with pan line indications (Figure 6.7). Or it may be shown by framing the beginning and end of the pan with sketched squares and indicating the direction of the move by dotted lines and an arrow (Figure 6.8).

☐ The speed of the animated movements determines the number of storyboard sketches needed to clarify each sequence. A greater number of sketches is required for fast action and radical visual changes than for a slow sequence. In extreme cases, as many as 20 or 30 sketches may be required for one minute of screen time.

☐ If the animation involves the teaching of a skill, present the material from a subjective camera angle; i.e., present the mechanism as it looks to the viewer's own eyes as he does

FIGURE 6.4 Storyboard: *Tree Improvement and Genetics*. Courtesy of the State University College of Forestry at Syracuse, New York.

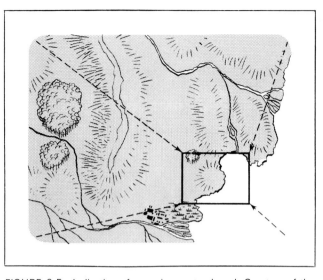

FIGURE 6.5   Indication of zoom-in on storyboard. Courtesy of the U.S. Air Force.

FIGURE 6.6   Indication of zoom-out on storyboard. Courtesy of the U.S. Air Force.

FIGURE 6.7   Indication of background pan in two sketches on storyboard. Courtesy of the U.S. Air Force.

Pan Line Indications

FIGURE 6.8   Indication of background pan in one sketch on story-board. Courtesy of the U.S. Air Force.

FIGURE 6.9   Two aircraft used in World War I. Courtesy of the U S. Air Force.

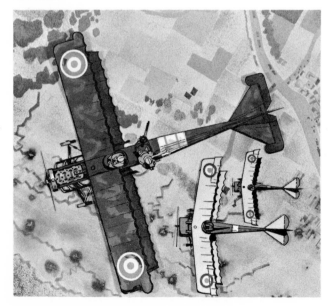

whatever it is he is learning. For example, if the repair or assembly of complex electronic gear is being taught, the assembly should be presented from the same perspective and from the same point of view that the learner will have to assume when he tries to make the assembly. If it is presented from another angle or from many angles in the mistaken notion that the learner will understand it better, the pattern of action may be confused and he may fail to execute it correctly on the job. When teaching a skill, teach it strictly from the learner's point of view.

☐   *Film style.* Film style is developed while making the storyboard drawings and is affected by four factors: the purpose of the film, the essential character of the subject matter, the target audience, and the will of the sponsor. The last is to some degree a matter of luck. Most sponsors have the good sense to let a qualified film maker exercise his own judgment. Some, however, consider themselves omniscient in their specialties, and the film maker can only struggle manfully for the right to use the style he feels is most appropriate.

☐   In general, however, the purpose of the film, the nature of the subject matter, and the educational background of the target audience should be the determining factors in selecting a film style. The nature of the content itself often dictates the style of animation as in films dealing with scientific or technological concepts. But there are other concepts which can be communicated with a wide range of interpretations.

☐   A realistic approach should be used in presentations which are to be taken literally by the viewer. This is especially true when objects are being studied for identification purposes, when an idea for a new structural concept is being projected or when a new skill is being taught.

☐   Figure 6.9 shows a scene from an Air Force film on the history of warplanes which depicts two types of aircraft used widely during World War I. Their structural configurations are crisply and clearly rendered for easy recognition and identification. Figures 6.10a and 6.10b show astronauts separating a cargo nose from the rocket which has carried it into space and assembling a space station. Tomorrow's realities are visualized for study today by "realistic" animation.

☐   The realistic approach is also preferable when the target audience has a low level of film literacy or a poor educational background. The less the viewer brings to the film, the closer to recognizable reality the style should be. It is worth remembering that films produced in a realistic style can be understood and interpreted correctly by almost everybody; each step away from realism may narrow the size of the potential target audience.

☐ Schematic interpretation is a step away from realism. Any departure from realism requires some film literacy and subject matter sophistication on the part of the viewer. The film maker's audience must already have a body of pertinent knowledge to which they can relate the new information. The film maker must therefore be aware of what the audience knows and is capable of understanding before he begins to interpret the subject with schematic forms.

☐ Perhaps the most common application of schematic film style is a cutaway to reveal hidden layers or the functioning of internal parts (Figure 6.11). A layman watching this animation may bring enough knowledge and film literacy to follow it in a general way, but only a trained technician will understand all the schematically stated ramifications.

☐ The use of symbols to represent functions and ideas is also characteristic of schematic abstraction (Figure 6.12). The diagrammatic treatment of the medical use of tracer atoms does not require a knowledge of anatomy for understanding, but does require a high level of film literacy and a background of cultural associations. To the average American or European the symbolism is simple and obvious, but to members of cultural subgroups and to persons in other parts of the world it may seem incomprehensible.

☐ In Figure 6.13, we go beyond commonly recognized symbolism and knowledge to a schematic interpretation of a piston engine which at first glance appears to be pure abstract art. The target audience of technicians for whom this film is intended is obviously qualified to recognize the subject and to absorb ideas related to it. But this animated interpretation is not comprehensible to the layman.

☐ A third type of cartoon style is the whimsical cartoon approach (Figure 6.14). In general, cartoons are most suitable for communicating ideas having emotional overtones, such as morals, manners, ethics and attitudes. Here the rate of development may quicken to a theatrical pace.

☐ Cartoons can be used to sugar-coat unpalatable subjects for children. For example, basic mathematics is simplified by showing the ''golden rectangle'' and demonstrating that the ancient Greeks applied its proportions in the Parthenon (Figure 6.15). This is followed by a scene in which Donald Duck tries to fit his own shape into the golden rectangle—and discovers to his dismay that his proportions are not golden (Figure 6.16).

☐ Cartoons are effective in drawing romantic analogies and

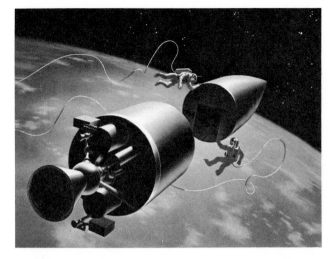

FIGURE 6.10a *Tomorrow the Moon.* Copyright © 1955 Walt Disney Productions.

FIGURE 6.10b *Tomorrow the Moon.* Copyright © 1955 Walt Disney Productions.

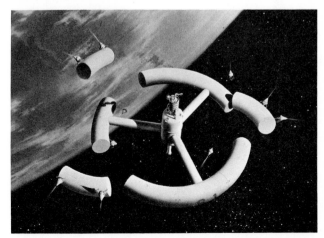

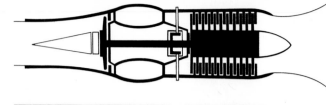

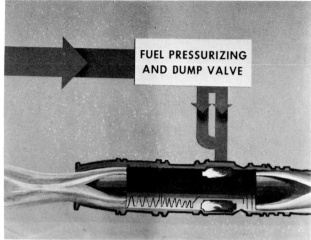

FIGURE 6.11   Cutaway. Courtesy of the U.S. Air Force.

FIGURE 6.12   *Our Friend the Atom*. Copyright © 1957 Walt Disney Productions.

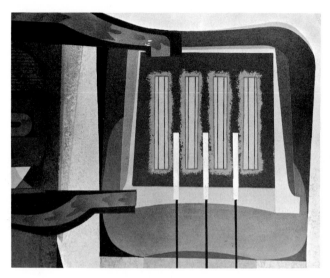

FIGURE 6.13   Piston. Courtesy of the U.S. Air Force.

FIGURE 6.14   *Animal Movie* by Grant Munro and Ron Tunis. Courtesy of the National Film Board of Canada.

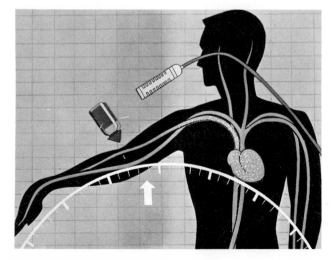

humanizing science. In *Our Friend the Atom,* atomic power is personified as a potentially destructive genie or a beneficent giant (Figure 6.17). The two interpretations are the basis of a generalized explanation of the principles of atomic power.

☐ Cartoons can make a strong appeal in public affairs programming. A sequence depicting the disgust of wild animals at the refuse left in the forest by litterbugs is likely to drum home the message (Figure 6.18). And a lecture bristling with statistics is probably less effective in reducing pedestrian mayhem than is the sight of Goofy beset by savage automobiles (Figure 6.19).

☐ *Storyboard critique.* This is the time to discover whether the film style, continuity, and visual presentation have worked out as anticipated. If they do not, the order of scenes and sequences may be changed; new scenes and sequences may be added and old ones deleted. One test of the pictorial effectiveness of the storyboard is its ability to communicate the essence of the content without recourse to the script. The more effectively the story is told in pictures the more certain it is that the film will achieve the film maker's purpose.

☐ There are several methods of predicting the effectiveness of the finished film. The storyboard panels may be photo-

FIGURE 6.15 *Donald in Mathmagic Land.* Copyright ⓒ 1959 Walt Disney Productions.

FIGURE 6.16   *Donald in Mathmagic Land.* Copyright © 1959 Walt Disney Productions.

FIGURE 6.17   *Our Friend the Atom.* Copyright © 1957 Walt Disney Productions.

FIGURE 6.18   *The Litterbug.* Copyright © 1961 Walt Disney Productions.

FIGURE 6.19   *Motor Mania.* Copyright © Walt Disney Productions.

graphed in filmstrip form and projected on a screen before a group representative of the target audience. A test given immediately after the screening will reveal whether there are any major gaps in their comprehension of the film's content. An alternative way, and one which more closely approximates the finished film, is to photograph the storyboard panels on the animation stand; each scene is photographed for the same length of time it will appear on the screen in the finished film. For projection to the sample audience, the film maker may narrate the commentary, or the film can have a magnetic strip applied to one side and the narration may be dubbed onto the film for the closest possible approximation to the finished production.

☐ Flexibility is the great advantage of the storyboard. It enables the film maker to explore different avenues of film style without a major investment of time. If the film does not measure up in terms of communication effectiveness, it is a simple matter to change things at this stage. It is far easier to modify a storyboard than to make changes in visual concept after production is under way.

☐ A word of caution about storyboards. Be careful to continue thinking in terms of motion. Do not become mesmerized by a series of attractive stills. A storyboard is a step toward the final film, but it does not have movement, spoken commentary, music, or sound effects. While doing a storyboard, it is easy to forget that nothing kills the vitality of an animated film more quickly than static images projected on the screen. If the movement stops, the film is dead. The viewer can be made to concentrate on an image through full or limited animation—*but make the image move!*

chapter 7
PLANNING AND DRAWING CARTOON ANIMATION

CARTOON short subjects in theaters and on television have conditioned almost everyone to anticipate a cartoon with pleasure. Cartoon animation is used in educational films to make people care, to involve them emotionally by presenting appealing characters in provocative situations.

☐ The key to effective cartooning is the appeal of the characters. A cartoon character should have attractive human qualities which make the viewer identify with him and experience his feelings. And because of the expense of full animation, the character should be simple to draw and quickly identifiable. In addition to being sympathetic and identifiable, the character should embody the idea being taught. Private Snafu of World War II fame was the essence of a soldier who could do nothing right—and had to pay the consequences.

☐ A cartoon character is most effective when he has had long exposure to the target audience and his personality has become well known. A certain peppery little duck has been used very effectively to teach safety practices (Figure 7.1). Nearly everyone is aware of his short supply of patience, and this common knowledge simplifies the job of making an educational point. With a known cartoon character, the film maker need only contrive a situation which the viewer can recognize and put the established character into it.

FIGURE 7.1 *How To Have an Accident at Work.* Copyright © 1959 Walt Disney Productions.

ANIMATED FILM

Many of us carry pictures in our mind of other persons, generalized in terms of age, sex, physical type, occupation, and clothing. The cowboy is thought of as a lanky, raw-boned man of action in a ten-gallon hat, swinging chaps, and jingling spurs. The professor is pictured as a plump, tweedy, introspective type, who trails pipe ashes and has a tenuous grip on reality. These stereotypes are caricatures which nevertheless often have a grain of truth in them. They afford a set of popular associations upon which to build easily recognizable cartoon characters.

☐ Not all scientists bear a marked resemblance to Albert Einstein, but a bald head and white mustache do help the viewer to identify a certain kind of person (Figure 7.2). Although all brainy young men do not necessarily dress trimly and wear horn-rimmed glasses, this popular stereotype can be useful to the animator (Figure 7.3). The typical teenage girl friend of the typical young intellectual may not sport a pony-tail, shorts, and sandals, but this image is a generally accepted stereotype (Figure 7.4). While all boys from the toddling to the trotting age do not have ovoid shapes and unruly mops of hair, these characteristics comprise a stereotype (Figure 7.5).

☐ A character's face and posture are often a mirror of his temperament. A happy, good-natured character can be suggested by a rounded, open countenance and an upright, positive stance (Figure 7.6). An irascible, tendentious temperament can be shown by pinched and shriveled features and a crouching, defiant posture (Figure 7.7). These are, of course, polar extremes; the many different styles of temperament and behavior can be shown by an equally wide variety of physical shapes and postures.

☐ Clothes make the character. In general, the jollier and happier the individual's nature, the lighter and gayer his clothing usually is and the jauntier is his manner of wearing it. Conversely, a gloomy, phlegmatic type is characteristically shown in dark, ill-fitting clothes. Clothing such as the uniform of a policeman or the space suits of astronauts identify the subject's occupation. And clothing, of course, places characters in their historical context (Figures 7.8a, 7.8b, and 7.8c).

☐ Remember to think about "types" when planning cartoon characters. Your audience will accept educational material more quickly when cartoon characters are familiar and easily identifiable. But keep in mind that a character should also be a unique individual endowed with distinctive details. If he is

FIGURE 7.2   Scientific type. Courtesy of Jiro Enterprises, Inc.

FIGURE 7.3   Young intellectual type. Courtesy of Jiro Enterprises, Inc.

FIGURE 7.4   Typical teenager. Courtesy of Jiro Enterprises, Inc.

FIGURE 7.5   Characteristic small boy. Courtesy of Jiro Enterprises, Inc.

FIGURE 7.6   Good-natured personalities. © Hanna-Barbera Productions, Inc., 1969.

FIGURE 7.7   Irascible temperament. Courtesy of United Productions of America and Columbia Pictures Corporation.

FIGURE 7.8a   Clothing and occupation. Courtesy of United Productions of America and Columbia Pictures Corporation.

FIGURE 7.8c   Clothing and stereotypes: *Victory Through Airpower.* Copyright © Walt Disney Productions.

FIGURE 7.8b   Clothing and historical context: *Man in Flight.* Copyright © 1957 Walt Disney Productions.

FIGURE 7.9   Jazz musician. Courtesy of Ernest Pintoff.

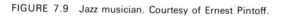

to excite the interest of the audience and be credible as a living creature, each cartoon character should have a unique face, physique, and manner of walking, talking, and gesturing. The musician being interviewed here is an unmistakable type from the smoke-filled world of jazz, but his features, stance, and expression give him the stamp of individuality (Figure 7.9). By giving generalized types unique personalities, we can present a set of widely differing characters who nevertheless suggest familiar human types. Exaggeration is the key to individuality, but exaggeration within the type.

PROPORTIONS

The proportions of cartoon figures vary according to whether the figures are drawn for theater or classroom projection or for television broadcasting. Since the viewing screen is quite large for theater or classroom projection, the cartoon characters often have proportions approximating those of a living person. But use of these same proportions on a small television screen results in a figure whose head is so small that it becomes difficult to distinguish his facial expressions.

☐   For television animation, therefore, the size of the head is often one-fourth to one-third the height of the entire figure. This ratio is generally accepted as the norm for television; it permits the film maker to express shades of meaning through facial expressions while at the same time indicating a full-length figure. The necessity of punching home a commercial in as little as 10 seconds has produced situations where the head is 50 per cent of the figure's height. There is little time for a build-up on television; the face is the all-important vehicle of communication and the body almost a vestigial organ.

MODEL SHEETS

While head-to-figure ratios may fluctuate from film to film and from character to character, each cartoon character should maintain consistent proportions within a given film, except at moments of extreme distortion for dramatic purposes.

☐   The head is the unit of measure for the rest of the body. The relative proportions of the trunk to the arms and legs, and the relationship of the limbs to each other, are planned in terms of the head units which remain consistent throughout the film. Once the proportions have been established, prepare a model sheet which should be referred to throughout the production (Figure 7.10).

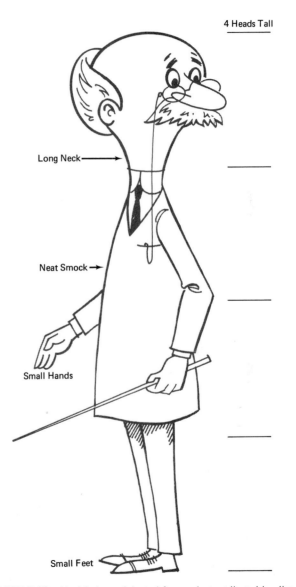

4 Heads Tall

Long Neck →

Neat Smock →

Small Hands

Small Feet

FIGURE 7.10   Model sheet. Adapted from cels contributed by Jiro Enterprises, Inc.

☐ The character must be recognizable from every viewpoint. Sometimes inconsistencies occur when planning a cartoon personality from the front and side. When the figure is animated, it undergoes a disturbing transformation when making a move which involves turning around. This usually happens when the film maker endows his character with clever details that are difficult to indicate clearly from different points of view. These features should be reduced to symbols which can be recognized from any angle.

☐ Remember that a cartoon character should be easy to draw. Even extensive use of limited animation and filmograph techniques does not completely eliminate the need for a large number of drawings and cels. Unless each detail is reduced to essentials, a character may require an overly long time to animate. Make up a second model sheet that shows each character in a wide range of emotional expressions and depicts each detail from a variety of angles (Figure 7.11).

☐ The relative sizes of the various characters should be consistent, except at dramatic highpoints, throughout the film. For this reason a third model sheet should be drawn which establishes the size and proportion of each character as he relates to every other character in the film (Figure 7.12). Thus, when each animator is working on his own sequence of the film, he will not modify the relative sizes of the various characters.

FIGURE 7.11   Model sketches of Magoo's face. Courtesy of United Productions of America and Columbia Pictures Corporation.

CARTOON STYLE

Theoretically, cartoon style is dictated absolutely by the individual film maker. But artistic fashion and the economic facts of life usually combine to encourage a style which is economically feasible while being acceptable to the largest possible audience. The pre-eminent finished cartoon style is seen in Disney productions (Figure 7.13). Using a style of romantic realism, every character, every layout, every move, and every shape, form, and rendered line is conceived and executed in full animation with maximum refinement.

☐ The styles which have emerged since World War II depart from this tradition of semi-realistic rendering and instead rely heavily on broadly designed forms and spontaneously executed lines (Figure 7.14). The new modes of cartooning range from slight modifications of form and perspective to expressionistic distortion (Figure 7.15). Rendering techniques have been developed in which the telegraphic line itself is an aesthetic factor and a means of communication and expression (Figure 7.16). These new techniques have proved exciting to many aficionados of cartooning techniques and have found limited use in television commercials. But few films done in this manner have enjoyed the wide popularity of the more finely rendered films. The style you choose depends greatly upon your budget, the purpose of your film, and the tastes of your audience.

LAYOUT

Layout in animation consists of determining where the subject will move and how it will look in relation to the background (Figure 7.17). Unless the subject and background are coordinated by the layout artist, the animated figure may not stand out distinctly or may appear, for example, to have a tree grow-

FIGURE 7.12 Comparative sizes model sheet. Adapted from cels contributed by Jiro Enterprises, Inc.

ing from the top of his head or branches sprouting from his ears. In limited animation films where decorative design is most important, the subject-background relationship must be carefully worked out for each aspect of a subject's move through every background.

☐ In animation, the traditional aspects of composition—formal and informal balance and so forth—do not truly apply except at points where the action pauses. Ordinarily, animation employs a type of informal balance—a dynamic subject balances a static area. Movement itself is treated as an element of the compositional balance. The compositional aspects of layout are dealt with in detail in Chapter 9.

FIGURE 7.13   Romantic realism: *Alice in Wonderland*. Copyright ©
.Walt Disney Productions.

FIGURE 7.14   Broadly designed cartoon style. Courtesy of United Productions of America and Columbia Pictures Corporation.

SPEED AND RATE OF EXPOSURE

Most animation is exposed at a rate of 2 frames per drawing, i.e., 12 drawings per second. We can, of course, get very smooth animation by doing 24 drawings for each second of screen time, but only in special cases does the difference in effect justify this doubling of work and expense. Exposing on ''twos'' suffices for all but the slowest and the fastest actions in animation.

☐ Where the animated object is moving at high speed, so that there is a substantial variation from one drawing to the next, as in the case of a flying object or a running figure, the animation is photographed on ''ones''—one frame of film exposed per drawing. The brief exposure aids the persistence of vision in bridging the gap between drawings. Where the subject is moving slowly, the variation between drawings is small, as in a sequence showing the journey of a snail, the animation may be photographed on ''threes''—3 frames of film per drawing. Errors in animation are easily detectable at a 3-frame exposure rate, and we should photograph on threes only when absolutely necessary. Moreover, movements whose individual components are held longer than 2 frames tend to have a slightly staccato flicker.

☐ The speed of the subject's move determines the number of drawings needed. A 2-second movement is animated with 24 drawings (photographed on twos). If the same movement is slowed down and made in 4 seconds, 48 drawings are needed to animate it. The slower the speed of the animated figure on the screen, the greater the number of drawings will be needed; the faster the speed of the figure on the screen, the fewer will be needed. At high speeds, however, there is a limit to the variation in drawings which persistence of vision can blend into a continuous flow of motion. When this point is reached, we animate "blurs" or speed lines to carry the flow of the action.

☐ This leads to the question of actual speed and illusionary speed. In many instances, the literal presentation of actual speed appears wrong on the screen. This is particularly true when two objects of radically different sizes are moving in relationship to each other, as where the moon circles the earth while the latter moves slowly in its solar orbit (Figure 7.18a). If the moon is animated to move at the same rate in proportion to its size on the far side of the earth as it does on the near side, it will appear to creep along the far side and then roar across the near side. Therefore, the moon's circuit of the earth must be presented at a less than natural speed on the near side in order to appear to move at a consistent and normal speed. Problems of this nature appear repeatedly when doing

FIGURE 7.15 Distortion in cartoon style. Courtesy of the National Film Board of Canada.

FIGURE 7.16 Calligraphic cartoon style. Courtesy of International Tournée of Animation.

animation for fields like astronomy, physics, and chemistry.

☐ A similar problem appears when depicting two objects moving parallel to each other across the screen (Figure 7.18b). Here four rockets are being fired simultaneously. If each rocket were animated at the same speed, the rockets in the foreground would appear to be moving much faster than those in the background. Only by proportionately exaggerating the speed of the distant rockets and understating the speed of the near rockets can the four be made to appear synchronized.

☐ How fast to make a given subject move across the screen so it appears to pass at the right speed is a matter of experience. But now is the time to become aware that apparent accuracy is sometimes a matter of unnatural distortion. One factor of speed to bear in mind is the size of the figure on the screen. The closer the action is to the camera, the bigger the subject looks on the screen and the less time it takes to traverse a given distance (Figure 7.18c). Conversely, the farther the action is from the camera, the smaller the subject appears and the longer it takes to complete its move.

FIGURE 7.17 Layout. Courtesy of FilmFair.

FIGURE 7.18a Apparent change of speed.

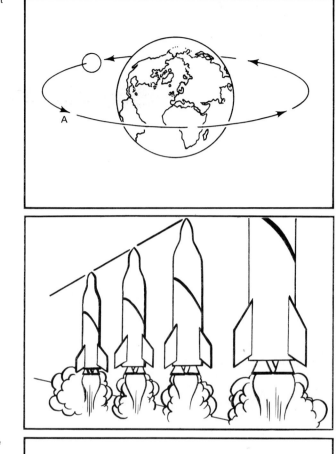

FIGURE 7.18b Proportional speed.

FIGURE 7.18c Distance and speed.

BEAT AND TIMING

A concept called "beat" is used to establish the tempo of animation. It is a measure of time which indicates the rhythm of movement in an animated sequence. A "24 beat" is simply one beat per second, or to put it cinematically, one beat every 24 frames. A "12 beat" is 2 beats per second, or one for every 12 frames. An "8 beat" is 3 beats per second, or one for every 8 frames. Tap your finger once a second, then twice a second, and then three times a second. Notice the radical increase in the tempo of the tapping. With each increase in the number of taps per second, there is a corresponding increase in the speed of the presented animation.

☐ A 12 beat is used for most conventional actions like walking about, climbing stairs, digging, and so on. A 9 beat or an 8 beat is used to show objects moving at high speeds or to generate emotional excitement. The beat of the animation is determined by the natural accents or cycles of the movement. An arbitary, even beat results in lifeless movement. A sense of rhythm is called for, a feeling for the "beat" of the movement.

☐ Imagine a boy of ten striding across the screen in a sprightly manner from point A to point B. Tap a finger every time the boy's feet touch the ground until you feel he has reached B. Using a stopwatch, repeat this imaginary sequence three or four times, and write down the average time for the movement and the number of finger taps. The number of finger

taps per second is the beat; you can then plan your drawings around this tempo. Fine gradations of tempo require a metronome, but for most nontheatrical animation a stopwatch will suffice.

☐ The concept of beat and movement becomes more sophisticated when animating a figure to convey subtleties of emotional meaning. When an animated figure walks across the screen, every one of his movements should be thought of in terms of who he is, what he is, where he is going, and why he is going there.

☐ A laborer crossing the screen hunches forward as if he were still using his shovel. A banker walks with solemn dignity. A youngster scurries here and strolls there, free to come and go as he pleases. A teen-ager bounces along with the jaunty manner of one who knows all the answers, though he has not heard the questions yet. A middle-aged man has the solid carriage of mature confidence. A senior citizen moves carefully, conserving whatever time is left to him.

☐ Where is the character going and why is he going there? If, like a chicken, a young man is merely crossing the road to get to the other side, his speed is affected only by traffic. If he is crossing the street to mail a letter, his walk is a bit more purposeful. If he is about to meet a young lady, his walk will be eager. If he is late for work, his walk is quick and nervous. Think about these psychological factors when planning the animation of a figure for even as simple an action as a walk.

☐ Different kinds of action call for different beats and timing, all conforming to the unique characteristics of each animated subject. With experience, the film maker will develop an instinct for the beat of different figures performing different actions under varying conditions.

PERSPECTIVE

In art, perspective is a method of presenting three-dimensional objects realistically on a two-dimensional surface. It is based on the fact that parallel lines appear to converge to a single vanishing point on the horizon (Figure 7.19). The chief methods of creating this illusion, in animation, are linear perspective and the systematic diminution in the size of objects and figures as they recede in the distance. A grasp of the principles of perspective is important; if the perspective in any animated sequence is slightly inaccurate, the error is immediately evident to the viewer.

☐ Perspective in animation is planned by determining the size

FIGURE 7.19 Perspective.

of the object to be animated at the beginning and the terminal points of its move. The distance between the two points is divided into increments which decrease in length as the subject departs toward the horizon or increase in length as the subject approaches the viewer. Because the actual movement on the drawings is small, there is a tendency to break down the distance into too few increments. The result may be a Bunyunesque character apparently capable of striding a hundred yards at a step. Be sure to make the increments proportional to the apparent distance in perspective.

☐   Many actions involving a change of relation to the horizon are not of the straight "railroad track to the vanishing point" variety. Most follow an irregular path, but the same principle applies. Establish the beginning and end positions of the move; draw a center line depicting the path the subject is to travel, and then mark off increments of diminishing length for the animated figure to follow. Irregular paths which are primarily horizontal are governed by the same principle; any variation in the subject's distance from the viewer must be reflected in a change of size corresponding to the changed relation.

☐   Perspective has dramatic uses. As a rule, any character viewed from a low perspective conveys an image of strength, power, and menace (Figure 7.20). And the closer to the animated character the view is photographed, the stronger is the connotation of power.

☐   Conversely, any character viewed from a high perspective presents an image of weakness and passivity. The greater the distance between character and viewer and the smaller the character is in relation to his environment, the weaker he will appear to be. A zoom-out from a medium or a close shot to a master scene conveys an impression of diminishing strength—especially if done slowly.

☐   Perspective can be distorted to dramatize an extraordinary situation or point of view. During one stage of Alice's travels through Wonderland, she found herself transformed into a giant. By first showing a worm's eye view of Alice jammed against the ceiling of a mansion, and then presenting a view of the nearby forest as seen through her eyes, perspective was used to make the unbelievable believable (Figure 7.21).

☐   In review, the following principles of perspective should be borne in mind when doing animation. A movement by the subject toward the horizon should be accompanied by a reduction in its size; conversely, a movement by the subject away from the horizon toward the viewer should be accompanied by an increase in its size. The apparent step sizes taken by a figure

FIGURE 7.20   Low perspective: *Education for Death.* Copyright © Walt Disney Productions.

FIGURE 7.21 Distortion through perspective: *Alice in Wonderland.*
Copyright © Walt Disney Productions.

should decrease or increase with changes in its relation to the horizon. A figure viewed from a low perspective projects power and strength; conversely, a figure viewed from above appears weak and impotent. A zoom-in or -out increases the dramatic effectiveness of the angle being used.

EXTREMES AND IN-BETWEEN

Animating a subject means drawing a series of sketches which progressively depict the action. But this progression is not created by adding a small amount to each new drawing with a wistful hope that it is the correct degree of added movement. Instead, the most expressive characteristics of the movement and its extreme points are sketched first in order to capture the spirit of whatever subject the film maker is animating (Figure 7.22). The in-betweens (drawings sketched in between the extremes) provide the flow of movement from point to point (Figure 7.23).

☐ How many drawings are needed in between any two extremes is determined by the speed of the movement, the distance between the two extremes, and whether the action is being photographed on ones, twos, or threes.

☐ As we know, most animation is planned to be photographed on twos and requires 12 drawings per second of screen time.

☐ In a movement taking one second, we have 2 extremes and 10 in-betweens. But the distance between the 2 extremes is not filled by making the 10 in-betweens equidistant; such an approach yields an effect as wooden as a zoom or a pan executed without appropriate eases. Instead, the equivalent of an ease-in and ease-out should be embodied in the spacing of the in-between drawings. A "spacing guide" is plotted to show how far each in-between drawing should be animated beyond its predecessor in order to portray a smooth and lifelike flow of action between the extremes (Figure 7.24). To make a spacing guide, the total distance between the two extremes is measured. As with zooms and pans, this distance is divided into increments with increase, remain constant, and decrease. The spacing guide customarily covers only half the actual drawing distance because distances between each drawing from the beginning extreme to the midpoint of the action are used conversely from the midpoint to the terminal extreme.

☐ In a traditional studio the animator responsible for a given sequence of action customarily draws only the extremes and most characteristic positions. An assistant cleans up his roughs

FIGURE 7.22 Extremes of an action.

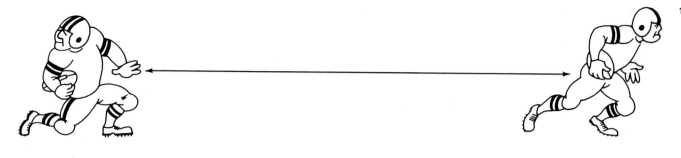

FIGURE 7.23 Extremes with in-between drawings.

and puts in the wide in-betweens. Then another artist, referred to as an "in-betweener," supplies the missing in-between drawings.

THE ANIMATION OF JOHN DOE

As a first exercise, let us animate a simple stick figure walking across the screen. He is "John Doe" of legal and statistical fame; he has no heart and no soul, but he does have two legs to carry him from one side of the screen to the other, two arms to swing as he walks, and a head to indicate which side is up (Figure 7-25).

☐ Let us presume that John is going to take his daily constitutional at a precise and tidy 12 drawings a pace. He starts off standing at screen left. This is the first extreme position. He is now going to walk from *A* to *B* by losing and catching his balance in the process known as "walking."

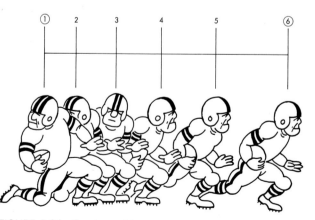

FIGURE 7.24 Spacing guide.

☐ The second extreme position shows John with his weight shifted forward and his left foot raised to the high point of its arc forward. John's right arm has swung back to counterbalance the body shift forward, and his left arm is swinging forward for added balance.

☐ The third extreme position shows the timely arrival of John's foot on the ground. Now the cycle begins with his other foot. His weight shifts forward, his right foot reaches the apogee of its arc toward the ground, his left swings back in counterbalance, and his right arm swings forward. The fourth extreme position shows his right foot on the ground. Now he is ready to begin another cycle of steps in his journey toward *B*.

☐ Once all the extreme positions have been drawn in John's journey from *A* to *B*, the in-between phases must be supplied (Figure 7.26). The number of in-between drawings necessary depends on the speed of the movement. Since in this sequence each step forward is a 12-drawing movement, there should be 6 drawings from the ground position to the extreme height of the arc, and 6 drawings from the height of the arc to the point where his foot steps on the ground. Are these drawings equally spaced? No. Look closely at the in-between drawings. The speed of the foot increases gradually from the beginning to the high point of the step, and then slows down gradually as it approaches the ground. Observe how the intervals relate to the spacing guide beneath the illustration.

☐ Notice the shadow under John's feet. Shadows confirm that the figure is indeed standing on the ground. But do not become involved in animating complicated shadow patterns unless they are needed for building a mood. Usually a small blob under a figure or an object is sufficient. Let the blob travel along with a minimum of fuss. If the animated subject leaves the ground, suggest this by reducing the size of the shadow.

ANTICIPATION, STRETCH, AND SQUASH

Animation requires that even the honest straight line be distorted to create the illusion of lifelike movement. A series of extreme positions may be observed as a basketball player dribbles a ball across the court, stops before the basket, and jumps up to throw the ball into the net (Figure 7.27). Examine the shape of the ball as it is being bounced across the floor. It is perfectly round only through the center of its path up and down. At either extreme, just before it reaches the floor or the player's hand, it stretches in the direction of the immovable object it is about to strike. The ball anticipates making contact and bulges in the direction of the impending counterforce. When the ball hits the floor or is bounced by the ball player's hand, it squashes and flattens to provide the force for the rebound. Notice, however, that the squash is exaggerated beyond what it would normally be. Notice that the stretch is repeated again when the ball leaves the ground. This distortion of "stretch" in anticipation and "squash" in reaction is an accepted technique of film animation. It is a necessary compensation for the loss of three-dimensional form. Distortion endows the flat image with vitality and dynamism.

☐ The distortions of anticipation, stretch, and squash also apply to animate subjects like the basketball player. Notice how the mass of the player's body contracts and thickens in anticipation as he crouches to begin dribbling the ball. As the player starts to run, his body extends itself and becomes attenuated as he races across the court until he pauses at a point before the basket. Again, as the player crouches in anticipation of the throw, his figure contracts and thickens. This pause preceding

FIGURE 7.25 Extremes of a walk.

an extreme action is important dramatically. The longer it is held, the more dynamic the action appears on the screen, and the greater dramatic impact it has. This pause of anticipation should be used before any strong dramatic action.

☐ When the player throws the ball, his body is transformed from a thickened compact shape to a strung-out extension of the path of the released ball. He lands on his feet and his body coils in a crouch—which extends again as he lunges forward to catch the ball now dropping through the net. In this sequence, the basketball player has repeatedly fluctuated in shape from extreme contractions to extreme extensions. Both extremities of action are based upon natural phenomena but are unnatural in their degree of distortion. But when photographed and projected on the screen, however, each extremity will appear to spring from the action—and be perfectly natural.

☐ To repeat, a figure drawn literally, without distortion to compensate for its flatness, appears ''unnatural'' when projected on the screen. Lines must be distorted in the direction of the action in order to appear natural to the eye; a rigid line, even if literally accurate, appears unnatural if animated without distortion. Shapes should also be distorted toward the main direction of the action to give the movement a natural flow and to aid the viewer's eye in bridging the gap between the drawings. When an animated figure or object is about to make contact with a counterforce or immovable surface, it stretches its shape in anticipation of contact. When the animated subject does hit the countervailing force, it squashes more than might be normal in order to appear to have the natural force for a rebound. When a strong dramatic effect is desired, a pause of anticipation is inserted before the action is completed. And

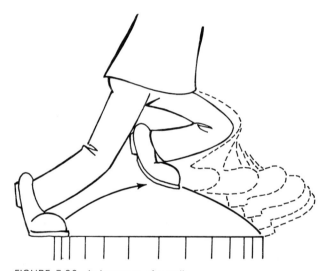

FIGURE 7.26 In-betweens of a walk.

FIGURE 7.27 Anticipation, squash, and stretch.

finally, the two extremes of an action can be exaggerated to give it greater force and vitality.

DRAMATIC DISTORTION

Distortion in cartooning is also used to exaggerate for dramatic effect. The more intense the dramatic moment, the more gross the distortion. In sequences of extreme violence characters may be stretched out like rubber bands or squeezed like putty. Distortion can be used to dramatize meanings and consequences. In *The Winged Scourge* an animated sequence portrays the transmission of malaria by the mosquito and depicts the consequences of infection to a family of farmers (Figure 7.28). The tiny mosquito which has been shown biting the forearm of the breadwinner in the previous scene becomes, through its power to carry a debilitating disease, a gigantic monster sucking the life blood and livelihood from the home of a once vigorous family.

FACIAL EXPRESSION

Facial expressions are formed by the whole face and not by the mouth alone. The shape of the face and the eyes say as much as the mouth about the emotions of the character, and every feature of the face changes with the mood of the moment. In order to give authenticity to the expressions of their characters, most professional animators set up a mirror beside their shadowboxes and act out the expressions they are trying to animate.

☐ When developing a cartoon character, experiment at length with facial expressions. Sometimes a character looks good from certain angles and with certain expressions, but does not lend itself readily to the expressions needed for the film. It is worth the time and trouble to work out all the kinks of personality and characterization; the character's face should be a fully pliable medium of expression before the animation is begun. Simplify the features so the face can pass through many hands without being subtly modified.

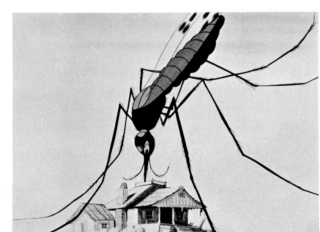

FIGURE 7.28 Dramatic distortion: *The Winged Scourge.* Copyright © Walt Disney Productions.

LIP MOVEMENTS

Simplicity is the secret of successful lip animation. The purpose of lip animation is not to imitate the realistic movements of living persons, but to present those movements in a visual shorthand that passes unchallenged by the viewer.

☐ Realistic or semirealistic cartoon characters offer the

greatest problems in precise lip movements, since they invite comparison with real people. The more fanciful the character, the greater the latitude we have in animating his facial expressions to suit our convenience and purposes.

☐ Lip movements are more than a matter of mechanically shaping the mouth to form words. The personality of the cartoon character and the unique shapes of his lips, eyes, and face are all important factors. Keep in mind when animating these lip movements that the emotional quality of the word has to be drawn too. A ''no'' shouted in a frenzied rage would be drawn differently from a ''no'' spoken in a whisper.

☐ Extreme accuracy in simulating lip movements usually results in overarticulation which appears forced and unnatural; in real life most people are lip-lazy. A simpler and more effective approach, therefore, is to use a visual pattern of vowel lip movements which are accented by consonant letters. Words requiring the pronunciation of *a, c, d, e, g, h, i, j, k, l, n, q, r, s, t, x, y,* and *z* are formed primarily by the tongue and do not require precise lip animation. A simple visual pattern in which the open lips generally match the open vowels of the sound track is usually sufficient (Figure 7.29).

☐ Consonants are the accents of animated speech because they call for closed lip movements. Here, pinpoint accuracy is important because the precision of the consonants gives credibility to the generalized speech patterns of the vowels. Perfect synchronization of words comprising letters like *b, m,* and *p* sharpens a line of dialogue and gives it the crispness of acceptable speech, even if the rest of the sentence is vaguely patterned.

☐ Letters like *o* and *w* call for shaping the mouth in an oval. *V* and *f* tend to make the character look cute because they call for tucking the lower lip under the front teeth. When *v* and *f* are needed in a sentence, underanimate them unless humor is needed.

☐ The first step in lip animation is to record the dialogue on magnetic film, analyze the sound track with a synchronizer and sound recorder or moviola, and transmute every word or syllable to bar sheets or exposure sheets (see Chapter 10). Once this is done, we can tell how much screen time the dialogue will take, and determine how many drawings to make by counting the number of frames within each word and between each word. The second step is to pinpoint the words having accented syllables, the *b*'s, *m*'s, and *p*'s, and the words having the distinctive shapes of *o* and *w*. Then, within these words, locate the frames where the lips meet. These are the cue points for the extreme drawings. The third step is to make the key

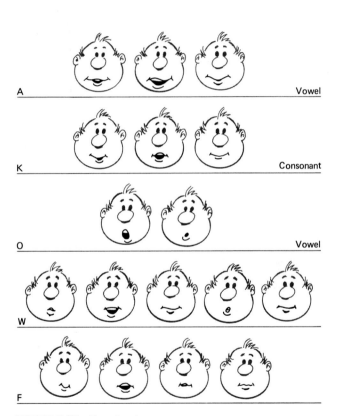

FIGURE 7.29 Lip animation.

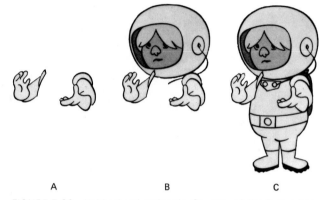

A   B   C

FIGURE 7.30 Held cel and cycle cels. Courtesy of Jiro Enterprises, Inc.

FIGURE 7.31 *Stipple effect.* From the film produced by the Encyclopaedia Britannica Educational Corporation.

drawings for these cue words in order to synchronize the lip movements with the consonants. The fourth step is to draw the in-between words with a simple visual pattern which approximates the rest of the spoken sentence.

CYCLING

"Cycling" is a technique for saving work when animating a figure which is moving at a steady gait. It involves drawing one complete cycle of movement for those limbs that are involved in the action, leaving the remaining portion of the subject in a separate drawing which is used again and again in conjunction with the sequence of cycled drawings. This is the "held drawing" (or held cel) concept (Figure 7.30). In the case of John Doe, one complete series of animated drawings for his moving legs and arms could be made as a cycle; his torso and head are drawn on a separate held cel. On the animation stand, each drawing of the animated leg and arm movements would be superimposed in turn over the held drawing of the head and torso. On the screen the animation appears to have been completely redrawn for each phase of the action.

☐ The held cel concept is very important in technical animation and in the popular limited animation technique. It eliminates the need to redraw, reink, and repaint an image which is held constantly on the screen. For technical animation in which there are flow lines to indicate movements of water, electricity, or materials through some mechanical fixture, it is common practice to put the fixture on a held cel and animate the movement with a cycle of flow cels which are photographed again and again, thereby indicating a lengthy process with only a few cels.

☐ Often a flow effect is desired when the material depicted does not move like water through a pipe, but permeates and seeps and oozes. In this instance the flow effect is better represented by a cycle of dots (Figure 7.31).

☐ The concept of the held cel and cycled movement is a time- and money-saver which has been used to the maximum on television programs. It is standard practice to put an entire figure on a held cel and then to animate the mouth and eyes or arms and legs with a cycle of cels. This very small number of cels is then used in conjunction with cuts, camera zooms and pans, and background pans to fill the greatest possible length of screen time with a minimum of artwork. Often a figure can be made to walk and talk for 60 seconds with no more than a dozen cels. Considering that full animation photographed on ones requires 1,440 cels for this single minute of screen time, cycling represents a considerable economy.

FLIPPING

As each 12-drawing cycle of animation is completed, test the smoothness of the animation of the in-between drawings by "flipping." Put all 12 drawings of each sequence over the pegbars of the drawing disc, with the first extremes on the bottom and the last extreme on the top. Allow each drawing to fall down steadily in sequence. This gives a general idea of how smoothly the action is being developed. However, flipping is not accurate enough to justify proceeding with inking and painting. There may be, and usually are, bumps and irregularities in the animation that do not show up in flipping.

□ Once the complete sequence of animation has been drawn as well as can be judged by flipping, the next step is to shoot a "pencil test." The animation is taken to the animation stand and photographed in the same sequence as the finished cels will be photographed, but with a difference in lighting. Pencil tests are usually lighted from beneath to make the pencil lines stand out strongly enough to be photographed.

□ Since the purpose of a pencil test is solely to determine the smoothness of the animated action when projected on a screen, it may be photographed with any inexpensive film. If the screened animation proves to be as smooth as anticipated, the cels can be inked and painted. A word of caution: The difference in the direction of the lighting requires a difference in the lens opening of the camera. The first time a pencil test is made, run a test to determine the optimum f/stop with one, two, three, and four sheets of animation paper.

□ The basic techniques of animation can be learned by any intelligent layman having the will to do so and an animation stand to work on. But to create cartoon animation with flair and personality, a film maker must either bring an artist's taste and training to the field or set about acquiring it. Mastery of technique does not enable the animator to create believable cartoons and infuse them with life. This takes a proficient and prolific artist; even a very short sequence of full animation requires many drawings and it is impossible to spend long hours niggling over each one. Facility with a pencil, brush, and pen is a prerequisite.

□ Cartooning can be learned by those who are determined to do so, but the path is smoother (as, alas, it is in every field of endeavor) for those born with the knack for it. Related to the talent for caricature is an instinct for dramatic effect. An animator must be able to "feel" the movements and mannerisms which enhance the personality of his cartoon characters. Finally, the nature of cartoon animation requires a talent for reducing characters to their simplest visual elements while retaining their appeal.

chapter 8
CELS: RENDERING AND SPECIAL USES

THE surface on which an animator renders animation artwork is a transparent plastic sheet, .005'' thick, called a ''cel.''* There are three basic types of cels, each differing in size according to its use.

☐ The standard cel commonly used in conventional animation is slightly larger than a 12 field and measures 10½'' × 13''. It is punched to fit over the pegbars of the shadowbox and the animation stand.

☐ The second type of cel has the same N–S dimension (10½'') as the standard cel, but comes in widths of 25'' and 40''—approximately twice and three times the E–W dimension of a standard cel. This cel is used when the wide range of movement of an animated subject across a stationary background would result in the edge of a standard cel moving into the photographed field. Extending the E–W dimension assures that the edge of the cel does not become exposed during the course of the animation movement.

☐ A third and entirely different kind of cel is the ''wild'' cel. This is a large sheet, 25'' × 40'' or 20'' × 50'', of unpunched acetate. The subject, usually a still or a mounted reproduction, can be moved freely under the camera without recourse to pegbars. This technique requires great care and unusual skill to execute successfully. It is used to create irregular movement patterns involving subjects which are extremely difficult to implement by calibration methods.

☐ The animation cel has a fragile surface which is easily smudged, nicked, bent, and scratched. These injuries tend to reflect under the optimum lighting conditions of an animation stand and are often photographed. Although each cel appears on the screen for only 2 frames in full animation, scratches, bends, or creases result in an annoying distraction of fine white lines and light kicks on the screen.

☐ The ounce of prevention here is a pair of the lintfree white cotton gloves used primarily by those who cut motion picture negatives (Figure 8.1). These gloves are inexpensive and can be purchased by the dozen from cinema supply houses. Cut the tips off the thumb and the first two fingers of the glove for your drawing hand; this permits direct contact with the pen or brush, while precluding direct contact with the cel.

INKING

Cels are inked by mounting the animation drawing over the pegbars of the shadowbox and laying the plastic cel over the

---

*It is sometimes spelled ''cell,'' but this has biological connotations which could lead to confusion when treating scientific subjects; the first spelling is preferable.

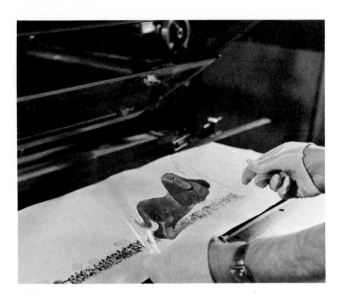

FIGURE 8.1   Gloves.

FIGURE 8.2   Rotating (drawing) disc.

drawing. Each line of the original animation drawing is then carefully traced in ink on the plastic sheet.

☐   A crow-quill pen or a brush is usually used for inking cels. For technical animation inking compasses and ruling pens can be used. The crow-quill pen is more widely employed in technical and educational animation because of the need for accuracy. A brush is used for inking cels when spontaneity and the spark of life is desired; here accuracy is subordinate. But many animators use a brush for precise technical work, and many others use a crow-quill pen for rendering cartoon subjects where a thick and thin line is not required. Choice of tool seems as much a matter of personal preference and skill as of subject matter.

☐   When a crow-quill pen is used, it is advisable to have a range of sizes on hand. Three different penholders, each holding a pen point with a different degree of flexibility and each distinctively marked, will expedite the inking of a wide variety of lines. For those who prefer to ink with a brush, any round sable hair brush capable of forming a fine point will do. The first three sizes, numbers 00, 0, and 1 are widely used. Again, it is wise to have a variety of brushes, each marked for quick identification. Pen points must be wiped clean from time to time or they will clog up. Sable hair brushes must be rinsed and wiped clean periodically, or they will become gummy and unmanageable. At the end of a working day it is important to cleanse a brush thoroughly, otherwise the brush may be left with two or three bristles that stick together permanently, rendering the brush stiff and unusable.

☐   Inking is a more difficult technique than opaquing. For this reason it is advisable for the beginner to use a pen rather than a brush. Everyone has used a pen in daily life, and thus will derive confidence and skill from its familiarity. The steel point provides a degree of substance when first attempting a controlled line; the brush provides no resistance and the slightest wobble of the hand is reflected in the line.

☐   The value of the rotating disc becomes evident when inking a cel. The relationship of the hand holding the pen (or brush) to the angle of the stroke being made on the cel varies constantly. Inking a line from an uncomfortable or unnatural angle results, as often as not, in a wobble toward the end of the stroke—and the cel is ruined. Either the film maker must accommodate himself to the angle of the line being traced, or the drawing and cel must be turned. If a rotating disc is available, it is a simple matter to turn the disc, containing pegbars and artwork, to a convenient angle (Figure 8.2). An investment in a disc yields dividends in ease of execution, better quality of workmanship, fewer ruined cels, and more rapidly completed work.

☐ India ink is used on cels for black-and-white-animation. But the conventional India ink used for illustration is not suitable in unmodified form; it does not readily adhere to the cel and cracks and peels off on drying. A few drops of a plastic adhesive called "noncrawl," however, enable ordinary India ink to adhere in a satisfactory manner. Virtually all of the ink manufacturers produce an ink constituted chemically for adherence to plastic cels.

☐ But even an experienced artist is in for a surprise when he tries rendering on plastic cels. Plastic is slick and smooth; it lacks the "tooth" normally found on painting surfaces which aids in drawing the ink from the pen or brush. In addition, the chemical additive which enables the ink to adhere to the cel also makes it flow slowly—sometimes it hardly flows at all. As a consequence of the smoothness of the surface and the density of the medium, the film maker must get used to rendering at a relatively slow speed. A supply of wiping rags and a reservoir of patience are valuable.

☐ *Colored ink lines.* Animation need not be inked in black outline only. Black is the most popular choice because it delineates the subject crisply and helps make it stand out from its background. In some kinds of animation, however, such conspicuous delineation may not be desirable. In these cases a line may be rendered in a color which matches the paint; such matching is called a "self-line." Animators sometimes mix colored inks with their black inks to strike a compromise between the two or to lend the body of black pigment to an excessively transparent colored ink. When the background is very dark it is sometimes preferable to use white ink to make the subject stand out distinctly.

☐ *Dry brush.* It was mentioned in the previous chapter that when the animated action is too fast for the eye to bridge when photographed on ones, we animate "blurs." These blurs can be drawn by dipping a flat sable brush into ink or paint, wiping it nearly dry, and then drawing the shape of the animated figure on cells with strokes in the direction of the movement. When these animated blurs are photographed, they will give an effect of furious activity and speed.

☐ *The dotted line.* A convenient way of rendering flow charts is to use charting tape, which comes prerendered with a wide selection of dots and dashes in a range of several widths. The tape is unrolled and pressed down on the cel along the path of the flow. With care in application, the tape can be aligned in each succeeding cel in a cycle to provide a progressive sequence of dots or dashes to render the flow.

☐ *Marking pencils.* Marking pencils that have been developed for writing on metals, china, and plastic provide an interesting alternative to the finely rendered ink line. These pencils yield a thicker and more textured line. The rough edges of the marking pencil rendering are very dynamic and reduce the need for painting cels or making a fancy background. Figures can be reduced to the simplest contours and still project a strong effect.

☐ *Xerox line reproduction.* Inking may be dispensed with in some forms of animation if a Xerox reproduction machine is available. The pencil drawing made on the animation paper can be printed directly onto a transparent foil. Simply superimpose the foil over the drawing, make an exposure, and remove the now "inked" foil for opaquing. A similar process is also feasible with an Ozalid foil machine, although it is more difficult to control the alignment of foil and drawing. This technique, whether used with Xerox or Ozalid, requires a strong, consistent pencil line whose tone is as black as possible. Unless the lines are consistently and conscientiously blackened throughout, they may vary in tone from drawing to drawing and foil to foil, resulting in animation which has vibrating outlines when projected on the screen.

OPAQUING

A cel is inked on one side and painted or opaqued on the reverse side. There are two reasons for this. First, the opaquer can paint up to the inked line without worrying about slopping over the edge. Second, in opaquing cels the paint must be applied heavily. This means that the cel would present an irregular surface to the lens of the camera if it were painted on the front. Painting the cel on the reverse side assures that the smooth face of the painted surface will be up and all irregularities hidden. This two-surface technique enables the film maker to present cleanly inked lines and a smoothly painted surface to the camera.

☐ To paint cels, do *not* dip a brush into the paint and wipe it at the edge of the jar and then proceed to stroke the paint on the plastic. This traditional technique does not provide an adequate supply of paint on the brush for opaque rendering, and the ordinary stroking technique yields a streaky result. Instead, when the brush is dipped into the paint, it is lifted up without wiping, and the paint is allowed to ''ball'' at the end of the brush. Then the paint is deposited in a blob on the area to be opaqued and pushed around until the surface is covered. Do not stroke it or streaks will appear on the front of the cel. As a general working system, have all the paints open at once and complete the painting of each cel as it comes along; this reduces the number of times each cel is handled and lessens the hazard of scratching the surface or of damaging the completed work.

MULTICEL LEVELS

The use of multicel levels is standard practice in animation. When cycles are used for repeated action, or when one subject is held while another is moved, it may be necessary to photograph several layers of cels at once.

☐ Placing one cel upon another has the effect of making the lower cels appear progressively darker. A cel of a given color placed at the bottom level of the four-cel pack will, when photographed, appear several shades darker than its original painted value. If a subject is supposed to be a consistent shade, and yet its place in the multicel levels shifts from scene to scene and sequence to sequence, its shade must be made darker or lighter according to the cel level at which it appears.

☐ A maximum number of four cels may be used simultaneously for any given exposure. This limit is established by the amount of darkening, light loss, and diffusion that is tolerable. There is a light loss of approximately 5 per cent with each cel thickness that has to be penetrated in photographing the lower cels. With a thickness of four cels, this means that there is roughly a 20 per cent light loss in photographing the value or color that is painted on the back of the bottom cel.

☐ A special problem arises when we plan a sequence using varying numbers of cels in its various scenes. Given the same background, if only one cel is used in the first scene, four cels in the next scene, and two in the scene after that, the result is a sequence which changes in density as the film progresses. In addition, the background will fluctuate in sharpness of focus and shades of gray. Therefore, the scene requiring the greatest number of cels determines the cel level for the entire sequence. If one scene requires four cels, then all the other scenes in the sequence must be maintained at this level by using blank cels for compensation. The cel level must be maintained at the same number throughout a sequence though it may change from one sequence to another.

☐ Number the cels according to the sequences in which they will be presented and according to their level in the cel sandwich. For example: in a layer of four cels, the cels would be numbered 1, 1a, 1b, 1c, beginning with the cel nearest the background. A fade-out, fade-in should be planned to separate sequences having radically different cel levels, if the backgrounds are similar.

BLACK AND WHITE PAINTS

The darkening effect of multicel densities on black and white paints is easily compensated for when working with commercial animation paints. Animation paints are sold graded in half-shade tones. To maintain a consistent shade in a given painted subject when it must be photographed at varying cel level positions, first determine what shade of gray is desirable on the top level cel—that is, the shade of gray that will appear in the photograph. Then, paint that subject one value *lighter* for every cel level down that the subject will be photographed in other scenes of the sequence. For example: If an animated subject is to be photographed at a consistent ''C'' shade of gray throughout a sequence, but the cels will appear on levels #4, #3, #2 and #1 in different scenes, then the cels should be painted C, B½, B, and A½ respectively. The result, when photographed and projected on the screen, will be a subject whose gray is visually consistent throughout the sequence, regardless of its actual position in the multicel levels.

☐ Commercial animation paints are more expensive than the average illustration and commercial art paints because they are compounded very carefully to be consistent, not only from batch to batch, but from year to year. In addition, these paints have the chemical additive which enables them to stick to a plastic surface. And finally, the consistency and fluidity of the paints are carefully prepared in order to cut down on the labor of opaquing. But, for the film maker on a limited budget and for whom these high-quality paints are prohibitively expensive, there is an alternative medium.

☐ Inexpensive photograph retouching grays can be bought in ten major shades of gray. As supplied, they will not adhere to plastic; but if a few drops of noncrawl are added and mixed in thoroughly, as when modifying India ink, they can be used satisfactorily. Their disadvantage is that the grays come in only the major shades of gray; shades for the various multicel levels will have to be mixed and graded carefully by the film maker before painting the cels. In practice, it is usually wise when using retouching grays to work in broad, simplified areas having only one or two cel levels. Grading a full spectrum of grays into consistent halftones is a tricky business, and may be more expensive in terms of time than buying the commercial grays.

COLOR PAINTS

Multicel densities have their most noticeable effects upon color. A color suffers not only from darkening and diffusing, but its "chroma" (intensity) is also reduced with each progressive lowering of its cel level position. If a subject is painted a color of the same chroma throughout, regardless of its cel level position, the density and darkening previously mentioned are exaggerated by changes in the intensity of its chroma.

☐ Every value of a given color must be represented by a palette of paints of four chroma levels, each chroma level to be used at a given layer in the multicel layers. In this way, whenever a color appears on the screen, regardless of its photographed cel level position, it will appear consistent.

☐ Color paints prepared for animation work are more expensive than their black and white equivalents. And color animation paints purchased in four chroma levels per color, to compensate for cel level losses, are even costlier. These paints are of optimum quality and are mandatory for commercial use. But for instructional purposes, there are less expensive and adequate substitutes.

☐ New vinyl paints specifically made for cel work can be purchased in tempera-size jars. They spread easily, can be removed with a wet rag if not yet thoroughly dried, and can be worked over when thoroughly dried. They are admirable for subjects—biological subjects, for instance—that need to be textured or rendered in an illustrative sense. But the vinyl paints have a major shortcoming—their chroma is much lower than that of the commercial animation paints, so that the colors of cels painted with vinyl paints appear relatively subdued when projected on the screen. This low chroma problem is compounded by the use of multicel levels.

☐ Casein paints can also be used. They adhere readily and the surface is relatively resilient. But the chroma level is even lower than that of vinyl paints; when multicel levels are used the lower colors are radically grayed down from their original chroma. The low chroma of vinyl and casein paints may be compensated for by using brilliantly colored photographic papers as backgrounds, against which the grayed chroma of

the paints will appear to be a form of artistic counterpoint.

☐ A complete spectrum of color-printed and silk-screen papers with a range of a half-dozen shades and chromas for each color can be bought at major art supply stores. Ask for a set of color swatches that can be thumbed through and compared before purchasing. Do *not* buy posterboard or ordinary colored construction paper; they will produce muddy colors. A word of caution—the surface of colored silk-screen papers is extremely fragile. A casual touch of the finger may be photographed for the audience to enjoy. Using a bright background of cutout paper to balance a subject runs counter to the practice in theatrical animation, where the backgrounds are usually grayed and the dominant characters dressed in bright colors. But the purposes of educational animation are different. If the subdued subject and the brilliant background are so arranged that each serves as an artistic foil to the other and if the content is being communicated effectively, there is no reason why the brilliant background cannot be used to enhance the visual impact of the instructional animation. A film maker with a flair for design can circumvent the low chroma level of vinyl paints and achieve a final result as brilliant, in its own way, as a film done with commercial animation paints.

SCRATCHOFF

Scratchoff is a technique used to create the illusion that a line or a word is being written across the screen by an unseen hand. Only one cel is needed to create most scratchoff effects; the words or lines are rendered in full as they are intended to look when completely "written across the screen." At the animation stand, the effect is created by scratching off a bit of the painted line with a wooden or plastic point, between each exposure, while photographing every stage in the removal process *in reverse*. When the film is projected on the screen in the normal *forward* direction, the painted line will flow magically across the screen to render cinematically whatever was originally on the cel.

☐ Scratchoff is one technique in which vinyl paints should not be used. Once vinyl paint is thoroughly dry it is so tough that it can scarcely be removed with a cold chisel. For scratchoff, use the more traditional commercial animation paints, and even here the use of a little soap worked into the paint helps to create an easily scratched-off line. Do not use a pen to create a scratch-off as it will usually leave a mark in the cel which will show up. Use a brush or an air-brush instead.

SUBJECT ZOOM

A conventional zoom is a progressive movement toward or away from the subject by the camera; this technique maintains the same proportional relationship between the subject and its background regardless of its distance from the camera. The converse of this concept is the "subject zoom." This technique involves having the subject grow progressively larger, or smaller, while the background remains a constant size.

☐ The subject to be enlarged or reduced in a subject zoom may be photostated, photocopied, or redrawn in progressively changing sizes—one for each exposure—for as many copies as are needed to complete a smooth subject zoom in the time desired. A subject zoom is plotted in the following manner. First, determine the beginning and terminal sizes of the subject in this zoom. Second, establish how much to enlarge (or reduce) the size of each succeeding copy over its predecessor for the length of the zoom. Third, have the subject photocopied and enlarged (or reduced) to provide a copy for each progressive change in the size of the subject. Fourth, cut out each copy and mount it on a cel, with each succeeding copy so positioned over its predecessor as to convey a subtle change in size; each must be precisely aligned so that there is no possibility of a jiggle on the screen when the film is projected. This technique finds only occasional use in educational animation, but is quite common on television commercials where it is used to create the illusion that a sponsor's product is leaping toward the viewer. A word of warning about making photostats or photocopies—variations in tone (greater than .02 in density) from print to print result in an intolerable flicker on the screen. The values must be constant from the first print to the last.

RENDERING FOR TELEVISION

How the animation will be projected affects how it should be conceived and rendered. Animation intended for a darkened room and a large projection screen can be conceived and executed in the manner so far described. Films intended for broadcasting over television require a somewhat different treatment. The television scanning unit does not reproduce the entire area of a given frame of film, but crops a certain percentage all the way around its perimeter. There is a limited area at the center of the frame within which all significant action should take place if it is to be visible on the television screen.

☐ Moreover, television and films have different distortions of the gray scale; television requires a narrower spectrum of grays. Low-contrast animation reproduces better over television than high-contrast work; pure black and pure white may produce "bloom," the complementary halo which forms around extreme values. Color television has less resolution than black and white and the communication of important information should not be contingent on sensitive textures or fine line details.

chapter 9
BACKGROUNDS AND TITLES

AN intimate four-way relationship exists between the script, the storyboard, the background, and the easy way of doing things. Animation backgrounds require a major expenditure of time and talent to execute, but with a little forethought this expenditure can be kept to a minimum.

☐ In the script and storyboard phases of production, plan to make the maximum use of a minimum number of backgrounds. In medium and close shots the viewer's eyes are held by the animated subject, and the background is often of negligible interest. Background forms, which are acceptable in shape, tone, and color and which are compatible with the content of the sequence, will pass uncriticized. (This is more true of black-and-white than of color films.)

☐ In addition, varying the field size extends the potential use of a single background. Zooms, pans, and compound moves permit a great deal of animation to be presented with a minimum amount of work. Before proceeding to the design and execution of backgrounds, we will examine the components of the animation stand which are specifically designed to handle the backgrounds.

TRAVELING PEGBARS

The primary means of mounting and moving backgrounds are the two sets of traveling pegbars (see Chapter 3). They are mounted on mobile tracks embedded in the surface of the animation table. The movable tracks on both top and bottom enable the film maker to mount a background from one side and cels from the other; each can therefore move independently of the other. This permits us first, to create the illusion that a subject is moving across a static background; second, to create the illusion that a subject is moving across a changing background; and third, to create multiple E−W movements (Figures 9.1 and 9.2).

☐ To create a static background, the pegbar holding the background remains in the same position throughout the action. The pegbar holding the animated subject begins in one extreme offscreen position and is then moved across the background to the opposite extreme position. In this instance, the background itself need be only the size of a standard cel, but the moving cel must have the E−W dimension of three standard cels to preclude showing a cel edge. The illusion created in the finished film is that the subject is entering the scene on one side and exiting from the other.

☐ To create a changing background, the subject is held in a static position while the background is moved. The pegbar holding the background begins its move by presenting one side of the background under the first cel of the animated subject. With each subsequent exposure of a cel, the pegbar holding the background is moved additional increments—depending on the speed the subject should appear to have—until the other end of the background is reached. The illusion created when the film is projected is that the subject has been moving across a changing landscape.

☐ When a number of horizontal actions are being depicted, the two traveling pegbars can be used in conjunction with the E–W and N–S controls to create multiple speeds of motion.

Those animation stands equipped with ''floating pegbars,'' clamped to the columns of the animation stand, allow the film maker even more flexible movement.

STILL AND PAN BACKGROUNDS

A still background is one which does not move at any time; therefore, it need be no larger than a standard size cel. Still backgrounds are used in three instances: first, when the subject is moving around within a background which need not be extended to depict the action; second, as a background to animated concepts which are being presented out of any recognizable context; and third, as a background for titles or other copy to be read. A still background may be a plain solid color or simple texture or a carefully detailed scene, depending upon the purpose of the film.

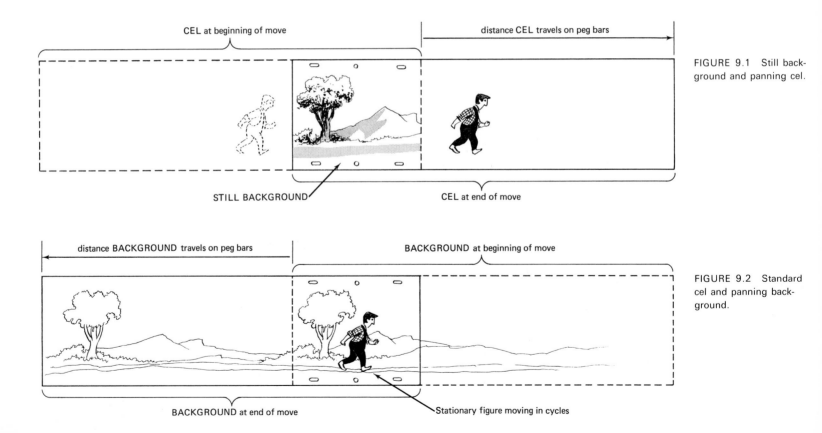

FIGURE 9.1 Still background and panning cel.

FIGURE 9.2 Standard cel and panning background.

☐ A pan background is used to create the illusion that the animated subject is traveling from one place to another. In practice, the background is moved while the animated subject is held in a stationary position.

☐ A pan background is moved by the traveling pegbars. Although use of the traveling pegbars theoretically permits construction of a pan background of almost indefinite length, the practical limit of length is about 40″, and for most purposes this is adequate. If, however, a series of pan backgrounds is used in sequence, to give the effect of one continuous background, the terminal and beginning areas of successsive backgrounds must obviously be identical; the transition between backgrounds is therefore not evident to the viewer.

DESIGN OF BACKGROUNDS

A well-designed background has no center of interest and therefore looks incomplete when standing alone. The real center of interest is always the animated subject which moves over the background and completes the picture. The background should be designed only to enhance and complement the animation; if the background can stand alone as an aesthetically satisfying picture, its center of interest will probably compete for attention with the animation. If the galleon were removed from the illustration shown, the background would have no center of interest and the picture would appear incomplete (Figure 9.3). This is as it should be—the animation must provide the center of interest. It is better to err on the side of simplicity and understatement when conceiving backgrounds than to make them overelaborate.

☐ The viewer must be shown where to look and what to look for. We cannot rely upon him to do more than sit with his eyes open; the picture itself must direct his perception. He must be guided by means of background design to the animation. Sweeping directional lines can rivet the eyes of the viewer on the animated subject (Figure 9.4). Design the background so that the main directional lines direct attention to the animated subject in its movement over the background. When the animation pauses, great care must be given to these lines to ensure that the viewer's eyes are directed to the correct center of interest.

☐ The amount of fine detail that should be included in a pan background depends upon the speed and purpose of the pan, and upon the relation of the subject to its background. When

FIGURE 9.3 Appropriate background. Courtesy of the U.S. Air Force.

FIGURE 9.4 Directional lines: *Man in Flight*. Copyright © 1957 Walt Disney Productions.

FIGURE 9.5   Pan background: *The Grain that Built a Hemisphere.*
Copyright © Walt Disney Productions.

the subject is moving quickly, finely rendered details in the background usually go unnoticed, and this may represent wasted labor. Moreover, strongly rendered details in a quickly moving background may set up a staccato visual pattern or strobe effect. Reduce the elements of this type of pan background to extremely simple but meaningful forms. It is sometimes wise to make the elements of a quickly moving background lean toward the direction of the move to further emphasize speed.

☐   When the animated subject is to move slowly before a recognizable landscape whose content is meaningful, the pan background must contain accurate details. For example, an Indian is shown stalking wild game amid stands of corn (Figure 9.5). The clumps of corn stalks are important and are conspicuously silhouetted in the background, and finely rendered for easy recognition. As a general rule, the more significance a pan background has the more carefully it is rendered in detail and the more slowly it is panned. It is interesting to note in this illustration that part of the "background" becomes "foreground," and is rendered on a cel which is positioned in front of the character. This cel will pan at a faster rate than the background to aid in creating the illusion of depth. This technique is commonly used to implement three-dimensional effects.

☐   Even when the background shapes are drastically simplified, as in a fast pan background, they must be meaningful; viewers are oriented by whole shapes and a subconscious recognition of contours in the background will help them to understand what is going on. Objects are recognized by their overall properties, their salient structural characteristics, rather than by details within their shape. When a pan background is being designed to move quickly there is a temptation to reduce it to aesthetically satisfying but uncommunicative abstract shapes, on the assumption that no one will notice the difference. Subconsciously, however, the viewer responds to shapes in the background and senses if they are related to reality or merely put in to fill space.

PERSPECTIVE

Perspective must be handled precisely in backgrounds. The same elements that were discussed in relation to animated subjects (Chapter 7) apply even more rigorously here, for errors in the perspectives of backgrounds are more painfully evident than errors in the perspective of animated subjects.

□ Strong perspective is often used in entertainment films or to evoke an emotional response (Figure 9.6). This use is justified whenever the emotional content contributed by the background is itself the subject of the scene. If perspective is intended to charge the emotional content of the picture, then use it boldly.

Lay in sweeping visual elements to give it excitement. Develop its impact with figures that recede decisively and raise the emotional temperature of the scene. When attempting to convey an emotion primarily through the background, it is better to err on the side of strength because you are dealing with an

FIGURE 9.6 Dramatic uses of perspective: *Gulliver's Travels.* Courtesy of Paramount Television Enterprises.

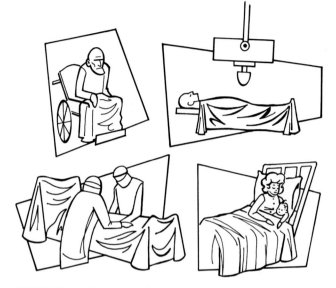

FIGURE 9.7 Simple background.

FIGURE 9.8 Sponge-textured background. Courtesy of the U.S. Air Force.

image that lasts only a short time. But keep in mind that this principle applies primarily when the ''subject'' of the scene is the emotional quality of the background.

☐ Use of strong perspective is of only minor importance in the fields of instructional and industrial films. In this area, backgrounds are usually simply the context within which the animated subjects function and need be given no more attention than is necessary to communicate instructional content.

BACKGROUND STYLES

A good general rule to follow in planning backgrounds is to plan no more background than you need (Figure 9.7). A background can sometimes be no more than a solid color. If the animated subject is quantitative or technological in character, then a simple flat pattern background is usually sufficient. A simple background which provides a little more in the way of visual stimuli is one that has been paint-textured with a sponge (Figure 9.8). Such a background is easily achieved by spreading the desired colors and values on a palette, dipping into them with a damp sponge, and dabbing the desired texture into the background. This can be carried a stage further by dabbing the paint into abstract or semirepresentational shapes. In the illustration the background was not needed to communicate an idea, create a mood, or provide a context for animation action; the area was simply ''filled'' with a textured pattern for the sake of interest.

☐ The briefest of sketches sometimes suffices for a background. A boy and a monkey sit in a tree whose structure is reduced to a few simple lines and whose leaves are indicated only by blots of water color (Figure 9.9). The viewer will use his imagination to fill in the forms and details of the tree.

☐ The highly stylized, decorative approach to background design is possibly the most widely used today (Figure 9.10). Three-dimensional visual elements are reduced to two dimensions; light and dark values are freely redistributed to form an overall pattern of modified but recognizable forms. The structural components become almost pure elements of design. Cutouts are frequently employed.

☐ Backgrounds may convey important ideas symbolically For example, this cartoon figure of an Indian is shown grinding corn on his metate before a background depicting North and South America (Figure 9.11). The three-dimensional effect of the continents is created by presenting them as one great, continuous cornfield. This background epitomizes the theme of

The Grain That Built a Hemisphere; it is not only aesthetically pleasing, but it also provides a factual and conceptual summing up.

☐ Related to the symbolic background is the topographical one, which is often used to establish the locale of a film. In *Victory Through Air Power,* a World War II film, one such background presented the topographical features and contours of China and Southeast Asia, labeled for clear recognition (Figure 9.12). The dark border along the coast of China signifies the area of Japanese control, the shuttle of planes over the Himalayas is fully animated. This background is a clear, succinct presentation of a problem of military strategy. Topographical backgrounds must, of course, be clear and accurate.

☐ A realistic background is most often used when the film maker wants to reach viewers of all ages and socio-economic levels. The realistic style may emphasize either form or line. When the background is intended to provide no more than a recognizable context for the viewer, forms are stressed. When the background is intended to provide subject matter information, forms become less important, and a linear, descriptive treatment with precisely articulated details is employed.

☐ Mood and atmosphere are all-important in an entertainment film; here we are not trying primarily to communicate an idea but to evoke a living experience. The background artist must feel the spirit of the characters and the needs of the story in order to prepare a believable environment in which the characters are to live (Figure 9.13). In every scene of the film, the background artist is expected to render the right dramatic mood for the actions taking place, with a consistency of approach which will give unity to the film.

RENDERING BACKGROUNDS

Backgrounds are usually rendered on illustration boards which are stiff enough to be handled freely while painting, and, in contrast to photographic papers, have surfaces that can be worked over with impunity. Strathmore, Crescent, Bainbridge, and a number of other companies manufacture and distribute a broad range of art surfaces that are suitable for backgrounds.

☐ The degree of "tooth" acceptable in the surface depends upon how fine the rendering should be. For coarse backgrounds rendered with an impasto technique, a cold-press surface is suitable. For fine backgrounds rendered with a detailed technique, a hot-press surface is preferable. For an

FIGURE 9.9 Sketched background: *How Animals Move.* Courtesy of the National Film Board of Canada.

FIGURE 9.10 Stylized background. Courtesy of the National Film Board of Canada.

FIGURE 9.11 Symbolic background: *The Grain that Built a Hemisphere*. Copyright © Walt Disney Productions.

FIGURE 9.12 Topographical background: *Victory Through Airpower*. Copyright © Walt Disney Productions.

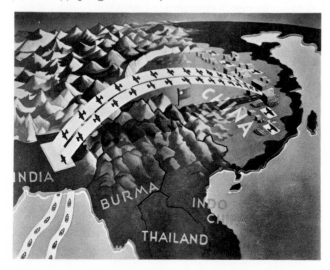

airbrush background, the tooth of the surface should be even finer. Avoid the high-gloss paper often used for pen and ink work. It lacks the proper tooth to take and hold water-base paints, and will be marred and warped by the penetration of the medium.

☐ Backgrounds are customarily rendered in muted colors so that brightly colored cartoon characters will stand out. As a rule, the longer the film the quieter the background; the viewer quickly grows weary of a succession of bright colors. There are several types of paint to use for backgrounds. Many professionals use Dr. Martin's Dyes. Others prefer Designer's Colors, which are manufactured in a wide array of colors. These paints can be handled like transparent water colors or laid on heavily like oil paints.

☐ For black-and-white flat-pattern backgrounds, tempera grays in jars are superior to tube paints for speed and ease of rendering. Their graded values enable a film maker to be consistent from one background to the next and to match his earlier work when retouching completed backgrounds. However, the tempera grays dry so quickly that modeling cannot be done except by cross-hatching or some other decorative technique. Impasto is out of the question, as any heavy application of the paint will result in cracking and flaking.

☐ For black-and-white backgrounds rendered in an impasto manner, casein paints are good. These are offered in a range of grays called "Ben Stahl" grays which are most often used for underpainting in oils. They have the texture of oils and have excellent handling qualities for a palette knife technique. Most caseins, however, build up impasto grooves, and their hard, coarse surface does not lend itself to reworking. Furthermore, the extreme hardness of the dry paint may rasp the bottom cel under the pressure of the platen.

☐ As mentioned in Chapter 8, silk screen paper can be cut out in a variety of shapes and combined to form brilliant backgrounds. Be sure to make every edge as sharp and clean as possible; even the smallest burr or turned edge will stand out as a white blemish in the background. Maps lend themselves particularly well to the use of the cutout technique. They can be given a three-dimensional effect by using an airbrush to accent their edges before they are mounted.

☐ Sooner or later every film maker must create the effect of a night sky filled with sparkling stars. This is done with a long panning cel, a black background, and underneath lighting. The panning cel is splattered with ink to create an overall mesh of ink dots and blotches. The black background is punched with small holes to permit pinpricks of light to show through from underneath. On the animation table, the cel is moved slowly over the background, with the splatters of ink alternately cutting off the dots of light and permitting them to show through, thereby creating the effect of twinkling stars in a night sky.

☐ All backgrounds should be carefully rendered. Sloppy workmanship will detract from almost any subject, particularly when treating a scientific or technological subject. And in the case of still backgrounds, in which the greatest part of the images being projected on the screen are static, everything visible to the naked eye will be photographed. Every nick, smudge, scratch, spot, fingerprint, rough-edged cutout, and streak of rubber cement will be faithfully reproduced on film.

TITLES

The practice of using beginning and end titles and screen credits means that lettering in some form must be used in almost every film. The design and composition of letters and words is an art form in itself. A film maker should have some knowledge of typography and composition in order to create the titles and labels for a complete film. When planning titles, it is worth the time and trouble to experiment with sketches in order to work out an attractive design and to examine different styles of typefaces to find the most appropriate style for the mood and character of a given film. Backgrounds for screen credits and labels should have simple patterns and textures. The busier and fancier the background, the harder it is to read the words. Credits are made to be read. Resist the urge to be arty unless it enhances the legibility of the credits.

☐ If the titles are being done for television, allowance must be made for cutoff around the perimeter of the picture. Titles should be placed near the center of the picture or composed with enough bleed to permit cutoff without partial or total amputation of important letters. Obviously, titles composed with compensation for television cutoff will appear too tightly clustered when projected on a movie screen.

☐ Black titles are commonly used when the background is a simple light value (Figure 9.14). If still photographs or a strongly textured background are used, however, black titles may blend with the background and become illegible. White titles are generally easier to read because their shadows help to sharpen the letters and separate them from the background. White letters stand out against all but the lightest backgrounds and are therefore the most widely used (Figure 9.15).

FIGURE 9.13   Mood and atmosphere: *Bambi*. Copyright © Walt Disney Productions.

FIGURE 9.14   Black titles. Courtesy of Vincent A. Molinare.

FIGURE 9.15   White titles. Courtesy of Vincent A. Molinare.

FIGURE 9.16   Dropped shadow. Courtesy of Vincent A. Molinare.

☐   When titles are to be superimposed over strongly patterned backgrounds, it is advisable to enhance the legibility of white type by means of a black shadow edge on one side, called a "dropped shadow" (Figure 9.16). Colored titles should be used against a simple dark background or made to stand clear with outlines or with a dropped shadow.

☐   Avoid using extreme or attenuated typefaces for screen credits and labels. Any type which is easy to read in print is usually legible when projected. The use of all upper-case or all lower-case letters tends to be more legible than a combination of the two. As a rule typefaces with serifs should be avoided because they tend to recede into the background.

☐   There are several ways of producing professional-looking titles and labels. Perhaps the easiest way is to use a hot-press machine to burn the selected letters of the chosen typeface directly into a cel; hot-press machines may be used to render letters in black, white, and a limited range of colors. Most hot-press machines offer a range of typefaces wide enough to meet almost any need. For those who lack lettering experience, the hot-press machine is invaluable.

☐   Another technique for producing credits and labels is to make use of letters which can be transferred to cels under pressure, using graph paper under the cel for the alignment of each letter. These letters are sold in large sheets, in a wide variety of typefaces. Pressure application letters are most practical for labeling items within a scene, and they can be positioned easily by the lay film maker. But the proper spacing of screen credits or other large bodies of copy by this method requires some lettering experience.

☐   A third technique calls for photographing strips of copy on 35mm film, mounting the copy on cels, and then transferring them to ozalid foils before photographing them on the stand. The letters of each word are photographed one letter at a time on 35mm film by a machine designed for this purpose. The strips of 35mm copy are trimmed and mounted on cels with nonreproducible tape, using the field guide for positioning and alignment. Then the cel with the mounted copy is aligned with an ozalid foil and the two are processed together in an ozalid machine. This machine transfers the words to an ozalid foil. Pegbar holes are then punched in the ozalid foil, and the copy is realigned with a field guide. This is done by slitting the cel between the punch holes and the photography area; then the two sections are taped together in the correct prepunched position. The credits are now ready to be photographed on the animation stand.

☐ The techniques so far discussed have dealt with "art" titles—lettering intended to be photographed with its background in a single-exposure run of the camera. White and colored titles may also be achieved by a multiple-run technique analogous to that used in the dissolve. In this technique, the background is photographed during the first run of the camera. The film is then reversed in the camera with the shutter closed until the starting point is reached. During the second forward run, the white titles (superimposed over a glossy black background) are held for the same number of exposures. To be sure of burning the white titles through the film emulsion, an alternate practice is to make a Kodalith negative of the titles and then photograph this negative on the stand with underneath lighting. Kodalith negatives are often made from photostats of the original printing, paste-up, or hand lettering in order to achieve maximum contrast and cleanliness. Colored titles may also be executed with a Kodalith negative; a colored gelatin is placed on the negative and both are then photographed. The technique of burning-in titles is treated at length in Chapter 12.

☐ A word about exposure. Overexposed titles will bleed and appear to be out of focus, whereas underexposed titles permit ghostly forms from the background scene to persist perceptibly through the letters. Once optimum exposure relations have been determined, record them in a log book.

☐ During a zoom-in to a detail it is often desirable to keep the letters of a label at a constant size while the camera proceeds to examine the subject in extreme closeup. A one-run zoom-in would of course result in the letters expanding on the screen along with the area selected for detailed examination. The technique for maintaining a constant label size is exactly the same as that for superimposing white titles on a still or live-action background. The artwork is photographed during the first run, making whatever zooms or moves are desired on the animation stand. Then the film is reversed in the camera with the shutter closed. Finally the white label is photographed from a fixed height over a black background and is thus burned through the previously exposed footage. When the film is projected on the screen, the zoom-in will result in an enlargement of the detail being examined while the label remains a constant size.

☐ Backgrounds and titles are often as important as the animation itself. Sometimes no more than black letters on a plain background is required. Sometimes the subject demands the use of original artwork in conjunction with hand lettering, Kodalith negatives, and hot press titles in one visual. But whatever is called for, do not slight the backgrounds and titles, for they can make an important contribution to the total impact of the animated film.

chapter 10
EXPOSURE SHEETS

THE exposure sheet is the roadmap of animation. On the exposure sheet is recorded all the material to be photographed—cels, backgrounds, zooms, pans, compound moves, and so forth (Figure 10.1). The exposure sheet makes provision for virtually every aspect of animation photography. The exposure sheet has not been introduced until this chapter because its components are meaningless without a fundamental knowledge of animation.

☐ In production the exposure sheets follow the film through all the stages of its creation. From the initial stages of recording the sound track and determining the timing of the animation, the exposure sheets pass through the hands of the director, the animators, the in-betweeners, the inkers and painters, the checkers, and finally the cameramen. Each contributes to or acts upon the instructions recorded in the exposure sheets according to his special function. Even in productions of less than feature length, any film maker who waits to fill in his exposure sheets until all the cels, backgrounds, zoom charts, and pantograph charts are finished will find himself in a fix. Even a short film has many elements which must be organized and coordinated. The work of animation is much easier and errors are less likely to occur if instructions are recorded on the exposure sheets while planning is in progress.

☐ Before proceeding with detailed examination of the exposure sheets, we must understand certain graphic symbols and procedures for organizing the cels and the backgrounds.

GRAPHIC SYMBOLS

The graphic symbol for a 36-frame fade-in shows two lines beginning at a common point and gradually diverging until they end at a point 36 frames down the exposure sheet (Figure 10.2). This graphic presentation makes sense when you think of its point of origin as the closed shutter and each frame-by-frame divergence as the progressive opening of the shutter. The symbols for fade-ins, fade-outs, and dissolves always extend the full length of the intended effects when indicated on the exposure sheet.

☐ A fade-out symbol is the reverse of the fade-in symbol (Figure 10.3). It is a graphic representation of the open shutter which progressively closes for each frame of the effect; the lines meet at a common point, signifying a closed shutter.

☐ The dissolve symbol is a fade-in symbol superimposed over a fade-out symbol (Figure 10.4). As we know, a dissolve is implemented by fading out on one scene, reversing the film in the camera with the shutter closed, and then fading in on the next scene. This is fully expressed by the dissolve symbol.

□ When entering fade and dissolve marks for sequences using multicel levels, always draw them in each column that represents a cel level being used in the given sequence. This should be done because certain cels and backgrounds may be retained while others are changed from scene to scene. Unless the presentation of each cel level is accounted for in every column, it is possible to make hard-to-correct errors. When inserting a pop-on symbol among other constant cels, circle the single change of cel to be sure that the change does not escape the notice of the cameraman (Figure 10.5).

NUMBERING CELS AND BACKGROUNDS

Every cel and background must be numbered sequentially according to its place in the planned animation. When photographing multicel levels, indicate the correct position of each cel in relation to its background. For example, the cels of the first scene to be photographed may be labeled 1c, 1b, 1a, and 1 to indicate their relative proximity to the background, and to convey the information that this is the first scene being photographed. The next would be labeled 2c, 2b, 2a, and 2; the

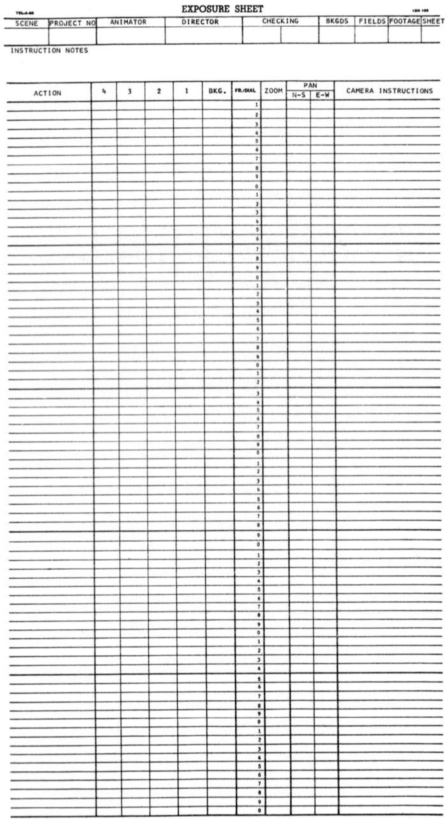

FIGURE 10.1   Exposure sheet.

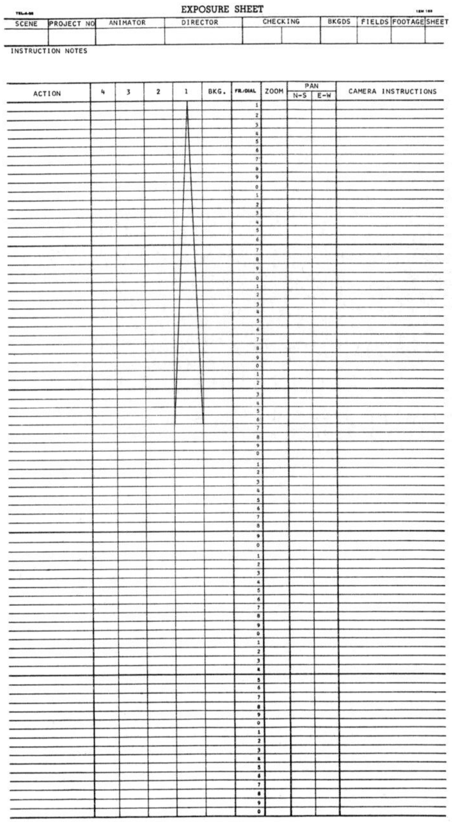

FIGURE 10.2   36-frame fade-in.

following set would be labeled 3c, 3b, 3a, and 3, etc., to the end of the sequence. Backgrounds are labeled according to the order in which they will be used: #1, #2, #3, and so on. Whatever system you choose for labeling the cels and backgrounds, be consistent or chaos will result.

THE EXPOSURE SHEET

The main body of the exposure sheet is divided horizontally and vertically by a series of parallel lines. Each horizontal line rep-

resents one frame of film. There are 80 horizontal lines on a page (representing 2 feet of 16mm film or 5 feet of 35mm), numbered from 1 to 10 eight times in succession.

☐   The vertical lines divide the page into columns in which are specified the moves to be made on the animation stand and the cels and backgrounds to be exposed.

☐   Across the top of each exposure sheet is a series of small squares used to register general information about the film. The first square on the left is labeled SCENE; scenes are numbered consecutively within each sequence. The PROJECT space

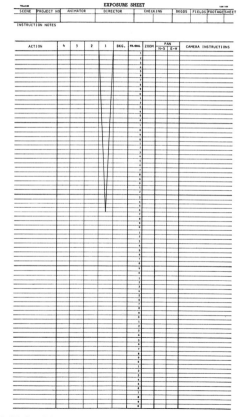

FIGURE 10.3   36-frame fade-out.

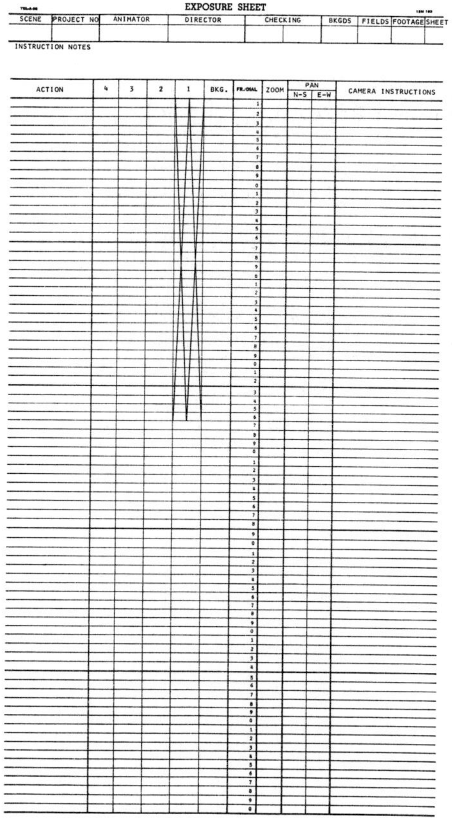

FIGURE 10.4   36-frame dissolve.

usually contains either the name of the sponsor, or the abbreviated title of the film. ANIMATOR and DIRECTOR are self-explanatory. On some exposure sheets, a double square marked CHECKING is used for the initials of those who double-check the accuracy of the exposure sheets and the numbering of the cels and backgrounds. SHEET is the page number of the exposure sheet.

☐ Below the series of small squares is a blank space extending the width of the page, which may be one inch to four inches deep. This may be used for any information the film maker considers relevant. It sometimes contains a synopsis of the content on that page. Or it may be used for technical explanations of a procedure on the animation stand, for ex-

ample, a reminder that a certain background must be taped to the animation table in order to free the traveling pegbars for use with moving cels. Anything requiring explanation for which no provision is otherwise made can be written into this blank area. But do not insert information here that belongs elsewhere! Otherwise, errors made through oversight will inevitably result.

☐ The column on the extreme left is the ACTION column. Here a phrase or two describing the action taking place in a new sequence enables the cameraman to see at a glance whether the artwork he is photographing corresponds to the brief description. This may seem like a nuisance for a short film, but an animated film even a few minutes long usually has

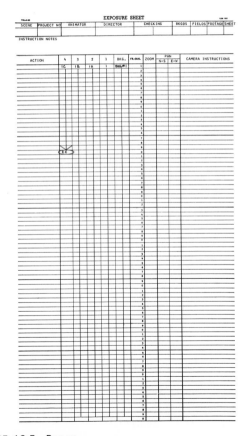

FIGURE 10.5   Pop-on.

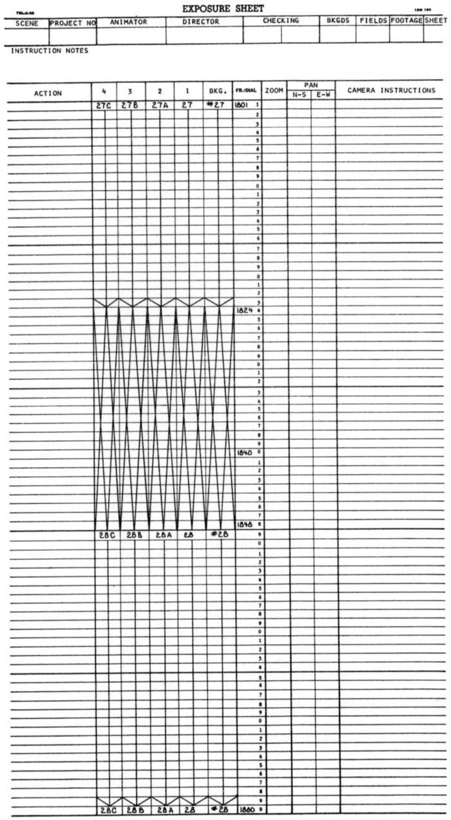

FIGURE 10.6   Cumulative numbering.

an impressive array of scenes and sequences. A cameraman who is working with strange material should have as much guidance and assistance as is feasible.

□ To the right of the ACTION column are four narrow columns numbered 4, 3, 2, 1, and an additional column with the abbreviation BKD. The first four columns represent four cel levels from top to bottom, and the fifth column represents the background. Each frame in these columns contain appropriate instruction from the first frame to the last exposure in the film. And each column must have its own separate indications of dissolves, pop-ons, and so on. There are many times when a change of cels at one cel level is required, while the other cels and the background remain constant.

□ To the right of the BKD column is the FR, or numbering column. Numbering on the exposure sheets is cumulative, as it is on the camera's frame counter, beginning with frame #1 and continuing to the end of the film. The two numbers—on the exposure sheet and on the counter—should correspond at all times. Every change from a continuous exposure should be indicated in the FR column. If a 24-frame dissolve begins at 1824 and ends at 1848, enter the beginning and end numbers in the appropriate frames (Figure 10.6). Zooms, pans, and compound moves must also have their beginning and end numbers entered in the appropriate frames.

□ Careful numbering on the exposure sheets expedites work on the animation stand. If the exposure sheet indicates that

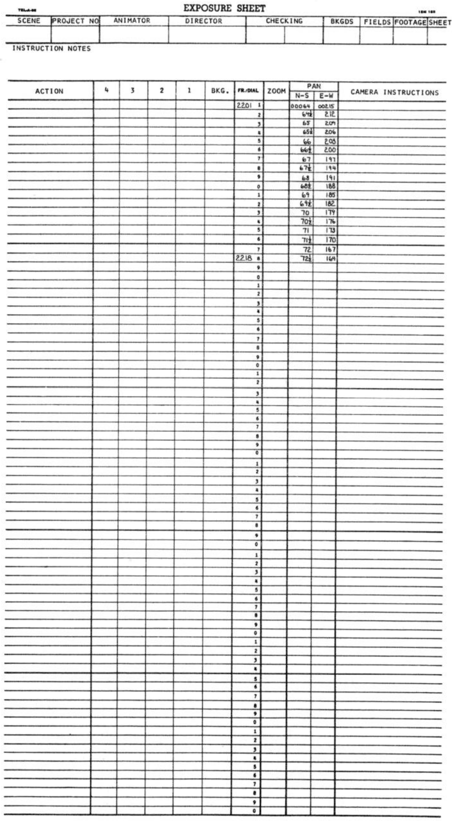

FIGURE 10.7   N–S and E–W numbers.

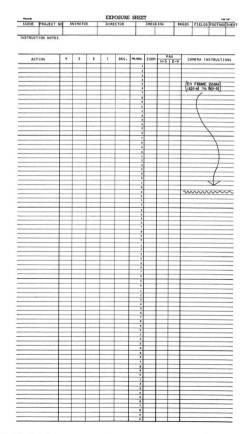

FIGURE 10.8   Camera instructions.

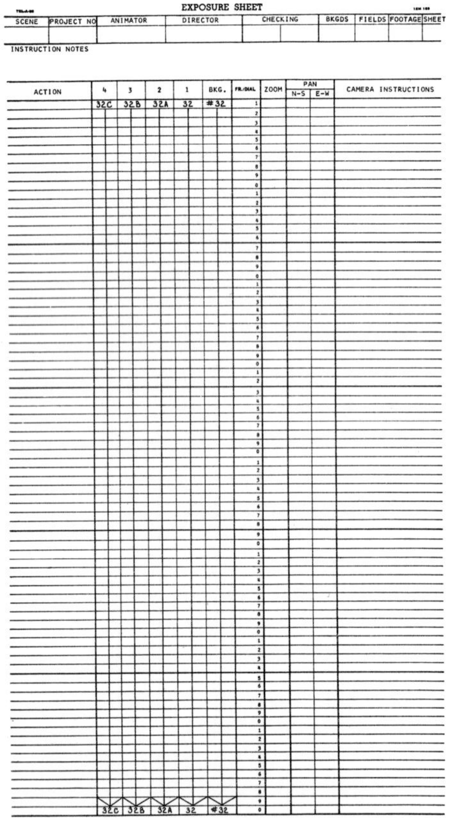

FIGURE 10.9 Continuous exposure lines.

there is a continuous series of exposures from one number to another, the cameraman can run the exposure quickly without having to check off each and every frame as it is exposed. He is alerted to changes not only by the graphic presentations in the columns, but by the cumulative numbers. He does not have to count the frames in a 40-frame dissolve—a glance at the beginning and terminal numbers enables him to set his controls accordingly.

☐ To the right of the numbering column is a double column labeled PAN, and subheaded N–S and E–W (Figure 10.7). These are used for indicating the calibration figures of the N–S and E–W counters when planning a pan or a compound move using the computation method. When a move is long in the number of frames exposed but short in terms of distance covered, it is prudent to state all of the calibration figures and check them during the move.

☐ To the right of the PAN column is the CAMERA INSTRUC-TIONS column, the last of the vertical columns. It provides instructions for zooms and other miscellaneous functions of the camera. When a 48-frame zoom is planned from a 12 field to a 6 field, it is described in this column and a line is drawn down the column to the frame at which the move is termi-nated (Figure 10.8). When zoom and pantograph charts are to be used, this column contains appropriate instructions.

☐ When no change is being made in a given column, run a continuous line down the page, and from page to page if necessary, until a change *is* made, at which point the line should terminate in an arrow (Figure 10.9). It is usually a good idea to indicate the cel numbers held at the bottom of each page as well as at the top.

WORKING PROCEDURES

It is worthwhile to number the midpoint and terminal frames cumulatively on each page for the entire length of the film before beginning to transfer cel and background numbers to the exposure sheets. These numbers provide convenient ref-erence points when filling in the sheet. As there are 80 frames represented on each exposure sheet, the first page would be numbered 40 at its midpoint and 80 at its terminal frame (Fig-ure 10.10). The second page would be numbered 120 at its midpoint and 160 at its terminal frame, and so on.

☐ The most practical working procedure at the animation stand is to have the cels, background, zoom charts, and pantograph charts arranged in order and close at hand. The exposure sheets should be arranged so that they can be seen easily and turned readily. The platen and glass insert should be cleaned before work begins, and the cels and backgrounds should be handled only with the lintfree white gloves used for inking and painting.

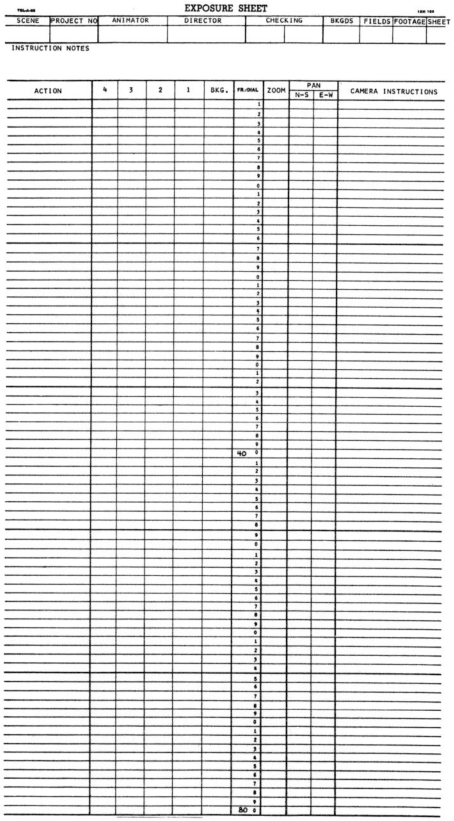
EXPOSURE SHEET
SCENE | PROJECT NO | ANIMATOR | DIRECTOR | CHECKING | BKGDS | FIELDS | FOOTAGE | SHEET
INSTRUCTION NOTES
ACTION | 4 | 3 | 2 | 1 | BKG. | FR./DIAL | ZOOM | PAN N-S E-W | CAMERA INSTRUCTIONS
40
80

FIGURE 10.10 Mid-page and end-page numbers.

chapter 11
SOUND RECORDING AND BAR SHEETS

TO provide sound to accompany animation, the film maker must complete two tasks simultaneously. The sound—dialogue, music, and special effects—must be recorded in the form of a "sound track" and the animation must be synchronized exactly with the appropriate syllable or musical note in the sound track.

☐ Sound for commercial motion pictures is usually recorded on perforated magnetic film. Many animators, however, do not have access to the expensive equipment required to record original sound on magnetic film, or the means to transfer ("dub") sound from tape or disc to film. In this instance narration or music is first recorded on quarter-inch magnetic tape; this tape can then be economically transferred to 16 or 35mm film by a commercial sound studio.

☐ The initial tape recording should be done on a machine equipped with a "synchronous pulse"—a system in which a regular inaudible beat is recorded on one track while the desired sound is recorded on another track of the same tape. This ensures that the sound will be recorded at a fixed rate equivalent to the projection speed of 24 fps, and eliminates unpleasant surprises when the narration, music, and effects sound tracks are combined in a mixing session. There are many commercial tape recorders on the market that have the synchronous pulse device. A recorder that does not have this feature can be adapted by a sound engineering firm specializing in the construction of custom recorders and sound systems. The rest of the equipment needed for producing and analyzing a sound track is relatively inexpensive and can be found in every motion picture studio.

EQUIPMENT FOR READING SOUND TRACKS

Visuals are more flexible than sounds. A line of critical narration or a melody cannot be changed readily to meet the needs of the picture; therefore, when producing animation that has a sound track, it has become standard practice to record the sound first and make the pictures match the sound track in order to assure perfect timing. This does not change the principle of the ascendancy of picture over sound; both are worked out carefully before the sound is recorded.

☐ The equipment needed to read a magnetic sound track and transcribe the information to bar sheets includes the sound reader and the synchronizer, used to pin point the location of each word; two rewinds with the magnetic sound film mounted on the left reel, emulsion side (dull side) up, and threaded on the right-hand reel (Figure 11.1). The film maker should also

FIGURE 11.1 Equipment for sound reading.

FIGURE 11.2 Synchronizer.

have a copy of the script, a pair of demagnetized scissors, a splicer, a felt-nibbed pen, and blank bar sheets.

☐ Let us examine the key components closely. The synchronizer is a four-channel unit used to maintain frame-by-frame registration between live-action footage and its accompanying sound tracks of narration, music, and sound effects, each of which is mounted on a separate channel (Figure 11.2). We will need to use only one of the channels to read a sound track.

☐ The film in each channel is mounted over a wheel having sprocket pins corresponding to the perforations found in 16mm film (or 35mm, in a commercial studio). Each wheel and channel is aligned exactly with every other wheel and channel, and when one wheel turns they all turn. The film is mounted in a channel by passing the release on the right side to open the head, mounting the perforated film over the sprocket pins and relocking the head.

☐ The wheel of the synchronizer makes one complete revolution for each foot of film. Each frame of this foot is indicated by a number on the near side of the closest channel. There are 40 frame numbers for a foot of 16mm film and a footage counter on the base cumulatively registers one additional foot revolution of the wheel. The wheel can be locked in place on any of the 40 frames.

☐ Under the head of each channel is a sound head like that found on a tape recorder which is connected by a cable and input jack to the *sound reader* (Figure 11.3). As the magnetic film passes through the synchronizer channel it goes under the sound head and any words or music on the track are amplified by the sound reader. The sound reader is activated by turning on the volume control, and the tone quality is modified by the tone control. If the sound reader picks up broadcasting signals from nearby radio stations, as happens from time to time, attach a ground wire from the sound reader case to a cold water pipe or radiator.

BAR SHEETS

The bar sheets account for every frame of sound from the beginning to the end of the film. The format for bar sheets varies, but is most often a series of horizontal lines running down the page (Figure 11.4a).

☐ In bar sheets for 16mm film, each line is broken into intervals of 24 frames, representing one second of sound. Every sixth frame is extended a bit longer than the others in order

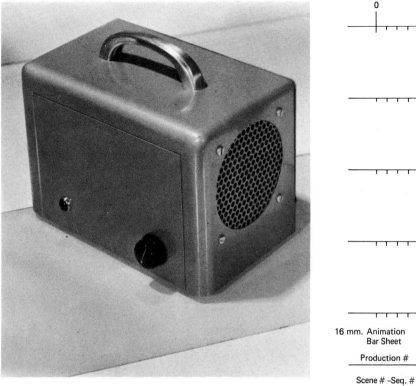

FIGURE 11.3   Amplifier–speaker of sound reader.

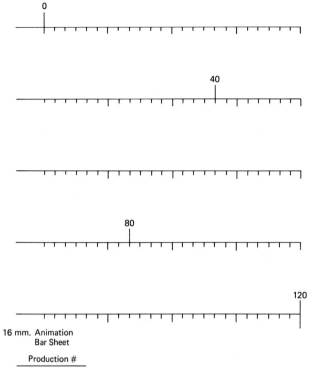

0

40

80

120

16 mm. Animation
Bar Sheet

Production #

Scene # –Seq. #

FIGURE 11.4a   Bar sheet for 16 mm single sound track.

FIGURE 11.4b   Bar
sheets for 35 mm "mixed"
sound track.

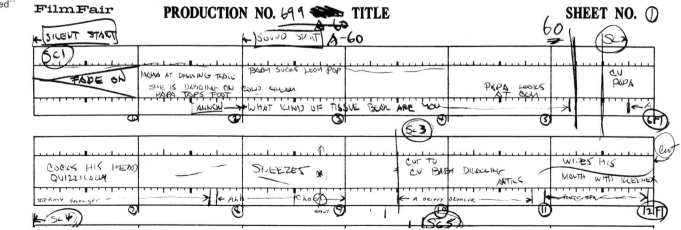

to divide the track into quarter-second units. The five lines on each page, represent five seconds of sound time and exactly three feet of 16mm film—or 120 frames. Bar sheets need not be bought; they can be drawn on ditto masters and duplicated at a cost of less than a penny a page.

☐ In 35mm film, bar sheets consist of five horizontal rows of paired sound paths presented in a double line to permit indications of dialogue on one line and music (or effects) on the other (Figure 11.4b).

☐ Bar sheets are numbered cumulatively in the manner of exposure sheets, but from left to right instead of from top to bottom. When doing the bar sheets for an animated film, determine how long the sequence is in terms of screen time and staple a sufficient number of sheets together to form a bar sheet unit large enough for this particular project. It is worthwhile to prenumber all the page units in advance, as in the exposure sheets.

SPLICING SOUND TRACK

Sometimes changes need to be made in the sound track before sound reading can begin. There may be a space of silence in the narration which is ½ second too long and we may decide to delete 12 frames. There may be a mispronounced word or poorly spoken sentence which needs to be replaced by a retake. Or the sound track may be accidentally torn and need repair before work can proceed.

☐ We must know how to splice magnetic film. For this we need a tape splicer, milar tape, and scissors. Let us presume that a second of sound is to be deleted. Overlap the first and the last frames that are to be cut, aligning the sprocket holes by eye, and cut *diagonally* between the sprocket holes. The reason for cutting diagonally instead of at a right angle is that it will soften any sudden dropout of sound. A right angle cut sometimes results in a wedge of abrupt silence as the sound head briefly loses contact with the film at the cut. Overlapping the first and last frames when cutting with the scissors assures that the film ends will butt together perfectly and be aligned when spliced.

☐ Cut a strip of perforated milar tape about two inches long and place it over the sprocket pins of the splicer, sticky side up. Carefully lower one end of the film down on *one half* of the milar tape, emulsion side up. Then do the same with the other end of film to be spliced, taking care to match the two cut ends perfectly on the milar tape. Lift the spliced film from

FIGURE 11.5 Film splicer.

the splicer and turn it coated side down; rub out all the air bubbles until there is complete adherence. The tape is now ready to be analyzed for bar sheets.

SOUND READING AND BAR SHEETS

To locate the words in a sound track we need only one channel, with a magnetic sound head. Insert the input jack in the amplifier, turn on the volume control, and when the amplifier warms up adjust the volume to an acceptable level. Press down the selected channel release and place the sound track over the channel wheel, feeding it from left to right, head out. While holding it in place, reach up with your thumb and lock down the sound head.

☐ Slowly run the film to the right under the sound head until the first word is heard—and stop. Maneuver it back and forth under the sound head until the first frame of the word, the first evidence of sound, is located. This frame is the reference point from which all subsequent words will be measured and marked on the bar sheets. Mark this frame with an "X" within a square (Figure 11.6).

☐ Unlock the channel release and temporarily remove the sound track. Turn the channel wheels until the frame number "0" is up and lock it into position by pressing down the lock lever beside the turning handle. Remount the sound track in its channel with the "X" frame aligned with the "1" frame; again reach up and lock down the sound head. Set the footage counter to read "0000." We are ready to begin reading the sound track.

☐ Have a copy of the narrator's script near at hand when sitting down to analyze the track. The script should have the narrator's cue marks, which will expedite the job of locating the important words. If the sound track is dialogue to be matched by the mouth movements of animated figures, then each and every word has to be located, measured for the number of frames it contains, and the information then transferred to bar sheets. If the sound track comprises off-screen narration and is cued to large moves such as zooms and pans, only key words need to be pin-pointed.

☐ As an example, let us assume that a line of narration in the sound track is, "The lure of California was gold." We are planning to begin a zoom from the first frame of the word "California" and end it on the last frame of the word "gold." We must locate the first click of the C in California and the last mumble of the d in gold in order to find the following informa-

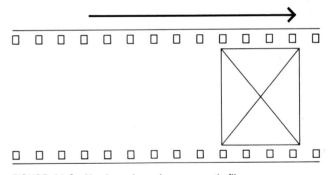

FIGURE 11.6 Head synch mark on magnetic film.

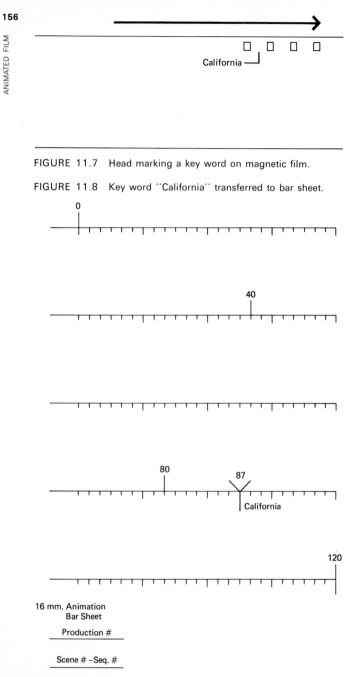

FIGURE 11.7   Head marking a key word on magnetic film.

FIGURE 11.8   Key word "California" transferred to bar sheet.

16 mm. Animation
Bar Sheet

Production #

Scene # - Seq. #

tion which we will need for our zoom chart: (1) How many frames after the starting frame the zoom will begin; (2) How many frames after the starting frame the zoom will end; (3) How many frames the zoom itself will require to begin on California and end on gold.

☐   The volume is on, the footage counter is set at 0000 and the synchronizer wheel number is turned to 0; the first sound is marked with an X, and is set on frame number "1" of the synchronizer wheel.

☐   Feed the film from left to right through the synchronizer and try to approximate a feed speed that will give a good audible sound. If the film is passed too slowly under the sound head, the sound will drag; if it is passed too quickly, the narrator will sound like Donald Duck. Experimentation will reveal an acceptable speed.

☐   When the word "California" appears, release the handles and take the sound track in your hands; move it slowly back and forth until the beginning of the word has been matched to the frame. Lock the wheel in place, and mark a right angle on the sound track to show where the word begins and on which side of the bracket the word appears (Figure 11.7). The word is written with a felt-nibbed pen for easy later reference. A sound track involving a few hundred or even thousands of words becomes a wilderness of brackets unless the key words are written in periodically. The frame numbers on the synchronizer wheel reveal that *C* falls on frame No. 7 of the third foot of film. We add 80 to 7 and find that the word California begins on the 87th frame of sound, and we transfer this information to the 87th frame interval on the first page of the bar sheets (Figure 11.8).

☐   Again, feed the sound track through the sychronizer until the word "gold" is heard. Take hold of the film and move it back and forth until the frame containing the sound of *d* is found. Mark the edge of this frame with a bracket facing the opposite direction from that used in *C,* and write the word "gold" on the other side for future reference. The footage counter reveals that the end of this word appears on a frame in the sound track which is a bit farther than 31 (120 frames) from the start mark. The frame number on the synchronizer wheel shows it to be the 15th frame into the fourth foot of film. By adding 120 to 15 we find that the word "gold" ends on the 135th frame of sound; this information is transferred to page two of the bar sheet.

☐   Here we can see the convenience of having each page numbered at the beginning and end. A glance at the corner reveals that at the beginning of this page we are 120 frames into the bar sheets. By counting 15 frames to the right we can easily locate the 135th frame which will coincide with the end of the zoom (Figure 11.9).

☐ Now we know that the zoom must begin at the 87th frame of the sound track and end at the 135th frame. By subtracting 87 from 135 we find that our zoom must be made in 48 frames, or two seconds, if we want it to begin on the first letter of the word California and end on the last letter of the word gold. We can plan our visuals to meet this time requirement, and transfer this bar sheet information directly to the exposure sheets as the artwork is finished. The procedure we have just described is adequate for most animation composed of filmograph techniques using only pans, zooms, cuts, and compound moves.

☐ The same procedure applies when analyzing a sound

FIGURE 11.9 Line for filmograph narration.

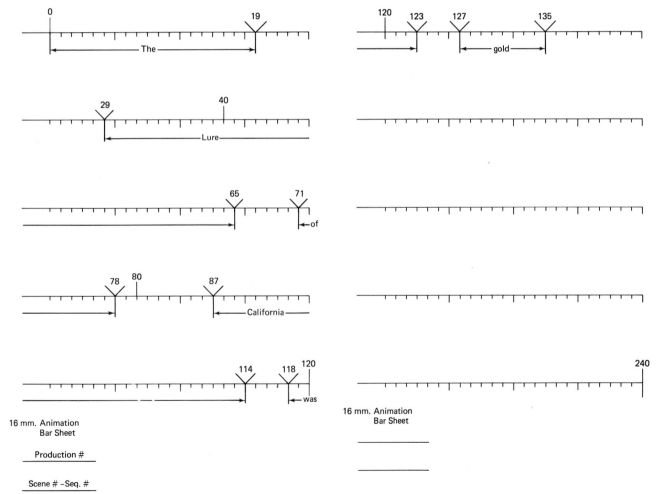

track of 35mm film to locate each and every word, as would be the case when doing cartoon animation; this requires perfect synchronization of lip movements, or action, with dialogue. Figure 11.4b shows how the bar sheets would look if a cartoon character were speaking a line of dialogue.

☐ Notice that every word is bracketed and, consequently, that the silent spaces between the words are clearly stated to the last frame. A film maker planning to match the lip movements of these words to their sounds would be able to tell, by counting the number of frames comprising each word, and by counting the number of frames between each word, how many drawings and cels would be necessary to match every vowel and consonant in perfect synchronization. The techniques of matching spoken dialogue to animated lip movements will be described in detail in the following chapter.

☐ If music is being used to provide the points of reference for the animation, use the high points of the music as reference points on the bar sheets to synchronize the picture with the music.

☐ Some knowledge of how to read music is required in order to write a statement on a bar sheet that makes sense. Those who lack this background would be better advised to use the beat of the music as a basis for the rhythm of the animation. When using this rhythm to pace the animation of a walking figure, however, be careful not to match each step to a beat in the music. Too rigid a synchronization will only create the grossest kind of burlesque.

☐ Once the bar sheets have been completed, the production can proceed in full confidence that the visuals will match the sounds to the last frame. The information on the bar sheets is transferred to the exposure sheet workbook that will accompany the creation of the animated film through all the phases of production.

chapter 12
MULTIPLE-EXPOSURE TECHNIQUES

A multiple-exposure technique is one in which the same frames of film are exposed more than once in order to incorporate two or more visual elements which could not be incorporated with a single run of the camera. Multiple-run techniques are often implemented with black mattes and masks—one portion of a picture is concealed so that it may be rephotographed later with the visual elements from another scene. Typical examples of effects achieved by multiple-run techniques are combining of animation with live-action footage, creation of titles with dark off-set shadows, superimposition of immobile titles and labels over moving backgrounds, and creating the ghostly illusion of superimposed images occurring simultaneously. Films treating modern scientific developments often require multiple-exposure techniques in order to visualize what has not yet been created or to protray what is too complex to photograph in live action.

☐ The execution of multiple-run effects derives from the same rerun principle used in the dissolve: the images of one scene are exposed first; then the film is run in reverse with the shutter closed to the starting point of the first scene, and then the succeeding scene is photographed. Some multiple-run effects are executed in the camera itself in the manner of the dissolve; more often the components of the desired effect are photo-graphed separately on the animation stand. A single print is then obtained by running these components through an optical printer or combining them by color-keyed videoelectronics.

MATTES

A matte is an opaque mask which covers a section of the artwork and thus prevents exposure of the corresponding area on the film emulsion. Mattes are used in multiple-exposure work to avoid exposing during the first run emulsion areas of a frame of film that are going to be exposed during the succeeding runs. Conversely, mattes during the second or third run are used to mask off areas of film emulsion that have previously been exposed. A matte may be cut to size from black card or other suitable material, or it may be created photo-graphically with high-contrast film.

☐ *Black card mattes.* The simplest use of the matte concept involves placing a black card directly on the artwork to mask off those areas of the scene that are not to be photographed during the first run. This split-screen technique is commonly used to depict simple cause-and-effect relationships or to show two events occurring simultaneously in different locales. We mask off the half that is going to be exposed during the second run, and then proceed to photograph the animation of the first run in the usual way. After the first half has been exposed, the shutter is closed and the film is run back to the beginning. The portion of the art work which has been exposed is then masked, and the area that was previously masked is now exposed. Since the second-run animation is not exposed in the previously matted out area, the images of two separate scenes are combined on the same strip of film.

☐ Satisfactory matte work requires that no exposure of emulsion occur in the blacked-out areas and that the camera registration is adequate for the job. While a relatively large black overlap can be seen easily in the finished film, minute overlap (1/32″ on a 12 field, for example) is almost undetectable. If necessary, a white burn-in boundary line made on one exposure can be used to hide registration discrepancies. If a definite black line is desired, however, it can be achieved by deliberately overlapping the two sides of the mattes.

☐ When making mattes of black card, avoid surfaces which catch or reflect light. These have a graying effect on the film emulsions. A clean, glossy surface of Flint paper, Pyro cover stock, or a black plastic sheet is preferable. Dull-finish blacks are unacceptable because their surface textures tend to reflect the ambient light and fog the film.

☐ A simple wipe can be created with two scenes shot at the

FIGURE 12.1 *Surveyor Lunar Module.* Courtesy of Jet Propulsion Laboratory.

same field by mounting a black card on the traveling pegbars, and photographing it at equal increments as it progressively masks the first scene. After the first half of the wipe has been photographed, the shutter is closed and the film returned to the beginning of the wipe. The second scene is introduced by inverting the black card procedure. The same directional movement is repeated with a second black card which, in this case, progressively reveals the incoming scene. This simple wipe is completed in the camera. But creating a precise wipe by this manual method is very difficult; if the two edges of the black cards are not aligned perfectly during both runs, a flickering line (''matte bleed'') may appear at the juncture of the two scenes in the finished wipe.

☐ A device for making soft-edged wipes can be installed over the lens mount of the camera; this device allows wiping to scenes shot at different fields and positions. Film makers who decide against photographing their own wipes can choose from a variety of standard wipes which are executed on order by commercial film laboratories (Figure 12.3).

☐ *Positive and negative photographic mattes.* Extremely accurate mattes for animation work can be created photographically. The camera is loaded with a high-contrast film to reduce the possibility of half-tones. The animation cel is placed on the tabletop, and the underneath lighting unit is lighted. When the cel is photographed, the underneath lighting burns off the film emulsion surrounding the artwork; the film will show the artwork as a clear silhouette on a black background. This is known as a clear-core matte. When a contact print is made of this film, a reverse image results which is called a black-core matte (Figure 12.4).

☐ Correct exposure of high-contrast film is important in the preparation of photographic mattes. The density of the black must be sufficient to prevent exposure of the accompanying raw stock in the matted areas when the two are printed together in an optical printer. For black-and-white work the mattes should have a minimum density of 2.6; for color, 2.3. Yet the high-contrast film cannot be overexposed to a density exceeding 3.0 or matte bleed will result.

☐ The photographic mattes must have silhouettes whose configurations match perfectly so they can be used to combine the images of the two selected scenes in a composite print without matte bleed. It is crucial that the registration pin systems in the animation camera, registration contact printer, and optical printer correspond in size as closely as possible. Experience has shown that when matching clear-core and black-core

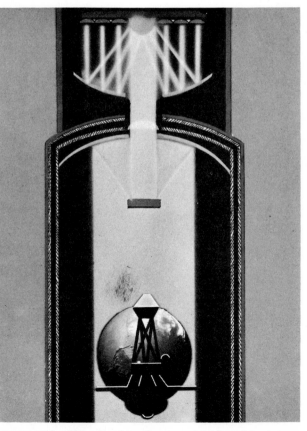

FIGURE 12.2 *Space Simulator.* Courtesy of Jet Propulsion Laboratory.

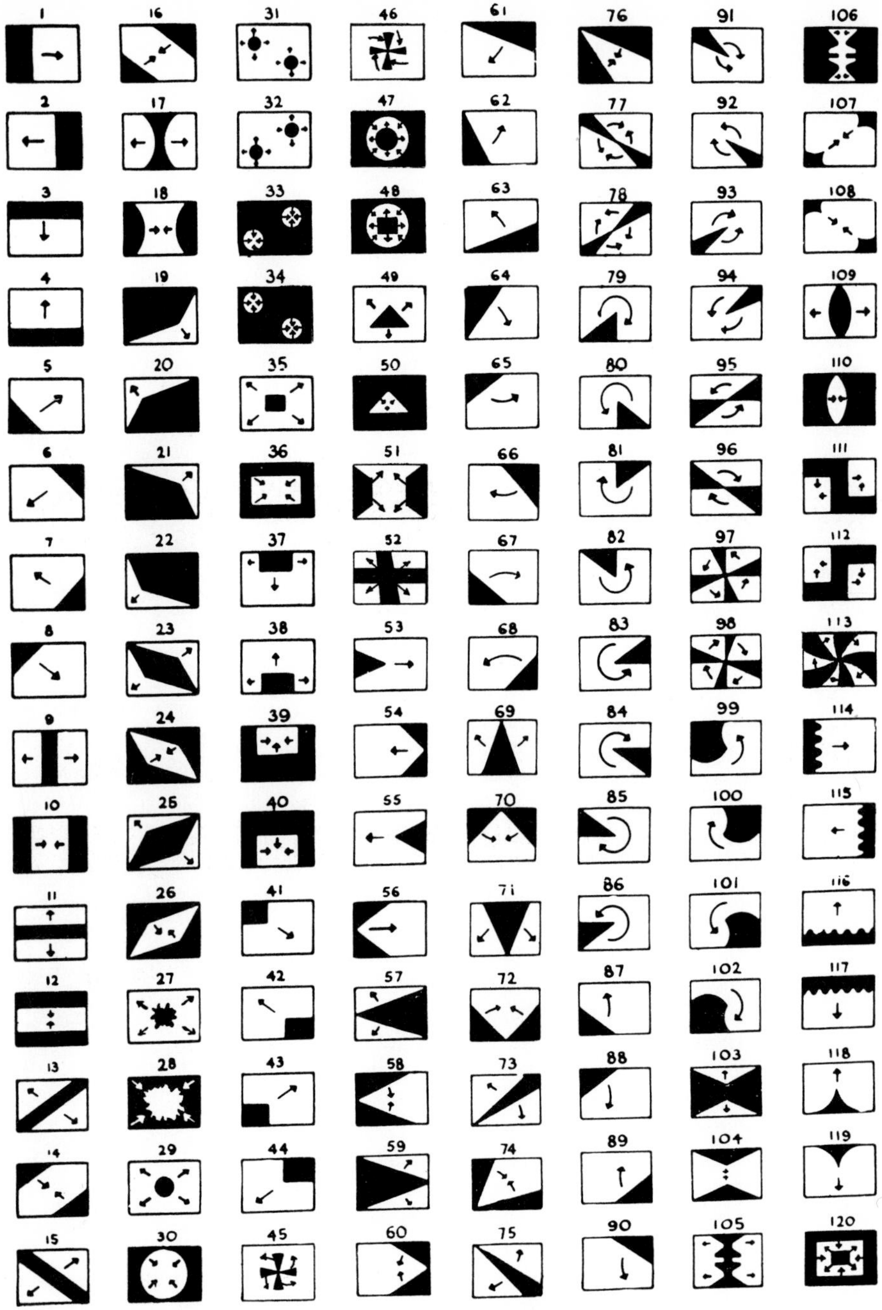

FIGURE 12.3 Standard wipe sheet.

mattes in 35mm production the maximum tolerable error of film positioning cannot exceed .0002''. The precision required for film matte work is difficult to obtain in 16mm cameras and film perforations.

☐ The stability of the film stock itself sometimes presents a problem in matte production. When a cel containing a large black area and a small clear area has been photographed, the silver emulsion may shift slightly toward the registration perforations during the developing process. This phenomenon does not seem to occur when the proportion of black to white is reversed; i.e., when there is a wide area of clear stock and a small area of black. Discrepancy of matte positions can be corrected on an optical printer where the operator can see and compare and fit the images to each other. Such realignment is not possible when printing bi-pack in the animation camera; this type of matte work is executed by cumulative frame count and the images being printed are not visible (*see* below).

☐ The clear-core and black-core mattes necessary for a given sequence are combined in the optical printer to produce a single print (Figure 12.5). When matte *A* and print *A* are run together through the optical printer, the opaque portion of the matte prevents the exposure of the corresponding raw film stock, while the clear areas of the matte permit the desired images to be printed on the film. When matte *B* and print *B* are run together through the optical printer, the already exposed areas of the previous run are protected by the black portions of matte *B*, and the formerly masked areas are now exposed with the images of print *B*. The images of print *A* are thus combined with the images of print *B* into one strip of film—print *C*.

ROTOSCOPING

When the film maker plans to combine cartoons or titles with live-action footage or to matte out images in live-action scenes, he often employs a technique called rotoscoping. Using a rotoscope unit, he projects each frame of the live-action background scene from the camera onto the animation tabletop. He can thus make layouts of drawings which correspond precisely to each frame of the live-action footage (Figure 12.6). The rotoscope unit is mounted behind the cut-out pressure

FIGURE 12.4 Photographic mattes.

plate of the camera and consists of a lighting unit and prism assembly which projects the images of the film through the open camera lens onto the animation tabletop. While rotoscoping, the live-action footage, fine grain positive and precision perforated, is mounted in the camera's shuttle in the taking position.

□ The rotoscope light is turned on, and the film footage is moved up until the first frame to be rotoscoped is projected on the tabletop. A sheet of animation paper is placed on the table pegs, and the necessary information is traced from the projected image. Each succeeding projected frame of film is similarly traced. The degree of precision in the drawings depends upon the planned relationship between live-action and animated elements in the final print. In some instances it may be necessary to have only every fifth frame in order to determine the general position of the live-action images. But when the live-action and animated images are intended to interact closely or when photographic mattes are being made, detailed and precise frame-by-frame tracings must be drawn.

□ An unpleasant "rotoscope wiggle" can sometimes result when mattes are hand drawn, frame by frame, to match very slow or tight moves, or irregular shapes. This is caused by variations in the rendering of the pencil lines or misinterpretations of projected image edges. Rotoscope wiggle can be avoided to some extent by tracing only every second or third frame and later creating a smooth flow of action by executing the in-between drawings on a drawing disc.

□ The live-action images should be as simple in form and clearly defined as possible. Live-action footage whose images move so quickly that their edges blur offer a serious problem in precise tracing. The live-action cameraman can reduce the magnitude of this problem by shooting with a high-speed camera and later skipping out frames to regain normal speed, or by closing down the shutter to sharpen the images. The problems offered by imprecise edges and inconsistent tracing are the primary shortcomings of the rotoscoping technique.

□ Using the technique of rotoscoping, we are able to make live-action and animated characters appear to coexist and interact. To obtain this effect, we compose the live-action sequence first, taking care to allow space in the composition for the animation to appear. Be sure to have the actor relate his eyes and his actions to the animation which will be added. Unless the back-and-forth relationship between live-action and animated characters is planned carefully, their combined images will appear unrelated even though they appear within the same picture frame.

□ Step two involves planning the animation. Record the dialogue, make the bar sheets, and plan the animation action

MATTE A   PRINT A   MATTE B   PRINT B   PRINT C COMPOSITE

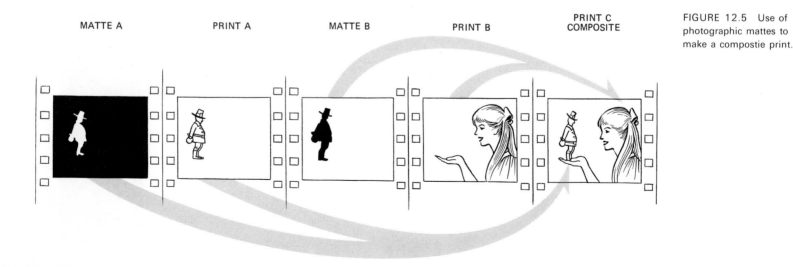

FIGURE 12.5 Use of photographic mattes to make a compostie print.

in synchronization with the actor's words and actions. Then, compose the animation in the area provided for it when the live action was exposed; using the rotoscope, project the live-action footage to be sure that the animation fits the live action.

☐ Step three requires photographing the animation by itself against a black background for the same number of frames that it is to appear in conjunction with the live-action footage.

☐ Step four is familiar. The animation is lighted from underneath to silhouette it and is photographed with high-contrast film to obtain film mattes. A word of caution—when painting cels to to be used for matte work be sure to apply the paint thickly to assure opacity. It is common practice to give such animation cels two coats of paint or to apply a coat of black after the regular opaque paint is thoroughly dry.

☐ The animation is then combined with the live-action footage in the optical printer. The black-core matte is printed with the live-action footage to mask off the area where the animation is to appear. When film is run through the optical printer a second time, the clear-core matte is printed with the animation to mask off the area where the live-action footage has already been exposed. The final result is a single strip combining the images of a cartoon and an actor who are mutually interacting as if both were living beings in the same environment.

BI-PACK

The animation camera can be used as a contact printer with mattes to achieve simple optical effects that are normally done on an optical printer. The bi-pack technique requires a magazine having four compartments with interlocked drive (Figure 12.7). Two of the compartments are used for loading the raw film stock and taking it up after exposure. The other two are used for loading and taking up the previously exposed and processed matte, whose images are now to be impressed upon the raw film stock together with any artwork being photographed on the table of the animation compound.

☐ Notice the film threading procedure (Figure 12.8). Both the processed film and the raw film stock pass through the camera drive system and shuttle simultaneously—with the matte on the *outside,* nearest the lens, so that its images may act upon the film emulsion. This means that the processed film should be loaded in the magazine nearest the camera so it can pass around the outside of the unexposed film. Wipes, surerimpositions, and the combining of cartoons with live-action back-

FIGURE 12.6 Rotoscope unit. Courtesy of Oxberry-Berkey Technical.

grounds can thereby be achieved by using photographic mattes in bi-pack for the processed film component.

AERIAL IMAGE PHOTOGRAPHY

The aerial image technique is essentially a form of rear projection—the animation camera photographs the projected image plus whatever titles or animation are superimposed over it. A film projector is positioned to the right of the animation stand and electrically interlocked with the animation camera (Figures 12.9, 12.10, 12.11).. Each frame of the previously exposed live-action footage is projected to a mirror under the table where it is reflected up through condenser lenses onto the raw film emulsion in the camera.

☐   An unobstructed aerial image can usually be seen only by means of the ground glass reticle in a through-the-lens viewfinder. But the projected aerial image can be seen on the tabletop if a translucent material is placed in the light path. It is here that animation or titles are planned—directly over the projected image. Positioned drawings can be made with paper mounted on the table pegbars for each projected frame of film. It may be necessary to do so for every animation drawing in the film if a need for precision requires it. The rotoscoped drawings can then be cleaned up and rendered on cels. A word of caution—great care must be taken in selecting cels for aerial image work because minute flaws reflect light and create undesirable flares.

☐   When the cels are placed in order of exposure, we return to the animation stand to photograph the animation and the live-action footage together. The film feed control of the projector is interlocked with the feed control of the camera mounted over the animation table; the aerial image unit is constructed with this interlock system to assure that there will be a frame of film moved forward in the camera with each new frame of film projected.

☐   The table is toplighted in the conventional way at the same time the live-action image is projected from the bottom. Each cel is placed in sequence over the corresponding frame of film from which the position drawings were made, and photographed. No more need be done. The aerial image unit automatically advances the film in the camera and projector after each exposure. When the film in the camera is processed the animation will be combined with the live-action footage.

☐   The aerial image is focused at tabletop level and can be photographed only when the camera lens is at a specific,

FIGURE 12.7   Bi-pack magazine. Courtesy of Oxberry-Berkey Technical.

preestablished field position level. It is therefore not possible to execute zooms on an uninterrupted aerial image because of the fixed height of the camera. If a zoom becomes mandatory, then a ground glass must be used to transfix the image for photography. Under this condition the image is no longer aerial. The room should be darkened as much as possible to reduce the loss of contrast through ambient light; top lighting may have to be eliminated entirely. A zoom-in to a ground glass image may be carried through to the 7-field position level, but any closer move may result in excessive graininess.

☐ The compound tabletop may not be moved during aerial image photography because such a move would misalign the optical projection system. Only E–W pans can be executed with the tabletop traveling pegbars. A floating pegbar unit can be used here to great advantage because it enables us to execute all the N–S and E–W moves we would normally implement with the compound controls which are now rendered immobile.

☐ Split-screen effects can be achieved by using the aerial image technique. Half of the aerial image area is covered with a glossy black surface, precisely and carefully positioned. The first live-action footage is projected and then photographed by the animation camera. The camera shutter is closed, and the live-action footage is run back to the first frame starting point. The opposite half of the aerial image area is then covered with black material, the shutter is opened to its normal position, and the second live-action film is projected and photographed for the same number of frames. When the exposed film is processed, the separate frame halves of the two live-action films will be combined in a split-screen effect within one film.

☐ The aerial image unit has manifold uses. Titles, trademarks, and animation may be added to live-action footage in a single pass before the camera. If a product changes its label design, those television commercials produced before the change can be salvaged by superimposing the new label over the area of the old by aerial methods with a minimum of time, effort, and money. The need for bi-pack filming is eliminated, as is the need for high-contrast positive and negative film mattes with their concomitant problems of registration and matte bleed.

☐ Another advantage offered by an aerial image unit is its flexibility in manipulating live-action scenes. As with an optical printer we can enlarge, reduce, or reposition individual frames from any given scene, or flop over the film and reverse its images. We can create a "freeze frame" effect by holding the

FIGURE 12.8 Bi-pack threading. Courtesy of Oxberry-Berkey Technical.

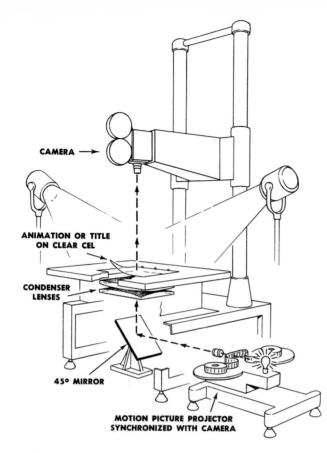

OXBERRY ANIMATION STAND WITH UNDERNEATH PROJECTION UNIT' AS 99

FIGURE 12.9 Aerial image photography. Courtesy of Oxberry-Berkey Technical.

same frame for repeated exposures or "skip frame" to shorten a film or lessen its projection speed. Special effects can be added by using such devices as the flip box, ripple glass, and split-screen prisms in conjunction with the aerial image unit.

☐ A disadvantage in aerial image work derives from its projection and optical system; films projected to a mirror and through a relatively large condenser system must almost inevitably show a slight degree of degradation, soft focus, and color fringing. Moreover, film stocks designed for original photography do not duplicate the photographic scale with the fidelity characteristic of film emulsions designed for direct reproduction. When the live-action scene is intended to be subdued in relation to the titles or animation, this loss of definition is no disadvantage. Despite this slight reduction in reproduction quality, an aerial image unit is an extremely valuable adjunct for any film maker planning to combine animation with live-action footage.

TRANSPARENT SUPERIMPOSURE

In certain instances, a film maker may wish to create a ghostlike or dreamlike sequence in which the images of the first or second run appear almost as a stream of consciousness. This effect is achieved by photographing the images during both exposures with the shutter partially closed or with the lens stopped down. Lens closure is more apt to give satisfactory results than shutter manipulation because on small shutter openings the slightest blacklash can cause flicker. The following table of relative exposure openings may be of aid in controlling and determining relative emphasis.

Percent Exposure	Cut in Lens Aperture Stops	Shutter Openings
100	0	170°
90	1/6	153°
80	1/3	135°
70	1/2	120°
60	2/3	100°
50	1	85°
40	1 1/3	68°
30	1 2/3	51°
20	2 1/3	34°
10	3 1/3	17°

Often it is impractical to include cels with white labels over backgrounds during a single run. If zooms, pans, or compound moves are being carried out with the animation photography, titles included on the first run would shift around with the rest of the artwork, and during a zoom these letters would enlarge and perhaps run off the screen altogether.

□　The procedure for superimposing white labels over moving animation is as follows: Plan in advance *where* the labels are to appear, determine from the bar sheets *when* they are to appear, and make up separate exposure sheets for the separate camera runs that will expose the labels. Be sure to match the timing perfectly because the animation will not be visible when titles are exposed. We are working from cumulative frame numbers only.

□　Photograph the animation or the background in the normal way; then close the camera shutter and run the film in reverse in the camera to the start of the first scene in which a super-imposed label appears. Set the film direction to "forward" again and open the shutter to its normal maximum. Remove all the cels and background materials that were used during the animation of the first run. Turn on the underneath lighting unit, mount the Kodalith negative titles according to the sequence of appearance indicated in the exposure sheets, and proceed to photograph the labels. The pure black of the negative surrounding the titles will not register on the background or animation exposed during the first run. But the clear titles with the light behind them will burn through the previously exposed subject of the first run and register as white. The combined result in the processed print is a film with clean white labels which remain in a stable position, superimposed over a context which may be shifting constantly. The same technique may of course be used for burning white titles into a still background for screen credits.

□　White titles become even more legible when the letters have dark, off-set shadows—called a "dropped shadow." This effect serves to separate the letters from their background and endow them with a three-dimensional character. When dropped shadows are created by multiple-exposure methods, the means of achieving the effects may be obtained either by photographing high-contrast positive and negative titles in separate runs, or by printing one to obtain the other. These mattes are ordinarily used in an optical printer where the dropped shadow effect is created by positioning the dark image slightly lower and to one side of the white.

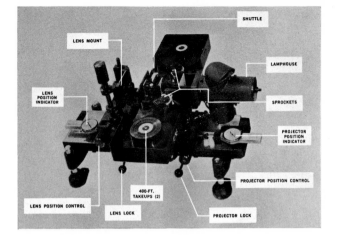

FIGURE 12.10 Underneath aerial image projector. Courtesy of Oxberry-Berkey Technical.

FIGURE 12.11 Optical layout of animation stand with underneath aerial image projector. Courtesy of Oxberry-Berkey Technical.

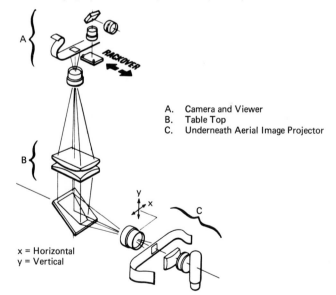

A. Camera and Viewer
B. Table Top
C. Underneath Aerial Image Projector

x = Horizontal
y = Vertical

☐ The same effect may be achieved in a bi-pack system on the animation stand if the camera has a very precise registration system, and if the artwork is positioned carefully. First, make a high-contrast black matte of the title; then load the matte in bi-pack with the raw film stock and photograph the subject on the animation table. The black matte titles prevent any light from reaching the emulsion it covers; if the operation ended at this stage there would be black titles only. Finally, position the white titles carefully over black and burn in the letters *without* the obstructing black title matte. If the white and black images have been offset correctly, the result will provide white titles with black shadows over the desired background.

FIGURE 12.12 Animation and live action scenes combined through multiple exposure and color-keyed videoelectronic methods. Copyright © 1969 Hanna-Barbera Productions.

chapter 13
ANIMATION OF OBJECTS, CUTOUTS, AND PUPPETS

ANIMATED film, as we have seen, is most commonly produced from a series of images rendered in one dimension on cels. There are, however, many other techniques and mediums which are widely used in animation. Every animator should be familiar with these methods and should be aware in particular of the effects which are achieved through animation of objects, cutouts, and puppets.

ANIMATING OBJECTS

The animation of objects is one of the easiest and least expensive forms of animation, and is frequently used to depict processes in business, industrial, and instructional films and to sell products in television commercials.

☐ The procedure for planning and executing the animation of objects is comparatively simple. As in other forms of animation, the first step is to determine the number of frames to be used to animate the object from the beginning to the end of its move. Then the object's path across the screen is established. If the effect consists of rearranging many objects between exposures, such as unscrambling letters to form screen titles, a separate path for each component should be worked out in much the same manner as a pantograph chart. Finally, each object's path is divided into increments representing one exposure apiece, with appropriate eases at the beginning and end of each move. The animation of objects is usually photographed on ''ones.''

☐ To execute the animation, the pattern chart may be traced onto the background. The objects are moved by eye to each new trace-mark for each exposure. The pattern can also be transferred to a cel which is mounted on floating pegbars or is hinged on the tabletop outside the photography area; the pattern is flipped forward to set each succeeding move. Or, last and perhaps least satisfactory, a pair of dividers can be set to the distance the objects are to be moved between each exposure and the pieces moved accordingly. All moves must be made carefully and consistently to prevent unsightly wobbles while the object is traversing its path. The faster the move, the harder it is to detect irregularities; the slower the move, the easier.

☐ A variation on this technique is the animation of titles. Plastic letters can unscramble themselves to form titles, and reform themselves into new words. But it is difficult to begin with scrambled letters and have them arrive at the right places at the right time in the right order and with correct alignment. The trick is to shoot the titles backward: Run the film through the camera with the shutter closed for the length of the effect. Align the titles in the desired final order. Set the film direction to "reverse," and proceed to scramble the plastic letters one increment at a time in the visual pattern planned. When the titles have been scrambled for the number of increments and exposures desired, the film will have arrived at the beginning of the effect. When the film is projected on the screen, the first frame photographed (showing the titles perfectly aligned) will be the last to appear. The effect will be that of scattered plastic letters rearranging themselves to form perfect titles.

☐ *Animation within objects.* A variation on the animation of objects occurs when an object unfolds itself, apparently without outside aid, to reveal its internal structure. A common use of this technique is in television commercials, where product packages unfold themselves to reveal their contents.

☐ This technique finds application in education. If time is short, and the expenses of conventional animation are too high, some scientific processes can be executed directly on the animation stand and photographed in progressive stages as they take place. For example, the dissection of a laboratory specimen can be photographed in slow careful steps. The incisions are extended minutely with each exposure, until the dissection technique has been completely demonstrated.

☐ Dissolves are useful in this type of animation; as in the filmograph, dissolves permit large but comprehensible moves. Double or "end to end" dissolves are particularly useful, but tend to produce a perceptible "beat," whereas a "triple" dissolve technique produces a feeling of flow. It is accomplished with special dissolve scales.

☐ When photographing three-dimensional objects, it may be necessary to adjust the follow focus cam. The focus cam is set for table level; because of its height, a three-dimensional object may suffer from soft focus. Some stands have adjustable cams which can be raised as much as 6" above the table and still permit a follow focus zoom. Otherwise, the lens may have to be focused manually.

☐ *Time-lapse photography.* This technique produces an animated effect without relying on conventional animation techniques. A camera is focused on a plant or on any object which changes too slowly for the eye to see; the shutter is tripped at widely spaced time intervals to record increase in size or other significant changes. When the finished film is processed, the plant appears to grow extremely rapidly from seed to maturity before the viewer's eyes.

☐ Time-lapse photography is best done with artificial light;

FIGURE 13.1 *Model of a sea bottom.* From the film produced by Encyclopaedia Britannica Educational Corporation.

if done by daylight, uncontrollable changes in natural light may result in an intolerable flicker in the finished film. Exposures should be as long as the emulsion can tolerate without sacrificing tone and color quality. For time-lapse work the intervals of photography should be controlled with an intervalometer.

☐ Some processes are so subtle that they can be depicted only with models and stop-motion photography. The illustration shows a transparent plastic model containing a specially designed sea bottom representing a schematic profile of the bottom of a sea at the delta of a river (Figure 13.1). The model was carefully designed to cause the moving dust particles to behave as much as possible like sand deposited by rivers in nature. A trap door is opened to release the flow of sandy silt (Figure 13.2). As in all animation of three-dimensional objects, special care must be taken to ensure adequate lighting (Figure 13.3).

☐ Perhaps the greatest single advantage of object animation is its quality of maximum realism. The advantages to the teacher (and advertiser) are twofold. When the viewer leaves the film, he will recognize the real thing immediately when he

FIGURE 13.3 *Lighting the model.* From the film produced by Encyclopaedia Britannica Educational Corporation.

FIGURE 13.2 *Flow of silt.* From the film produced by Encyclopaedia Britannica Educational Corporation.

sees it; he will not have to bridge the differences between an artistic rendition and an actual object. And, having seen the process take place as it really happens, the viewer should be able to duplicate it whether the process in question is dissecting a frog or unwrapping a package.

ANIMATION OF PUPPETS

In many respects, puppet animation is more closely related to live-action filmwork than it is to animation. The more successful the traditional puppet becomes in simulating lifelike motion the greater reason there is to ask oneself whether live-action photography might not be a better medium than puppet animation. Puppets have their feet on the ground; they exist in and are limited by three-dimensional reality. The flights of fancy made possible by the imagination of an artist and the capabilities of an animation stand are generally not possible with puppets. Realistic puppets invite comparison with reality and in this comparison they may become somewhat macabre. Caricature endows puppets with charm. And if placed in a world of fairy tales, a world of unabashed pretending, it is easy to become absorbed in and be entertained by their lives of make-believe. The more refreshing form of puppetry is that which makes little pretense of imitating life but instead uses a collage of materials in a nonrealistic way to make a personal statement (Figure 13.4).

☐ Puppets are animated by moving the limbs in small increments between each exposure. The principle is the universal rule of animation—movements must be small enough so that when the film is projected on the screen the images appear to be moving smoothly and of their own accord. Puppet animation requires the same kinds of planning necessary to other forms of animation. A script should be written and storyboarded, with all close-up, medium, and long shots worked out carefully. The narration or dialogue is then recorded, and bar sheets are made from the sound track to time the movements of the puppets from one part of the scene to the next. Accurate model sheets are made for the artisans who produce the puppets, and these are related to the settings in which the puppets will be photographed. Once the puppets and sets have been constructed, acceleration and deceleration charts should be made for the puppets' limbs in order to give them smooth and natural movements.

☐ The cameras for photographing this make-believe world should have facilities for tracking and tripod heads geared for

FIGURE 13.4 Collage puppets: *A Study in Paper.* Courtesy of Loyd Bruce Holman.

slow motion. All camera equipment should be devoid of the slightest vibration; this is close work and any shakiness will be visible on the screen.

☐ *Puppet construction.* Because puppets are moved a fraction of an inch between each exposure for many, many exposures, they need certain structural properties. The solid portions of the figure must be really solid in order to take constant handling without changing shape or breaking. The joints must be constructed of material which will not wear out quickly or become slack. The wires used to give "spine" to the limbs must be durable enough to be bent repeatedly without breaking. These requirements narrow down the number of materials usable for puppet making.

☐ The traditional material used for the head and torso is wood. Once wood is carved into its final shape, it will not change unless broken. Wood can be painted and touched up with a fine finish to cover small blemishes, which, with the great magnification used in this kind of work, would become apparent on the screen. When the puppets are made of wood, the limbs usually have ball-joints.

☐ Many puppets are now being constructed in part of rubber, plastic, or other synthetic materials (Figure 13.5). These figures are usually clothed from head to toe, with only the heads, feet, and hands showing. The torso and limbs are constructed almost entirely of multistrand wires, which are easily bent and controlled. Some puppets are constructed entirely of plastic, with no attempt to conceal the artificial joints, and their clothing is painted on from head to toe.

☐ Papier-maché figures can be made of wet paper spread over a wire substructure. Clay is impractical; the type of clay which remains malleable readily loses its shape with repeated handling and the type that hardens tends to crumble. Baked terra cotta is usable but brittle; a casual bump may chip or break it. Wax is sometimes used because it is so malleable, but it tends to soften under the lights.

☐ Changes of facial expression are difficult to achieve with puppets. If many expressions are required, it is necessary either to make a series of papier-mâché masks to indicate changes of expression, or to make the features themselves of plastic or other malleable material that allows progressive adjustment. A jointed lower jaw, such as is found in ventriloquists' dummies,

FIGURE 13.5 Plastic puppets: *Hansel and Gretel.* Courtesy of Michael Myerberg Productions.

FIGURE 13.6 Interior set: *Hansel and Gretel.* Courtesy of Michael Myerberg Productions.

FIGURE 13.7 Exterior details: *Hansel and Gretel.* Courtesy of Michael Myerberg Productions.

can be used to simulate the speech of the sound track. Hands can be made of plastic or rubber over a wire skeleton, but it takes experienced eyes and practiced fingers to animate a puppet's hands in an acceptable way—particularly in close-up shots.

☐ *Sets.* The sets for puppet animation offer problems similar to those used in theatrical production, but they should be executed with the same degree of caricature as the puppets themselves. Tables, chairs, and all the paraphernalia appropriate to the story must be constructed in three dimension; these are most easily made of balsa wood, which can be readily carved and joined (Figure 13.6). Exterior landscapes can be constructed of papier-mâché spread over a wire or cardboard substructure, and painted. Trees and shrubs can be made of pieces of sponge, dyed green and mounted on sticks of balsa; fences and buildings are made of balsa, too (Figure 13.7). Take care to fix everything down firmly. It is a good idea to have pins mounted in the legs of the set pieces which can be pressed into the floor of the set to anchor them.

☐ In addition to the three-dimensional pieces for the foreground and middleground, a distant background is usually needed as well. For interiors, it can be the open-top, three-sided square of the conventional theater, painted and decorated according to the mood of the story. For exteriors, a diorama may be more effective in creating the sweep of an outside landscape; a diorama is simply a flat sheet of illustration paper, bent in a semicircle across the back of the set, and painted with the appropriate scenery (Figure 13.8).

☐ After the puppets are made and the sets completed, the stage must be lighted with small floods and spotlights (Figure 13.9). The play of light over the puppets should be tested as they are put through their paces on the set. Move the puppets from one point to another and see whether unexpected dark ''holes'' or ''hot spots'' require one or more lights to be shifted. Work out the lighting continuity first. Once shooting has begun, you cannot stop in the middle of a move to relight the action; the change would be evident in the completed film.

ANIMATION OF CUTOUTS

Animating cutouts can be lots of fun, and this technique has a definite place in art education—all the way down to kindergarten. Figures are most often the subjects for cutout animation, but animals and objects can be animated too. There are three basic types of cutouts for animation.

1. The painted cutout with jointed limbs, which is lighted from the top of the animation stand in the conventional way.

2. The black cutout with jointed limbs, which is lighted from beneath (as with pencil tests) to throw the animation into silhouette.

3. Painted cutouts which are mounted on unphotographed sticks.

☐ *Painted and jointed figures.* In this type of animation, the head and torso and limbs can be made of any reasonably durable kind of paper or cardboard. Cut out each part separately, paint it with opaque water-color paints or cover it with colored paper, and assemble it with metal joints (available at any school supply store). The joints will show and be photographed unless the cutouts are designed with some kind of an overfold. One way to avoid evident joints is to punch a circular hole centered at the pivot point of the limb. The punched-out circle is reinserted in its hole. A circle of cel material which is slightly larger than the hole is glued to the back of the punched-out circle; the limb to be moved is glued to the front of the punched-out circle, thereby making a three layer "sandwich" that holds the limb to the figure while permitting the limb to be moved.

☐ The backgrounds for toplighted cutout animation are the same as those used for conventional animation. As jointed figures are inevitably unsophisticated, we can afford to be spontaneous and unpretentious and have fun in executing them.

☐ This animation can be planned as simply or as completely as is desired. We can work out movement and timing from recorded sound and make acceleration and deceleration charts for the cutouts' movements. Or we can make a simple silent film, moving the figures by eye through a little sequence of pantomime.

☐ The illustration shows how simple it is to animate jointed cutouts. A cutout figure is shown dumping a basket of leaves. The film-maker has merely bent the figure with his hands and spread the cutout leaves with a pointed instrument for short distances between each exposure (Figure 13.10).

☐ This is fun and it need not be fancy fun. If the film is being made from cutouts produced by elementary school children, just the sight of their cutouts going through their paces on the screen will delight them and spur them on to do more. Cutout animation can also be used for more serious purposes. Quantitative mathematical concepts, chemistry formulae, and basketball and football tactics can be taught by painting sym-

FIGURE 13.8 Exterior landscape: *Hansel and Gretel.* Courtesy of Michael Myerberg Productions.

FIGURE 13.9 Lighting the set: *Hansel and Gretel.* Courtesy of Michael Myerberg Productions.

FIGURE 13.10 Cutout animation. Courtesy of the National Film Board of Canada.

FIGURE 13.11 Stick cutout on a cycling template.

FIGURE 13.12 Silhouette cutouts. Courtesy of the National Film Board of Canada.

bols on cardboard squares and moving them about under the camera. In this instance, the techniques for moving and aligning them are the same as those used in animating objects.

☐ *Stick cutouts.* The second type of cutout is widely used on television to avoid the necessity of painting cycles of figures as they appear through a landscape or a room. These cutouts have only the top half showing, and are mounted on a stick extending down to a point. A small cycling chart is mounted under the point of each stick, and each puppet is moved a point for each exposure in a continuing cycle as the background is panned in the conventional way (Figure 13.11). Or, the stick can be run along a heavy cardboard template that has been precut to provide the desired path of movement.

☐ A version of this stick cutout can be made with jointed arms, hands, torso, and head, and photographed with this portion showing, in the manner of hand puppets. While the wild pantomime possible with completely free puppets is impractical, short sequences with a great deal of charm can be created.

☐ *Silhouette cutouts.* Silhouette cutouts have the same jointed structure as painted cutouts, but the figures are made from black cardboard, or painted black, to make as sharp a silhouette as possible (Figure 13.12). Even the metal joints are painted so the camera will not photograph highlights picked up by indirect reflection. This form of cutout animation is lighted from beneath and photographed on high-contrast film.

☐ Oddly enough, silhouettes are inherently more sophisticated and require a higher degree of skill on the part of the artist than do painted cutouts. Painted cutouts are obviously mere painted pieces of paper held together with metal joints, but only the outlines of silhouette cutouts are seen. These contours must have grace and articulation or the figures will appear to be little more than animated sandbags. Lotte Reiniger, of Germany, has carried silhouette cutting to the level of high art in her films; the exquisite cutting of each part is worth careful study on the part of the film maker planning to do this kind of animation.

☐ The carefully cut contours of the figure must have their qualitative counterparts in the backgrounds. If translucent effects for clouds or distant landscapes are desired, they can be achieved by cutting their shapes out of Bourges sheets or some other transparent but toned material. Compose the figures and their backgrounds carefully to prevent confusion, or a black figure may blend with a black background and produce an incomprehensible blank.

chapter 14
UNUSUAL ANIMATION TECHNIQUES

THE overwhelming majority of animated films are made with cels, models, and puppets in the ways described up to this point. But a whole world of techniques remains unknown to many who might make use of them. Some of them are far less costly in time and materials than conventional techniques, and many of them offer entirely new avenues of expression.

PASTEL ANIMATION

Norman McLaren of the National Film Board of Canada has devised a form of animation which he calls the "pastel method." Its concept is best described in his own words:

*In doing oil paintings myself, and in watching other painters at their canvases, it often seemed to me that the evolution . . . from its virgin state to (in my own case) its soiled and battered conclusion, was more interesting than the conclusion itself. Why not, therefore, consciously switch the focus-point of all the effort from the end condition and spread it over the whole process? In other words, do a painting, but put the emphasis upon the doing rather than the painting—on the process rather than the end product.**

* "Animated Films," *Documentary Film News* (May, 1948).

FIGURE 14.1 Pastel animation: *La poulette grise.* Courtesy of the National Film Board of Canada.

☐ McLaren's idea was to create an animated film by photographing each progressive change in a single drawing, instead of photographing many drawings in the form of cels to achieve the effect of change. This technique has application in art classes where conventional animation may be too costly, but where the students have time enough to spend doing pastel drawings. He described his technique in making *La poulette grise* ("The Little Grey Hen") as follows:

. . . *I stuck a bit of cardboard about 18 inches by 24 inches upon a wall, placed rigidly in front of it a tripod and camera loaded with colour film. To avoid reflection and waiting-to-dry trouble, I used chalks and pastel rather than paint.*

The picture then grew in the normal way that any still painting grows, being evolved from moment to moment, and each stage being very dependent on the stage before it. About every quarter of an hour the evolution was recorded on the film mainly by short, continuous dissolves. For three weeks the surface of this one bit of cardboard metamorphosed itself in and out of a series of henly images, and at the end of it, all I had was one much worn bit of cardboard with an unimpressive chalk drawing on it, and 400 feet of exposed film in the camera. In a sense the film was the by-product of doing a painting.

Of course, the sound track had to be marked up first and the dope (cue) sheet made out in much the same way as for the hand-drawn technique, but once again the creative part of the job happened in one and only one concentrated binge, unhampered by technical headaches and frustration. Also of importance was the fact that here again the movement evolved in its natural sequence, and as a result I had a chance to improvise everything at the moment of shooting.

As this particular technique lent itself more readily to creating visual change rather than to action (side to side, and to and fro displacement of image on the screen), I intentionally avoided the use of action, particularly because it suited the theme, and partly out of curiosity to see if change in itself could be a strong enough cinematic factor to sustain interest.

*The technique also invited me to take chiaroscuro out of its usual role as a dead element in the ,decor of animated films, and put it to work as the foremost factor with a life of its own. In this I hope that perhaps I am on the way to bridging the gap that has always existed between painting proper and the animated film.**

*Ibid.

☐ Pastel animation can be carried out more securely and conveniently when taped down upon a standard animation table. The animation stand will not move, as a tripod would if bumped, nor will the drawing work loose from the horizontal animation table as it could work loose from a vertical wall. And finally, the optimum level of lighting has been pre-established for the animation table, so there is no need of using an improvised lighting arrangement, as with a camera and a tripod. The animation stand already provides the optimum situation for pastel animation.

☐ Mr. McLaren developed two variants of the pastel technique. One method calls for making minute changes within a single drawing, which is photographed a frame at a time for each change until the drawing and the film are completed. The other method calls for using a series of pastel drawings, combined with zooms and dissolves, to create the illusion of continuing three-dimensional movement.

☐ The single-drawing pastel method requires fewer materials than the other. We make only one basic sketch which then undergoes progressive changes. This sketch is most easily done on a black surface, since black provides a background against which it is not necessary to render an entire drawing; significant changes can be implied by only a few touches. If the drawing is made on a white background, the whole surface has to be rendered and changes may have to be made over many parts of the picture between each exposure. An additional advantage of black is that it dramatizes color and enhances its chroma level, while white tends to bleed and wash out colors. Whatever painting surface is selected, mount it on illustration board or some other surface sturdy enough to endure a great deal of handling and reworking.

☐ Pastels vary in chroma level and range of selection; they vary also in fragility. Soft pastels are easier to apply than hard pastels and can be rubbed and smudged with facility; but they break easily and can become a nuisance. Harder pastels require more pressure to apply but stand up better. The only other instrument needed is a smudger or durable fingertips.

☐ The procedure for pastel animation at the stand could not be simpler. The pastel paper, mounted on a stiff board, is punched and mounted on the pegbars. Since the material will be handled a great deal before the animation is completed, it is worthwhile to avoid wear and tear around the pegbar holes by taping down the edges of the sheet with masking tape.

☐ As the first step, draw the basic pastel sketch on which the changes will be made. If the photographed transitions from point to point are to occur within a given time, make a tracing paper overlay indicating in a general way how far the rendering and smudging should progress within a given number of frames. When working on the animation stand, work with the platen open or remove the glass. Once we have faded in on the original drawing, minute changes are made with pastel or smudges, exposing one frame after each change until the entire pastel sequence is finished.

☐ If cels indicating symbols or concrete objects are to be superimposed over the pastel drawing, it is advisable to use mattes or an aerial image unit to combine the two. Cels can, of course, be superimposed on the pastel drawing, but this necessitates lowering the platen on the drawing. The pressure may cause undesirable smudging which will gradually soften all the sharp edges in the drawing. Fixative can be sprayed over the drawing only after the pastel drawing and film are finished.

☐ The first and most obvious use of this pastel technique is in art education. Any student who can make a pastel drawing and press an exposure button can make an animated film in the pastel technique.

☐ An equally promising area is the biological sciences, where gradual growths and changes can be depicted at a low cost. A typical example would be the progressive growth and development of a foetus within a womb. Each major stage of development would be rendered and photographed. Each change to a new drawing would be made by means of a long dissolve, and the gradual development within each phase would be drawn and smudged in pastels. A half dozen pastel drawings could be used to depict the whole process of evolution from conception to birth. In the physical sciences, the illusions of gas and air flow or chemical combinations, can be achieved easily and inexpensively in pastels. If these processes were depicted by conventional animation, it would cost thousands of dollars in time, labor, and materials. With the pastel technique the cost of materials is negligible and the time and labor required is a fraction of that necessitated by conventional animation techniques.

☐ The second variation of the pastel technique in which a series of drawings is used was also developed by McLaren: In *C'est l'aviron,* an animated film inspired by a French Canadian folk song, a sequence of drawings simulates the views a canoe

FIGURE 14.2 Zoom and dissolve: *C'est l'aviron.* Courtesy of the National Film Board of Canada.

FIGURE 14.3 Worktable for painting on film. Courtesy of the National Film Board of Canada.

FIGURE 14.4 Film-holding block. Courtesy of the National Film Board of Canada.

voyager would have as he paddled down a Canadian stream (Figure 14.2). The film is a series of zooms from long shots to close-ups of each of these pictures; every transition to a new drawing is made by a dissolve. The continuous zooms and the repeated dissolves beautifully re-created the smooth gliding movement of the canoe and the spirit of the song. These zooms are logarithmic—to keep the rate of approach constant. The illusion is further heightened by cutting a piece of cardboard into the shape of a canoe prow and moving it rhythmically up and down to the beat of the song.

☐ This zoom-dissolve pastel technique has an other-worldly quality. It can also be used to create the illusion of limitless space; a series of dissolves to changing patterns of stars is often used to make the viewer feel that he is traveling through space or time.

PAINTING ON FILM

The technique of painting directly on clear film stock has been developed by McLaren. Thus animated film is created without using an animation stand or even a camera.

☐ Painting directly on film requires specialized equipment. The film maker works at a table having a tilted board surface, which has a vertical slit cut in the board to let the light through from behind (Figure 14.3). The slit should be about 2'' wide for 35mm film, and long enough to illuminate 24 frames of film at a time. A channel for feeding the film over the slit is formed by nailing a thin strip of wood on each side of the slit.

☐ It is awkward to hold the film with one hand while painting on it with the other; the film slips and slithers with every attempt to slide a new frame forward. It is a convenience, even a necessity, to construct a film holder from a wooden block which will hold 24 frames of film. This block should have a slot the actual width of the 35mm frame and a frosted glass insert to provide a solid but transparent support (Figure 14.4). The block should be grooved, with an overhanging lip on each side to hold the film in place securely, but not so tightly that it cannot be pulled readily through the groove. The block should have serrations or pegs on one side; these are put on the right-hand side for left-handed artists, and on the left-hand side for right-handed artists. They enable the artist to push up the block with one hand as he paints on the film with the other.

☐ If the film maker wants to animate a shape progressively, for even as short a time as one second, some means of assuring consistent controlled animation from frame to frame is necessary or only erratic blobs will flash by on the screen. The simplest solution is to scratch a registration grid—analogous to a field guide—in the surface of the holder glass (Figure 14.5). The grid can be inked, but inked lines tend to intrude upon the creative act of painting, asserting themselves as a compositional element which tends to mislead the eye. The projected film will not show these lines and the results may not be those that were anticipated. A scratched line will catch the light sufficiently for registration purposes.

☐ The roll of blank film being painted is most conveniently hung on a rod fixed below the table. Suspended between the film maker's knees, it is out of the way while painting and can be readily unrolled as new frames of film are fed forward. There should be a bin for catching the painted film on the far side of the table. The bin can be made of cardboard, cotton, or any other materials that will not mar the film. The bin must be kept clean at all times.

☐ The materials needed for actual painting include a roll of clear, blank film called "machine leader." The film can be 90mm, 70mm, or 35mm wide (or 16mm, if you do not mind eye strain) for the original painting. In printing it will be reduced to a practical projection size, such as 16mm. The development of the wider film stocks has made direct film painting practical. Other needs include transparent inks or dyes (Craftint, Higgens, or Pelikan), brushes and pen points, white cotton gloves to keep the film clean and a damp cloth for wiping off disasters before they dry. For those planning to work on 16mm clear film, a magnifying glass is mandatory. Holding a glass by hand is very awkward, and the constant wobbling is annoying. A better solution is to have a magnifying glass mounted on a jointed arm which can be set in a given position.

☐ The procedure for painting on film is as follows: Keep inks, brushes, pens, and rags ready at hand. Determine which side of the film is the base side and which is the emulsion side; paint on the emulsion side, which has a duller surface. If in doubt, dab a little paint or ink on each side. If the medium flakes off readily when dry, it is the *wrong* (base) side; paint on the side to which the inks readily adhere. Thread the blank film through the groove of the wooden block, pushing through enough film to provide some leader at the head, and align the frames with the 24 registration grids.

☐ Now begin to paint whatever figures or abstract shapes are desired on the frames of film, working from top to bottom. It is preferable not to paint each frame completely and then proceed to the next, in comic strip fashion. This tends to result

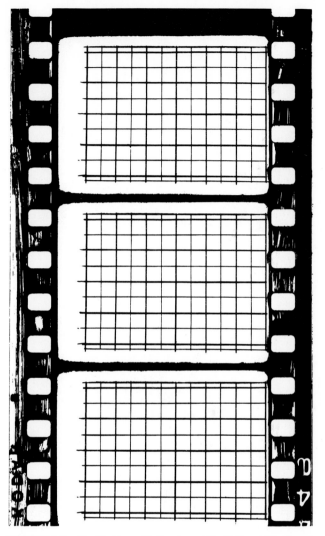

FIGURE 14.5   Registration grid. Courtesy of the National Film Board of Canada.

FIGURE 14.6 Technique of painting film lengthwise. Courtesy of the National Film Board of Canada.

FIGURE 14.7 Etching black emulsion. Courtesy of the National Film Board of Canada.

in a series of individual ''pictures,'' rather than embodying the progressive changes of shapes in motion. And motion is the heart of the medium.

☐ Instead, paint one of the larger elements of the picture (backgrounds, for example) through its 24-frame sequence, changing its position slightly in each frame, keeping the shape and its movement under control by glancing at the scratched registration grids. When this element is painted, go back to the first frame and add whatever other elements or details are desired for the same 24 frames. When they have been painted, move the film up until the last painted frame is at the top and the next 24 frames are aligned with the registration. We are ready to begin painting again, and hopefully, can maintain a reasonable continuity of shapes and colors.

☐ There are two approaches to painting on film, and the two can be combined. One way is to paint the frames one at a time for each 24 frame sequence, as just described. A second way is to ignore the individual frames and to paint in long sweeping abstract shapes (Figure 14.6). Tape the film down on a long table and paint it lengthwise with long strokes which vary in shape, size, and texture. Each length of film can be worked over again and again, adding shapes and textures, drips and blobs, for as long as the transparency holds out. And once dry, the inks can be scratched into with a knife. This technique obviously will appeal to nonobjective artists who want to add the element of motion to their work.

☐ This technique can also be used to provide backgrounds for films which will later have recognizable shapes rendered on them, with the 24-frame system described earlier. Once the background colors and shapes have been painted and the inks or dyes have dried, the film is threaded through the holding block on the rendering table and rendered a frame at a time for 24-frame sequences as before. This is a good way to expedite what might otherwise be a long, tedious process of background painting.

☐ A variant of the direct painting technique is the etching technique. The inks and paints applied directly can be textured with additional designs and patterns which are cut and scraped with a scratch-board point or with one of the many mat cutting knives on the market (Figure 14.7). This concept can be carried a step further by using a leader coated with a black emulsion which can be scratched off—but because the leader is opaque, it is difficult to relate the engraved shapes to the underlying registration grid.

☐ Never project the original painted film, for this is an invitation to irreparable damage. If the film gate of the projector has one speck of grit in it, a scratch may be gouged into the inks and dyes for the entire length of the film—ruining it. Roll up the original as gently and carefully as possible and send it to a film laboratory for processing. They will make an internegative from the original, and then make a print from the internegative. If the original was painted in a size larger than 16mm, the laboratory can reduce the print to 16mm or to whatever projection size is desired.

□ The technique of painting directly on film stock may have wide application to making educational films in underdeveloped countries where money for equipment is scarce, and where there may be a lack of electricity for lighting. It was tried out in China in 1949 under the auspices of UNESCO. Chinese artists were taught to make simple animated films by the direct painting method about such topics as conservation techniques, the benefits of reforestation of exhausted land, and the consequences of drinking polluted water (Figure 14.8). This initial fieldwork in China was followed up by more intensive training of Chinese artists by McLaren at the Film Board of Canada. Whether this kind of work is being continued in China under the Communist regime is unknown, but the effectiveness of the work which was done in China suggests possible applications for this technique in other underdeveloped parts of the world.

HAND-DRAWN SOUND

Mr. McLaren has developed a technique for inking on the sound track; he "draws" the music and sound effects in the same way that he draws the animation. He creates music and sounds having a tonal quality which is without counterpart in the world of conventional musical instruments and natural noises; they are, quite literally, out of this world. He described his technique for hand-drawn sounds as follows:

I draw a lot of little lines on the sound-track area of the 35mm film. Maybe 50 to 60 lines for every musical note. The number of strokes to the inch controls the pitch of the note; the more, the higher the pitch; the fewer, the lower is the pitch. The size of the stroke controls the loudness: a big stroke will go "boom," a smaller stroke will give a quieter sound, and the faintest stroke will be just a little "m-m-m." A black ink is another way of making a loud sound, a mid-gray ink will make a medium sound, and a very pale ink will make a very quiet sound. The tone quality, which is the most difficult element to control, is made by the shape of the strokes. Well-rounded forms give smooth sounds; sharper or angular forms give harder, harsher sounds. Sometimes I use a brush instead of a pen to get very soft sound. By drawing or exposing two or more patterns on the same bit of film I can create harmony and textural effects.*

□ Here are some examples of hand-drawn sound, and a sample of etched sound (Figures 14.9a and 14.9b). Modifications can be made of all the described characteristics by varying the transparency of the inks used. The lighter and more translucent the medium, the more delicate the sounds. By varying the shapes, sizes, character, translucency and distances between the marks, a tremendous array of unique sounds can be mustered to create music and sound effects. The field of hand-drawn sounds and music offers a rich potential for experimenters.

□ McLaren has also developed a system for creating the notes of melodies by drawing on the sound track. He uses a series of registration grids which, he has discovered by experimentation, yield certain notes in the musical scale. By making marks corresponding to the tune of a melody on the points indicated by the grid, he knows that the results will yield a certain song. Listening to *Frère Jacques* in hand-drawn music is an experience. For those who have access to educational film libraries and are interested in the potential of hand-drawn music and sounds, I suggest viewing and listening carefully to *Pen Point Percussion and Loops* and *Neighbors*, both done by Norman McLaren and distributed by the National Film Board of Canada.

ANIMATION ON PAPER

Another expedient developed in China is the substitution of cheap typewriter paper for expensive animation cels. The paper is extended still further by being cut into quarters. The registration of the quarter-sheets was controlled by fitting all the sheets into an "L" mounted on both the drawing table and the improvised animation stand. The loss of precision caused by this method of registration precludes any sophisticated work. Because there is so much latitude and lack of precision in this method, it is advisable to draw and photograph on ones.

*"Dots and Loops," British Broadcasting Corporation, November 22, 1951. Quoted from William E. Jordan, "Norman McLaren: His Career and Techniques," *The Quarterly of Film, Radio and Television*, VIII, No. 1.

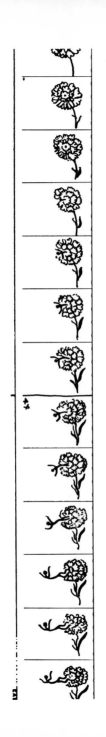

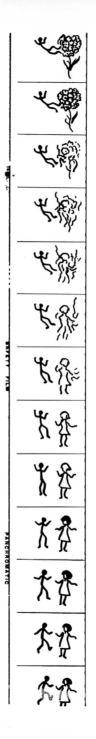

FIGURE 14.8 Painting on film by Chinese students. Courtesy of the National Film Board of Canada.

☐   The principle of paper animation is the same as that of full conventional animation, except that "hold cels" and "cycles" are impractical because of the opacity of the material. The light from beneath the table is usually sufficient to enable the film maker to see through two or three sheets of paper and thereby make a smooth progression of animation. The drawings can be inked with a dark Flomaster pen, having interchangeable felt-tipped points, or with a Pentel pen, whose points are not interchangeable, but have the virtue of being dark black, readily flowing, and inexpensive (Figure 14.10).

☐   In a static shot the grain of the paper is not at all noticeable. But when photographs of typewriter paper are projected at 24 frames per second there is a rapidly fluctuating or "boiling" effect all over the white areas of the screen. By experimenting with different kinds of film stocks and exposure rates, McLaren and his group in China found that high-contrast stocks aggravate this effect, and low-contrast stocks almost eliminate it. It can be totally eliminated by slightly overexposing a low-contrast stock.

☐   The Chinese artists used the paper method to draw animated films showing how to prevent tuberculosis, dysentery, and trachoma. Later, a group of artists from India made animated films in the same way; their films taught how to care for orange trees, how to spin and weave, and how to prevent diseases by correct hygienic practices. What this technique lacks in sophistication it makes up, to some extent, in low cost. And it has a place in art education courses where the class may wish to get the feel of animation and to see whether they want to continue at a more advanced level. Even small children can enjoy this kind of work.

COMPUTER TECHNIQUES FOR ANIMATION

A computer-controlled system for producing simple animated films has been developed in prototype form. The concept is essentially that of photographing in stop motion the illumination of a cathode tube in accordance with signals fed to the tube by a computer. Computer cards are programmed by the planning engineer; then computer output is displayed on the face of the cathode ray tube in graphic form (Figure 14.11). The images are best photographed on high-contrast film. Since the images are under direct programmed control, film mattes may be shot and the images combined with standard animation and optical effects in the optical printer or videoelectronically.

☐   This technique offers promise in areas of animation requir-

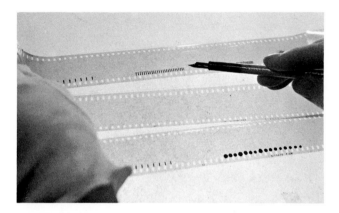

FIGURE 14.9a   Inked sound track. Courtesy of the National Film Board of Canada.

FIGURE 14.9b   Etched sound track. Courtesy of the National Film Board of Canada.

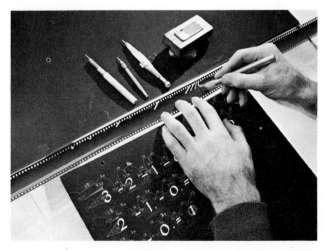

FIGURE 14.10 Flomaster rendering on typing paper. Courtesy of the National Film Board of Canada.

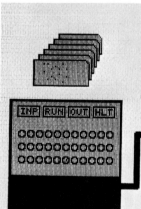 

Instructions for the desired movie enter the computer as a deck of punched cards.

ing the maximum of mathematical precision, such as plotting trajectories and depicting complex physical relationships. Pictures may be programmed to move in accordance with the laws of perspective, at any desired speed and following any set of rules or formulae.

ULTRAVIOLET FLUORESCENT ANIMATION

An ingenious solution to the problem of animating complex models without revealing their manipulative rigs has been developed by William Millard. The essence of the techniques is that everything to be photographed is coated with a fluorescent surface and everything else is painted a flat black. The animation is then photographed under an ultraviolet light source and only the fluorescent animation registers on the film emulsion. The rigs can therefore be improvised and structured without regard to their appearance because they are painted black and will not be photographed. Each movement of a model is made by an assistant wearing black gloves and arm shields, so it is possible to have a hand within the scope of the camera without it appearing on film. The illustrations show how the structure of a torus appeared when photographed conventionally (Figure 14.12a), and when photographed in motion under ultraviolet light (Figure 14.12b).

☐ A 250 watt (3600 Å ''Black Light'') light source is used; because all films are quite sensitive to this wave length an ultraviolet filter must be used over the lens. Continuous motion filming is practical up to 8 frames per second. The camera can be as far as 5′ from the subject, with an aperture range of from f/1.5 to f/2.5 for color film with an ASA rating of 25. Normal techniques for determining the correct exposure are not applicable to ultraviolet lighting. The only way to determine the correct exposure is to run a series of f/stop tests with the kind of color film and filters to be used in the final film.

TRANSPARENCY AND COLOR-AID PAPER FILMOGRAPH

An interesting and inexpensive technique for producing color filmographs has been developed at the University of Southern California. Essentially, it consists of superimposing photo-

FIGURE 14.11 Computer animated image. Courtesy of Bell Telephone Laboratories.

graphed transparencies of illustrations over abstract patterns of Color-Aid paper.

□ All the illustrations to be included in the finished filmograph are prepared for photographing on an animation stand or on a filmstrip stand. Photograph the selected pictures on black and white 35mm *negative* film. Then, enlarge the images to at least 8" X 10", to allow maximum zooming and panning range within them and print them on Kodak Fine Grain Positive Film (a low-speed, blue-sensitive emulsion for printing positive transparencies from continuous-tone or line negatives). The illustration reproduced on the transparency will be reduced in its half-tone densities and its line quality just enough to permit the colors of the underlying paper to show through brilliantly.

□ The next step is to make a selection of colored papers and plan their arrangement. If the filmograph is treating a technical subject, then the spectrum of colors may need to be naturalistic and their design quality limited to pleasing compositions. But if the filmograph is intended to have emotional impact, then the colors and designs should be planned abstractly to enhance the emotional quality of the story. In either case, the color scheme ought not to be improvised from scene to scene, but should be conceived for the entire filmograph in order to tighten the overall continuity of the film and build to a climax.

□ The final phase in this technique is to combine the transparencies and their backgrounds and to plan and execute the filmograph moves that will give the film its final form. A typical completed scene is shown comprising a transparency, an abstract pattern, and their appearance when combined* (Figures 14.13a, 14.13b, and 14.13c).

□ It would seem that similar effects could be achieved by placing translucent color overlays *above* black and white prints, but this traditional printing concept does not work in animation. Each layer of color tends to obscure the illustration beneath, and the darker the color the greater the opacity. The use of more than one color compounds the problem by darkening the values still further and by canceling or modifying lower levels of color. Moreover, there may be endless problems of exposure. This technique is promising and practical only if the color is beneath the illustration.

*The Story of Dentistry. A film designed and directed by Herbert Kosower.

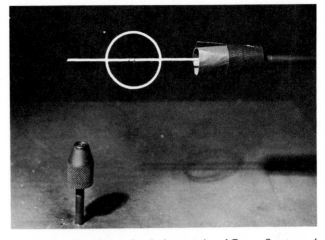

FIGURE 14.12a Conventional photography of Torus. Courtesy of William L. Millard and Rensselaer Polytechnic Institute.

FIGURE 14.12b Ultraviolet photography of Torus. Courtesy of William L. Millard and Rensselaer Polytechnic Institute.

FIGURE 14.13a Transparency. Courtesy of Herbert Kosower and the University of Southern California.

FIGURE 14.13b Background. Courtesy of Herbert Kosower and the University of Southern California.

FIGURE 14.13c Combined. Courtesy of Herbert Kosower and the University of Southern California.

FIGURE 14.14 Pinhead shadow animation. Courtesy of Contemporary Films.

PINHEAD SHADOW ANIMATION

An exotic form of animation developed by Alex Alexeieff is called ''pinhead shadow animation'' (Figure 14.14). Rows of pins are pressed into a board and strongly cross-lighted. For each exposure of a frame of film, the pinheads are raised to catch the light or lowered to throw it into shadow. Hundreds—sometimes thousands—of pinheads must be raised and lowered for each exposure of film.

VISUAL SQUEEZE

A popular technique in television commercials uses related still photographs presented in rapid-fire order. Actors, products, props, and backgrounds pop on and off the screen in staccato sequence. When conventional animation, pans, zooms, and intercut live-action scenes are incorporated with visual squeeze techniques the result transfixes attention. Bar and exposure sheets are a must because of the tight correlation between picture and sound in short television commercials.

PIXILATION

''Pixilation'' is a flickering, tricky effect becoming popular in experimental film circles. In one form, actors move from point to point and pause en route to be photographed a frame at a time. In another form the actors are photographed in continuous action with varying camera speeds. The resulting footage is then modified by skip-frame and stop-frame techniques, optical printing, or aerial image manipulations.

chapter 15
THE PRODUCTION SEQUENCE

THE techniques of animation treated in this book were presented in an order designed to simplify them and facilitate learning. But this order of presentation is not the sequence in which animated films are customarily made. The following ten phases present in skeletal form the order in which most animated films are produced, subject to variations depending on whether the film is intended for sales, instruction or entertainment:

1. SCRIPT-STORYBOARD

The script-storyboard phase of a film determines its form and content. At the inception of a nontheatrical film, the sponsor and the film maker meet to discuss the target audience and the behavioral objectives of the film. With these clearly in mind the writer completes several synopses offering a variety of approaches to the same film. The sponsor then selects one approach, and the writer proceeds with his research, completes a treatment, and writes the final script when the treatment has been approved. The script is then given pictorial form in a storyboard which receives a final critique from the sponsor and all concerned before production is begun.

☐   In theatrical animation the story may be written largely in storyboard form because of its emphasis upon entertaining characters and situations rather than upon content. The shorter television commercials also may be telescoped into storyboard form for their initial presentation to the sponsor.

2. SOUND RECORDING AND BAR SHEETS

Animation techniques most often require that the sound be recorded first and the animation be drawn afterward in order to synchronize the sound-picture relationship. The voice track, effects track, and music track are usually recorded on magnetic tape and later transferred to magnetic film. (These three sound tracks are subsequently combined into one track during a "mixing" session in a sound studio.) The magnetic film is locked into a synchonizer and sound reader, or the sound head of a moviola; the sentences and words or notes of music are measured in frames; and the information is recorded on bar sheets. These bar sheets represent every frame of film in the complete production and are used to synchronize the picture and sound tracks.

FIGURE 15.1 Script and storyboard conference. © Hanna-Barbera Productions, Inc., 1969.

FIGURE 15.2 Designing cartoon characters. © Hanna-Barbera Productions, Inc., 1969.

3. CARTOON CHARACTERS

In theatrical and television animation, and when cartoons are used in nontheatrical film, the development of cartoon personalities to embody and tell the story is all-important. Their physical characteristics and personalities, their quirks and idiosyncracies, all must be worked out before the film can proceed. This is always done in conjunction with the work of the layout men and the background artists.

4. LAYOUT

Working from the storyboards, the layout artist redesigns, cleans up, and scales the drawings to a workable size for animation. He is the man who is primarily responsible for the overall design of the film. In traditional cartoon animation, all the elements of background composition—architecture, props, color, and perspective—are the layout man's concern. And the cartoon characters also are his concern because their idiosyncracies affect the planning of moves across the background. In nontheatrical work the layout artist needs to apply the same principles to make the graphic information as clear and dynamic as possible, and as artistically satisfying. He must be familiar enough with the problems of the animator to know, for example, if it would be wiser to zoom into a small field, or to cut to a larger scale background of the small area, even if it means an extra background. The layout artist also plans where the camera will pan and zoom and, with the animator, establishes the approximate length of hold scenes to determine the amount of detail they will need. The rhythm, the mood, the tempo, the color key, and the final effect of the film are to a large extent in the hands of the layout man. His work must be done before the animators and background artists can get on with the business of drawing animation and painting backgrounds.

5. BACKGROUNDS

The background artists work hand in glove with the layout men in planning backgrounds. Only when the layout men have defined where the animation is to move and how it interacts with its environment can the background artist proceed with drawing and painting. He designs the compositional components to meet the exigencies of the layout and animation and follows a color key created by the director or layout man

FIGURE 15.3   Laying out an animation scene from a storyboard. ⓒ Hanna-Barbera Productions, Inc., 1969.

FIGURE 15.4   Painting the background for a cartoon scene. ⓒ Hanna-Barbera Productions, Inc., 1969.

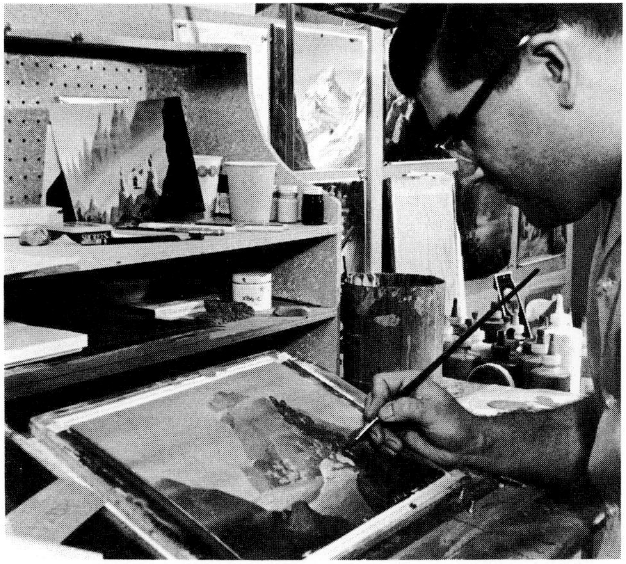

FIGURE 15.5   Animating cartoon characters. ⓒ Hanna-Barbera Productions, Inc., 1969.

FIGURE 15.6   Following instructions from an exposure sheet. ⓒ Hanna-Barbera Productions, Inc., 1969.

FIGURE 15.8 Animation photography. © Hanna-Barbera Productions, Inc., 1969.

FIGURE 15.9 *Moonbird.* Hubley Studio, Inc.

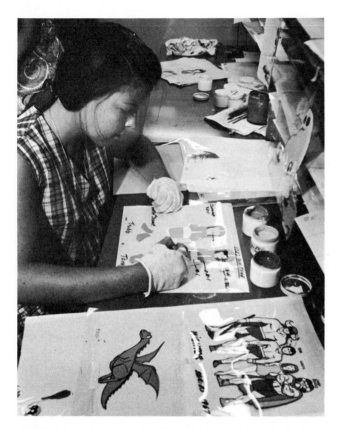

FIGURE 15.7 Painting an inked cel. © Hanna-Barbera Productions, Inc., 1969.

to build the emotion of the scenes, yet conform to the overall tenor of the film. He is primarily a renderer and as such must conform to the overall style and techniques of the layout and direction of the film. Frequently, because they both function largely in the realm of design and artistic technique, the layout man and the background artist may be the same person, but the functions he performs in each category are clearly defined.

6. ANIMATION

After the general movements of the animation across the background are planned, the animator makes his extreme drawings and spacing charts for each action. The assistant animator and the in-betweener then complete the drawing of the action and test the smoothness of the movements by flipping. When all

FIGURE 15.10 *Moonbird*. Hubley Studio, Inc.

the drawings are completed, they are photographed in a pencil test for a final critique of the flow of animation. If flaws are evident the drawings are redone and rephotographed until an acceptable degree of animation smoothness is achieved.

7. EXPOSURE SHEETS

Exposure sheets are made up by the animator before he hands his work over to his assistants. The length of the exposure

FIGURE 15.11 *Adventures of an Asterisk.* Hubley Studio, Inc.

sheet workbook is determined from the length of the bar sheets. The exposure sheets accompany the production of an animated film around the studio from its inception to final photography. All of the specialists concerned—directors, layout artists, animators, in-betweeners, inkers and painters, background artists, checkers—refer to the exposure sheets to get the information pertinent to their aspect of production. When the production is ready for camera, the exposure sheets are handed to the cameraman with the appropriate cels and backgrounds.

8. INKING AND PAINTING

After the final pencil test the animation drawings are sent to the inkers and painters. The drawings are traced onto cels in ink and numbered. These cels are then painted on the reverse side with opaque colors.

9. ANIMATION PHOTOGRAPHY

A checker examines everything to be photographed be sure each item is in correct order according to the exposure sheets. All the finished cels and backgrounds and titles are then sent to the animation cameraman together with the exposure sheets. The exposure sheets advise the cameramen of the correct sequence of cels and backgrounds to use for each frame of film, including complete instructions regarding zooms, pans, and any matte or optical effects to be done in the camera. The exposed film is sent to a laboratory for processing, most commonly as a series of separate scenes, each carefully slated.

10. THE WORK PRINT AND THE COMPOSITE PRINT

A print of the processed film footage is put together for the entire length of the film and is projected in an interlock with the mixed magnetic sound track. If everyone concerned approves this work print and the picture-sound relationship, the original film is cut to match exactly the approved workprint, and is sent to the laboratory together with an optical transfer of the sound track to produce final composite release prints. If, however, the film requires any optical effects, positive duplicating elements are prepared from the original and from various precision high-contrast shootings, and are combined according to complete and detailed instructions which are written out on

FIGURE 15.12   *The Hole.* Hubley Studio, Inc.

the work print picture by the editor. The result of the optical combining will be a dupe or internegative, which will then be sent to the laboratory as it is. Or, if it represents an entire film that when printed with the optical track will provide the composite print, or if it represents only a portion of the entire film, it will be treated in the same manner as the rest of the original and be cut into its proper place in the film with the composite being pulled as before.

☐   There is a new electronic system for combining several images into one which is displacing the use of an optical printer in productions where precise registration is not a critical factor. In color productions for television it is feasible to combine live action subjects with animation by videoelectronic production of traveling mattes, and electronic editing, to achieve a composite picture in videotape form. The electronics involved are outside the purview of this book, but a brief statement of its principles is in order.

☐   This is a color matrix system based upon the capacity of a chroma key unit to electronically supress all luminance information of a given portion of the spectrum. For example: if a live action subject is photographed against a blue-screen background—when blue is the color suppressed by the chroma key unit—the background will remain an undeveloped area prepared to accept the images of the animation footage and its background. Editing is done electronically while viewing each visual element over television picture monitors. The images of the live action subject (with blue-screen background) and the images of the animation are channeled through the chroma key unit and the special effects amplifier to a videotape recorder, where the animated images are electronically imprinted into the blue-screen area of the live action background to become an integrated composite picture on videotape—ready for broadcast over television.

BIBLIOGRAPHY

☐ Agbe-Davies, Anthony Akintunde, ''Film Activities of African Colonies Under Four European Powers, 1946–1951.'' Unpublished Master's thesis, The University of Southern California, Los Angeles, 1960.

☐ Alberti, Walter, *Il Cinema De Animazione, 1832–1956.* Edizioni radio italiana. Torino, 1957.

☐ ''Animated Films.'' *Documentary Film News* (May, 1948).

☐ Anonyme, Service d'information de l'ambassade, *Le Cinéma et la Production cinématographique en Yougoslavie,* 1960.

☐ Arnheim, Rudolph, ''What Do the Eyes Contribute?'' *Audio-Visual Communication Review,* Vol. X (September–October, 1962), p. 19.

☐ Babitsky, Paul, and Paul Rimberg, *The Soviet Film Industry.* New York, Praeger, 1955.

☐ Baker, Everett Burgess, ''A Method for Controlling the Posing of Three Dimensional Figures Used in Making Animated Model Films.'' Unpublished Research Report, 1945.

☐ Barnouw, Erik, *The Television Writer.* New York, Hill & Wang, 1962

☐ Battison, John H., *Movies for TV.* New York, Macmillan, 1950.

☐ Benayoun, Robert, *Le Dessin Animé Apres Walt Disney.* Paris, Pauvert, 1961.

☐ Bernardet, Jean-Claude, *Cinèma Tschecoslovaco.* São Paulo, Cinemateca Brasiliera Grafica Editora Hamburg, 1964.

☐ Bocek, Jaroslav, *Jiri Trnka: Artist and Puppet Master.* Prague, Artia, 1965

☐ Brons, Herk, *Filmtitels en Trucfilms.* Haarlem, Focus, 1963.

☐ Bulleid, Henry Anthony Vanghan, *Special Effects In Cinematography.* London, Fantain Press, 1954.

☐ Castello, Giulio Cesare (G.C.C.), ''Walt Disney.'' *Enciclopedia dello Spettacolo,* Vol. IV, ed. Le Maschere, Rome, 1957.

☐ Chevalier, Denys, *J'Aime le Dessin Animé.* Paris, Denöel, 1962.

☐ *Cinema Cecoslovacco Ieri e Oggi.* Rome, Edigioni dell' Ateneo, 1951.

☐ Cinema TV Promotion, *Dessin Animé* (January, 1960).

204

BIBLIOGRAPHY

□ Collin, Philippe, and Wyn, Michel, *Le Cinema d'Animation dans le Monde*. Paris, IDHEC, 1956.

□ Cook, Olive, *Movement In Two Dimensions*. London, Hutchinson, 1963. 142 pp.

□ Cramer, Lucilla I., *Tekhnika proïvodsta moultiplikatsionnik filmov v'amerikanikh studiakh*. La Technique de Dessins animes dans les Studios américains. Moscow, 1934.

□ *Der Sowjetische Film*. Discussion of animation by Ivanov-Vano in German. Berlin, Dietzverlag, 1953.

□ Disney, Walt, and Staff. *The Art of Animation*. New York, Simon and Schuster, 1959. 192 pp.

□ Disney-Miller, Dianne, *The Story of Walt Disney*. 1958. Trans. from *L'Histoire de Walt Disney*. Paris, 1960.

□ Service d'information et publicité à l'Office national du film du Canada. *Le Cinema Image par Image*. Brussels, 1958.

□ *Elements of Color in Professional Motion Pictures*. Society of Motion Picture and Television Engineers. New York, 1957. 104 pp.

□ Epstein, Alvin, *How to Draw Animated Cartoons*. 1945.

□ Falk, Nat, *How to Make Animated Cartoons*. New York, Foundation Books, 1941. 79 pp.

□ Field, Robert Durant, *The Art of Walt Disney*. New York, Macmillan, 1942. 290 pp.

□ Finn, James D., Perrin, Donald G., and Campion, Lee E., *Studies in the Growth of Instructional Technology, I: Audio-Visual Instrumentation for Instruction in the Public Schools, 1930–1960: A Basis for Take-off*. A Report prepared for the Technological Development Project of the National Education Association of the United States. Occasional Paper No. 6, 1962.

□ Foster, Walter, *Animated Cartoons*. Hollywood, California, 1942.

□ Gamburg, E. A., *Secrets of the Drawing World*. Moscow, Soviet Artist, 1966. 116 pp.

□ Ghirardini, Lino Lionello, "Walt Disney e il disegno animato in America." *Storia generale de Cinema*, Vol. II, Chap. XVI. No. VI, ed. Marzorati, Milan, 1959.

□ Gianeri, Enrico, *Storia del Cartone Animato*. Milan, Editrice Omnia, 1960. 279 pp.

□ Ginzburg, *Drawing and Puppet Films*. Moscow, Iskusstvo, 1957. 284 pp.

□ Gomez Mesa, Luis, *Los Films de Dibujos Animados*. Madrid, Compania Ibero-Americana de Publicaciones, 1930.

□ Gordon, Jay E., *Motion-Picture Production for Industry*. New York, Macmillan, 1961.

□ Gromo, Mario, *L'Arte di Walt Disney*. Torino, Instituto del Cinema, 1960.

□ Groschopp, Richard, *Der Filmtitel: Seine Technik und Gestaltung*. Saale, Fotokinoverlag Halle, 1958, 154 pp.

□ Halas, John, ed., *International Animated Film*. London, British Film Academy, winter journal, 1956–1957.

□ ———— and Roger Manvell, *Design in Motion*. London, Studio, 1962.

□ ———— and Roger Manvell, *The Technique of Film Animation*. New York, Hastings House, Inc., 1959. 348 pp.

□ ———— and Bob Privett, *How to Cartoon for Amateur Films*. London and New York, Focal Press, 1958.

□ Hardeg, Walter, *Film and Television Graphics; an international survey of film and television graphics*. Zurich, Graphics Press, 1967.

□ Heymann, Robert, *Der Film in Der Karikatur*. Berlin, O. Stollberg verlag g.m.b.h., 1929.

□ Hoban, Charles F., Jr., *Focus on Learning*. Washington, American Council on Education, 1942. 172 pp.

□ ———— *Movies that Teach*. New York, The Dryden Press, Inc., 1946. 189 pp.

□ ———— and van Ormer, Edward B., *Instructional Film Research, 1918–1950*. Pennsylvania State College, Instructional Film Research Program, 1950.

□ Jacobs, Lewis, "L'avventurosa storia del cinema americano." *Virtuosismo ai Walt Disney*, ed. Einaudi, Chap. XXIV, Torino, 1952.

□ Jaspen, Nathan, *Effects on Training of Experimental Film Variables, Study II: Verbalization, "How It Works," Nomenclature, Audience Participation, and Succinct Treatment*. Technical Report SDC-269-7-11, Instructional Film Research Program, Pennsylvania State College. Port Washington, Long Island, New York. Special Devices Center, March, 1950.

□ Jenkins, C. Francis, *Animated Pictures*. Washington, H. L. McQueen, 1898. 210 pp.

□ Jordan, William E., "Norman McLaren: His Career and

Techniques." *The Quarterly of Film, Radio and Television,* Vol. VIII, No. 1.

☐ Kautsky, Oldrich, *Le Film de Marionnettes et le Dessin Animé Tchécoslovaque,* set, 0-1087-53.

☐ Kessler, Pierre, *La Technique modern du Dessin Animé.* Paris, Revue, 1938.

☐ Kircher, Athanasius, *Ars Magna Lucis et Umbrae.* Rome, 1646.

☐ Knight, Arthur, *The Liveliest Art.* New York, Macmillan, 1957. 352 pp.

☐ Knowlton, Kenneth C., *A Computer Technique for Producing Animated Movies.* A Report Prepared by the Technical Information Libraries, Bell Telephone Laboratories, Inc. Murray Hill, N.J., Bell Telephone Laboratories, Inc., 1964.

☐ Krows, Arthur Edwin, "Motion Pictures—Not for Theaters." *The Educational Screen Magazine* (September, 1938).

☐ Laks, Simon, *Le Sons-titrage de Films: Sa Technique, Son Esthetique.* Paris, Propriete de L'Auteur, 1957. 61 pp.

☐ L'Association France-Tchecosloveuie, *Le Cinéma tchécoslovaque.* Paris, 1957.

☐ Laswell, Harold D., Lerner, Daniel, and de Sola Pool, Ithiel, *Comparative Study of Symbols.* Stanford, California, Stanford University Press, 1952.

☐ Levitan, Eli L., *Animation Art in the Commercial Film.* New York, Reinhold, 1960. 128 pp.

☐ Lo Duca, *Le Dessin Animé.* Paris, Prisman, 1948.

☐ Los Angeles County Museum, *A Retrospective Exhibition of the Walt Disney Medium.* Racine, Wisconsin, Whitman Publishing Company, 1940. 22 pp.

☐ Lumsdaine, A. A., Sulzer, R. L., and others, "The influence of simple animation techniques on the value of a training film." Report No. 24, USAF Human Resources Research Laboratories, Washington, D.C., April, 1951.

☐ Lutz, George Edwin, *Animated Cartoons.* New York, Scribner's, 1920. 261 pp.

☐ Lutz, George Edwin, *Der Gezelchnete Film. Ein Handbuch für Filmzelchner und die es werden wollen,* trans. by Konrad Wolter. Halle, Knapp, 1927.

☐ Malik, Dr. Jan, *Les Marionnettes tchécoslovaques.* Prague, Orbis, 1948.

☐ Mandara, Lucio. "La caduta degli angeli (Ininerario walt-disneyano)." *Bianco e Nero,* Vol. XII No. 6, Rome (June, 1951).

☐ Manvell, Roger, *The Animated Film.* London, Sylvan Press, 1954. 64 pp.

☐ Martin, Andre, "Norman McLaren, ou Le Cinema Des Deux Mains," *Cahiers du Cinema.*

☐ Mascelli, Joseph V., *American Cinematographer Manual.* Hollywood, American Society of Cinematographers.

☐ May, Mark A., "The psychology of learning from demonstration films." *Journal of Educational Psychology* (January, 1946).

☐ ———— and Lumsdaine, Arthur A., and others, *Learning From Films.* New Haven, Yale University Press, 1958. 357 pp.

☐ McLaren, Norman, "Cameraless Animation: A Technique Developed at the National Film Board of Canada." In UNESCO, *Fundamental Education: A Quarterly Bulletin,* Vol. I, No. 4, October, 1949.

☐ McMahan, Harry Wayne, *The Television Commercial.* New York, Hastings House, 1954. 177 pp.

☐ ———— *T.V. Tape Commercials.* New York, Hastings House, 1960. 110 pp.

☐ Meierhenry, W. C., *Enriching the Curriculum Through Motion Pictures.* Lincoln, Nebraska, University of Nebraska Press, 1953.

☐ Miller, Neal E., ed., "Graphic Communication and the Crisis in Education." *Audio-Visual Communication Review,* Vol. V, No. III (1957). 120 pp.

☐ Norberg, Kenneth, "Introduction to Supplement 5, Perception Theory and A-V Education." *Audio-Visual Communication Review,* Vol. X (September–October, 1962), p. 4.

☐ Nossam, Sam, *Le Dessin Animé et sa Technique.* Paris, Revue, Ciné, Amateur, 1939.

☐ Office of the Coordinator of Inter-American Affairs. *History of the Office of the Coordinator of Inter-American Affairs.* Washington, U.S. Government Printing Office, 1947.

☐ Pittaro, Earnest M., *TV and Film Production Data Book.* New York, Morgan and Morgan, 1959. 448 pp.

☐ Poncet, Marie Thérèse, *Dessin Amimé; Art Mondial.* Paris, Le Cercle du Livre, 1956.

☐ ———— *L'Esthetique du Dessin Animé.* Paris, Librarie Nizet, 1952.

☐ ———— *Etude Comparative des Illustrations du Moyen Age et des Dessins Animés.* Paris, Nizet, 1952. 150 pp.

BIBLIOGRAPHY

Quigley, Martin, *Magic Shadows*. New York, Quigley Publishing Co., 1960. 191 pp.

Ranieri, Tino, "Walt Disney." *Filmlexicon degli autori e delle opere*, Vol. II, ed. *Bianco e Nero*, Rome 1969.

Regnier, Jean, *La Technique du Dessin Animé*. Paris, Nouvelles Editions Film et Technique, 1947. 28 pp.

Reichow, Joachim, *Zaubereix auf Zelluloid*. Berlin, Henschelverlag, 1966. 173 pp.

Reid, J. Christopher, and MacLennan, Donald W., *Research In Instructional Television and Film*. Washington, U.S. Department of Health, Education and Welfare, Office of Education, 1967.

Reusch, Jurgen, and Kees, Weldon, *Nonverbal Communication*. Berkeley, California, University of California Press, 1956.

Reynaud, Maurice, *Emile Reynaud, Les Maitres du Cinéma*. Paris, Cinematheque Francaise, Office Francais d'edition, 1945.

Rider, Howard Edward, "The Development of the Satire of Mr. Magoo." Unpublished Master's thesis, University of Southern California, Los Angeles, 1965.

Riding, Laura, *Len Lye and the Problem of Popular Films*. Dejá, Majorca, Seizen Press, 1938. 46 pp.

Ross, Wallace A., *Best T.V. Commercials of the Year*. New York, Hastings House, 1967. 190 pp.

Rotha, Paul, Road, Sinclair, and Griffith, Richard, *Documentary Film*. London, Faber and Faber, 1952. 412 pp.

Saettler, Paul L., *History of Instructional Technology, II: The Technical Development of the New Media*. Los Angeles. Technological Development Project, University of Southern California, 1962. Occasional Paper No. 2, p. 23.

Schickel, Richard, *The Disney Version*. New York, Simon and Schuster, 1968.

Schott, Gaspar, *Magia Universalis Naturae et Artist*. Wurzburg, 1658.

Sharps, Wallace S., *Commercial Television*. London, Faber and Faber, 1935. 326 pp.

Spaulding, Seth, "Communication Potential of Pictorial Illustrations." *Audio-Visual Communication Review*, Vol. IV (Winter, 1956), pp. 31–46.

Spottiswoode, Raymond, *A Grammar of the Film*. Berkeley, California, University of California Press, 1950. 328 pp.

————— *Film and Its Techniques*. Berkeley, California, University of California Press, 1951. 516 pp.

Stephenson, Ralph, *Animation in the Cinema*. New York, A. S. Barnes & Co., 1967. 176 pp.

Taylor, Deems, *Walt Disney's Fantasia*. New York, Simon and Schuster, 1940.

Thomas, Bob, *Walt Disney: Magician of the Movies*. New York, Grosset & Dunlap and Rutledge Books, 1966.

Toeplitz, Jerzy, *Historia Sztuki Filmowej*, Vol. III, Chap. IX: *Mistrz Filmu Rysunkowego*—Walt Disney, Wydawnictwa Artystyczene i Filmowe, Warszawa, 1959.

Turfkruyer, Marc, "Walt Disney en de Tekenfilm." *Geschiedenis van de Film*, Vol. 1, Antwerpen, Uitgeverij Onwikkeling, 1958.

Turney, Harold Merrill, *Film Guide's Handbook: Cartoon Production*. Hollywood, California, Film Guide, 1940.

VanderMeer, A. W., "Relative effectiveness of color and black and white in instructional films." Technical Report No. SDC 269-7-28, Special Devices Center, Port Washington, New York, 1952.

Vano, Ivanov I., "Cartoon Film in the Soviet Union," *The Journal of the British Film Academy* (Winter, 1956–1957).

————— *The Drawing Art of Film*. Moscow, 1950.

Vernon, M. D., "Presenting Information in Diagrams," *Audio-Visual Communication Review*. Vol. I (Summer, 1953), pp. 147–158.

Wagner, Robert Walter, "Design in the Educational Film: An Analysis of Production Elements in Twenty-One Widely Used Non-Theatrical Motion Pictures." Unpublished Doctoral dissertation, Ohio State University, 1953.

————— "Motion Pictures and the University." *Journal of the Society of Motion Picture and Television Engineers*, Vol. LXXII (April, 1963), p. 290.

Waldron, Gloria, *The Information Film*. New York, Columbia University Press, 1949.

White, Eric Walter, *Walking Shadows*. London, Hogarth Press, 1931. 31 pp.

Wisdom. Vol. XXXV (November, 1960).

Wright, Quincy, *Symbols in Internationalism*. Stanford, California, Stanford University Press, 1952.

Zuckerman, J. V., "Predicting film learning by pre-release testing." *Audio-Visual Communication Review*, Vol. II (1954), pp. 49–55.

FILMOGRAPHY

☐ *A Short History of Animation: The Cartoon* (60 min., b/w). A history of animation, 1907–1935. Museum of Modern Art Film Library.

☐ *Animated Cartoons: The Toy That Grew Up* (17 min., b/w). A history of the precursors of animation, from the Thaumatrope and persistence of vision studies through the beginnings of the animated cartoon. Film Images Collection.

☐ *Animation Goes to School* (15 min., color). Depiction of the Horace Mann Project in which high school students and teachers produce animated films for teaching and creative arts purposes. The Oxberry Corporation.

☐ *Animation Techniques* (25 min., b/w). A demonstration of how each major part of the animation stand functions. The Oxberry Corporation.

☐ *Artwork In Motion* (13 min., color). Demonstrations of such fundamental animation techniques as cycling, scratch-off, etc. Calvin Productions.

☐ *Behind the Scenes at Walt Disney's Studio* (27 min., color). All major stages of the production of a feature length animated film. Walt Disney Studios.

☐ *Biography of a Motion Picture Camera* (27 min., color). Early history of cinematography. Film Images Collection.

☐ *Date with Dizzy* (10 min., b/w). A satire of television commercials in which John Hubley displays his skills in animation to create a television commercial. Brandon Films.

☐ *Dingbat Story, The* (15 min., color). A humorous approach to the matter of film titling in which animation techniques are demonstrated. Calvin Productions.

☐ *Dots* (2½ min., color). An experimental film in which sound and visuals are rendered directly upon the film with ordinary pen and ink. Film Board of Canada.

☐ *Film Interlock, The* (2½ min., color). The mechanics and uses of the interlock shown in animation. Calvin Productions.

☐ *Filmograph, The* (6 min., b/w). Uses of the filmograph as an audio-visual aid. Cinema Department, University of Southern California.

☐ *How You See It* (8 min., b/w). An animated explanation of persistence of vision and its relation to image projection. Jam Handy Organization.

☐ *Ideas and Film* (11 min., color). The uses of motion pictures in communication, including animation and time lapse photography, presenting its applications to educational and scientific purposes. British Information Services.

☐ *Loops* (2 min., 43 sec., color). Sound and visuals are

rendered upon film leader with pen and ink. Film Board of Canada.

☐ *Make a Movie Without a Camera* (6 min., color). Students draw and paint directly on clear film leader in the technique developed by Norman McLaren. Bailey.

☐ *Making Films That Teach*. The role of animation within the context of planning and producing an effective educational film. Encyclopedia Britannica Films.

☐ *Man In Motion* (10 min., b/w). A film history of man's study of human and animal locomotion, using animation techniques. University of Southern California.

☐ *Movie Magic* (14 min., b/w). The use of models and miniatures, with single frame exposure techniques, to create a "battle" scene. Sterling.

☐ *Pen Point Percussion* (6 min., b/w). Norman McLaren explains and demonstrates how to create synthetic sound on film (see also *Dots* and *Loops*). National Film Board of Canada.

☐ *Naked Eye, The* (71 min., b/w and color). The techniques of making motion pictures with still photographs are demonstrated by Louis C. Stoumen in this documentary on photographers from Dauguerre to Steichen. Film Representation.

☐ *Origins of the Motion Picture* (21 min., b/w). The development of cinematography from the "camera obscura" to the contributions of Edison and others. DuArt Film Laboratories.

☐ *Smathering of Spots* (11 min., b/w). A series of animated commercials created by John Hubley. Brandon.

☐ *Window on Canada: An Interview with Norman McLaren* (31 min., b/w). A presentation of several new animation techniques created by Norman McLaren in his experimental work. National Film Board of Canada.

☐ *Your Name Here Story, The* (10 min., color). The satirical story of a film which attempts, at the insistence of the sponsor, to do everything, and in the end succeeds in doing nothing. Calvin Productions.

GLOSSARY

ABERRATION. Any image distortion caused by a defect in a component of an optical system, such as a lens or a mirror.

ACADEMY LEADER. A format for the head and tail leaders of release prints, designed by the Academy of Motion Picture Arts and Sciences, accepted as standard throughout the motion picture industry.

ACTION. The movements of characters and objects which constitute the events of a film.

AERIAL IMAGE. A technique which combines the images of processed film with images on cels by rephotographing them together. A projector is focused at the level of the compound tabletop. When cel images are interposed in the path of the projected images, a combined image is presented to the lens of the camera and is photographed.

ANGLE. The point of view in drawing perspective.

ANIMATED ZOOM. A zoom effect achieved by making progressive changes in the sizes of artwork, rather than by moving the camera toward or away from the subject as when making a conventional zoom on an animation stand. *See* Zoom.

ANIMATION. The arts, techniques, and processes involved in giving apparent life and movement to inanimate objects by means of cinematography.

ANIMATION BOARD. A drawing board adapted for animation drawing by the addition of registration pegs.

ANIMATION, COMPUTER. A system of photographing in stop motion the illumination of a cathode tube in accordance with signals fed to the tube by a programmed computer.

ANIMATION, CUTOUT. A technique in which subjects, cut from cardboard and sometimes having jointed limbs, are moved manually between single-frame exposures.

ANIMATION, ETCHING. A technique in which the emulsion of black leader or inks and paints applied to clear leader are scratched off to produce animation effects.

ANIMATION, ON FILM. A technique in which the animator inks and paints directly on clear film stock.

ANIMATION, FLUORESCENT. A variant of object animation in which the objects to be photographed are coated with a fluorescent substance. The background and extraneous ob-

*Terms followed by * are reprinted from the USA Standard Nomenclature for Motion-Picture Film Used in Studios and Processing Laboratories, PH22.56-1961 and PH22.56a-1964, copyrighted 1961 and 1964, copies of which may be purchased from the United States of America Standards Institute, 10 East 40th Street, New York, N.Y. 10016.

**Terms followed by ** are reproduced by permission of the University Film Association.

jects are painted flat black; the animation is then photographed under an ultra-violet light source. Only the objects coated with a fluorescent substance appear in the finished print.

☐ ANIMATION, LIMITED. A technique in which the cel images are animated only in part, but appear to be rendered in full animation because of added movement contributed by pans, zooms, cycles, and other effects.

☐ ANIMATION, OBJECT. The movement or manipulation of three-dimensional objects, photographed by single-frame exposure.

☐ ANIMATION, PASTEL. A technique in which chalk, pastel, or charcoal is the chosen medium of rendering movements to be photographed on the animation stand.

☐ ANIMATION, PINHEAD SHADOW. A form of animation in which rows of pins are pressed into a board, and the board is cross-lighted. The pinheads are raised and lowered to catch or lose the light for each frame of film.

☐ ANIMATION, PUPPET. A technique in which three-dimensional figures are moved, an increment at a time, and photographed with single-frame exposures.

☐ ANIMATION STAND. A mechanical device for holding and photographing artwork. An animation stand comprises a comera mounted on a movable carriage, one or two vertical columns supporting the camera and carriage, and a compound tabletop on which the artwork is mounted beneath the camera for photography.

☐ ANSWER PRINT. The first combined print of picture and sound.

☐ ANTICIPATION. A technique of animation drawing in which the movement preceding an accented action stretches toward the high point of dramatic accent in order to give it greater emphasis.

☐ APERTURE. 1. *Lens aperture:* The orifice, usually an adjustable iris, which limits the amount of light passing through a lens. 2. *Camera aperture*: In 16mm cameras the mask opening (0.410″ × 0.294″), which defines the area of each frame exposed. In 35mm cameras the mask opening (0.631″ × 0.868″) which defines the area of each frame exposed. 3. *Projector aperture:* In 16mm projectors the mask opening (0.380″ × 0.284″) which defines the area of each frame projected. 4. *Printer aperture***: The limiting orifice through which light passes to expose the film to be reproduced.

☐ APPROACH. *See* Zoom.

☐ ASA INDEX. A measure of the film emulsion's receptivity to light. *See* Film Speed.

☐ ASTIGMATISM. An optical distortion in uncorrected lenses which tends to resolve a single point in the subject not as a point, but as short vertical or horizontal lines.

☐ ATMOSPHERE SKETCH. An impressionistic rendering of a location for the exploration of an appropriate mood, which is later developed into a finished background.

☐ AUDIO. All matters pertaining to sound or to sound recording.

☐ A-WIND. A term used to designate the emulsion position of rolled film stock in which the film unwinds downward from the *right* side of the roll when the perforated side is nearest the viewer.

☐ BACKGROUND. The setting against which the cels are photographed.

☐ BACKGROUND, HOOKUP. A pan background whose terminal features correspond to the beginning features of the succeeding pan background, so that a transition may be made from one to the next without a break in pictorial continuity.

☐ BACKGROUND, PAN. A background whose width is twice or three times the E–W dimension of a standard cel, thus permitting a wide range of horizontal movement without revealing an edge.

☐ BACKGROUND, STILL. A background which is not designed to move and therefore need be no larger than a standard cel.

☐ BACKLASH. Incorrect stopping position of a shaft caused by looseness in the mechanism.

☐ BACK PROJECTION. *See* Rear Projection.

☐ BAR SHEETS. A written record of the sound track of a film showing the frame position of each syllable of every word recorded in the sound track.

☐ BARN DOORS. Metal gates mounted on hinges around the perimeter of a light source to control its beam.

☐ BASE, FILM. The transparent, flexible material bearing the photographic emulsion.

☐ BEAM SPLITTER. A device used in reflex viewfinders which permits the subject to be viewed while the motion picture film is being exposed.

☐ BEAT. A measure of time used to given consistency to a sequence of animation, with a given number of drawings allotted to each beat.

☐ BI-PACK PRINTING. The use of the animation camera with

photographic mattes to achieve simple optical effects normally done in an optical printer.

☐ BLACK AND WHITE. The photographic rendering of all images in a noncolor monochrome.

☐ BLANK. An unrendered cel used to maintain a constant number of cels in a given sequence.

☐ BLEED. The area of artwork or photograph extending beyond the scope of a camera.

☐ BLOOM. The complementary halo which may form around extreme values in a subject on the television screen.

☐ BLOW UP. The process of enlarging selected areas in frames of motion picture film, by means of an optical printer, for the purpose of presenting a larger screen image of some desired detail, or of deleting unwanted areas of the original frames of film.

☐ BLURS. Animated speed lines rendered softly to carry the flow of fast action.

☐ BOTTOM LIGHTING. The reverse of conventional lighting— the subject is lighted from beneath the compound table, through opal glass, instead of from the top, and is thereby thrown into silhouette.

☐ BREAKDOWN. *See* In-Between Breakdown.

☐ BURN-IN. A multiple-exposure technique in which the images to be burned in, usually titles, are exposed until they remove the emulsion within their own image area.

☐ B-WIND. A term used to designate rolled film stock in which the film unwinds downward from the *left* side of the roll when the perforated side is nearest the viewer.

☐ CALIBRATION. The way in which a measuring instrument is graduated; for instance, the controls of the compound are calibrated in hundredths of an inch.

☐ CAM. *See* Follow-Focus Cam.

☐ CAMERA, ANIMATION. A motion picture camera having special adaptations making it suitable for animation photography. These adaptations most often include a single- and continuous-exposure control, forward and reverse directional movement of film, a shuttle movement and registration system, a variable opening shutter with fade scales, and a rackover or reflex viewfinder to permit direct viewing of the animation artwork.

☐ CAMERA CARRIAGE. Any mobile device mounted on the column or columns of an animation stand, used for transporting the camera up and down.

☐ CAMERA, LIVE-ACTION. Any motion picture camera de-

signed to make continuous exposures of its subjects and not having the special adaptations required in animation photography.

☐ CAMERA PROJECTION. *See* Rotoscoping.

☐ CAMERA TRACK. British term for "zoom."

☐ CEL. A transparent plastic sheet used as the surface for inking and painting images in full and limited animation. Animation cels are usually punched with three holes, outside the photography area, intended to fit over registration pegs which are identical on both the drawing disc and the surface of the animation table.

☐ CEL LEVEL. The position of a given cel when several cels are placed one on top of the other.

☐ CEL, PAN. A transparent plastic sheet whose width is twice or three times the normal E–W dimension of a standard cel, permitting a wide range of horizontal movement without revealing an edge.

☐ CEL SANDWICH. The simultaneous use of more than one cel in animation photography to a maximum of four to combine the images of separate cels within a single frame of film.

☐ CEL, STANDARD. A transparent plastic sheet whose dimensions are slightly larger than a 12 field; the type most commonly used in animation artwork.

☐ CEL, WILD. A large sheet of unpunched transparent plastic on which the rendered subject is moved about under the animation camera without the use of pegbars or compound controls.

☐ CEMENT, FILM. Bonding solvent used for splicing film.

☐ CHARACTER. An animated cartoon personality.

☐ CHARACTER SKETCHES. Pictures of an animated cartoon personality which specify his features, proportions, expressions, and clothing.

☐ CHARTS. British term for "exposure sheets" and "bar sheets."

☐ CHECKER. The person in an animation studio assigned to examine the materials to be photographed on the animation stand to assure that everything is ready and in order.

☐ CHROMA. The intensity or brilliance of a given color.

☐ CHROMATIC ABERRATION. The failure of a lens to focus different wave lengths of light at the same point.

☐ CINCH MARKS. Scratches on motion picture film caused by pulling the film to tighten the roll, or by the abrasive action of foreign particles caught within the roll of film.

☐ CINEMATIC TIME. A condensation or extension of actual

time for the purposes of drama, by means of cinematographic techniques.

☐ CINEMATOGRAPHERS. Personnel associated with motion picture photography, including the director, cameraman, and assistant cameraman.

☐ CINEMATOGRAPHY.** Motion picture photography. Loosely, the entire complex of activities involved in the staging, direction, photography, editing, and presentation of motion pictures.

☐ CLEAN UP. Removal of dirt and dust from cels.

☐ CLOSE-UP. A photograph of a detail within a larger picture on the animation stand.

☐ CODE NUMBERING. The practice of inking an identical series of numbers on two or more lengths of film in order to synchronize them.

☐ COLOR. (1) The retina of the human eye perceives wave lengths of light between 400 and 700 millimicrons; the capacity to discriminate between the various wave lengths within this purview results in the impression of color. (2) Subjects rendered photographically in a spectrum of natural colors in contrast to subjects rendered in black and white.

☐ COLOR BALANCE. A color value relationship usually defined in terms of a film emulsion and a light source. For example, if a given film emulsion, or a given light, is color balanced for 3200° Kelvin, then the light source or film used with it must be identically balanced in order to obtain good photographic reproduction.

☐ COLOR CAST. *See* Chromatic Aberration.

☐ COLOR COMPENSATING FILTER. A filter mounted in the path of a camera lens in order to modify the color temperature of the light falling on the subject, so that it will conform to the color temperature of the film emulsion.

☐ COLOR CORRECTION. The use of light filters in a camera or an optical printer to modify colored subjects.

☐ COLORER. *See* Opaquer.

☐ COLOR KEY. Color assignments, or color swatches, used to assure the color consistency of every subject and background in a given sequence.

☐ COLOR MODEL. *See* Color Key.

☐ COLOR PHOTOGRAPHY. The photographic rendering of all subjects in the closest possible approximation of their actual color.

☐ COLOR TEMPERATURE.** A concept formulated for the purpose of standardization of light sources. When a so-called "black body," such as a fragment of carbon, is heated to the

point where it begins to emit light, the color of the light it emits varies directly with the temperature of the black body, when the temperature is expressed in degrees centigrade beginning at absolute zero (Kelvin scale).

☐ COLOR TEMPERATURE METER. A device for measuring the color temperature of a given light source.

☐ COLORTRAN. The trade name of a system for boosting the voltage delivered to an incandescent light source in order to raise its color temperature to meet the demands of a given color film emulsion.

☐ COMBINED MOVE. *See* Compound Move.

☐ COMPOSITE NEGATIVE. A film negative bearing synchronized picture and sound which is intended to be used as the master for printing film positives.

☐ COMPOSITE PRINT. A film positive on which picture and sound are synchronized.

☐ COMPOSITE REVERSAL DUPE PRINT.* A composite reversal dupe print is a reversal dupe print having both picture and sound tracks on the same film.

☐ COMPOSITE REVERSAL ORIGINAL.* A composite reversal original is a reversal original which has both picture and sound on the same film.

☐ COMPOUND MOVE. A move on the animation stand in which a zoom and a pan are combined into one continuous movement.

☐ COMPOUND TABLE. That part of the animation stand on which the artwork is placed.

☐ COMPUTER ANIMATION. *See* Animation, Computer.

☐ CONTACT PRINTING.* Contact printing is that method of printing in which the raw stock is held in direct contact with the film bearing the image to be copied.

☐ CONTINUITY. British term referring to "storyline" or "plot."

☐ CONTINUOUS EXPOSURE. The transport of frames of film past the exposure aperture of a camera without interruption until the motion picture scene has been completely photographed.

☐ CONTINUOUS PRINTER. An optical printer or a contact printer designed to move film past the exposure aperture at a constant rate of speed.

☐ CONTRAST.** 1. *Lighting Contrast*. The ratio between the maximum and minimum intensities of the incident light on the subject, or of the radiated and/or reflected light from the subject. 2. *Photographic Contrast*. In terms of negative or positive film, the ratio between the optically most dense and least dense areas, expressed in terms of gamma—the tangent of the angle formed by the straight-in line portion of the D log E curve and the log E axis. 3. *Subject Contrast*. The scale of tonal values exhibited by a subject. If the scale is short, it is called "flat," whether generally dark or generally light. If the scale is reasonable long, with good graduation from black to white, it is regarded as normal. When the scale is extensive, and intermediate tones are relatively lacking, the subject is termed "contrasty."

☐ CONTROL PANEL. A console consisting of switches and dials which activate and control the mechanical functions of the animation stand.

☐ CORE. A center of metal or plastic around which raw film stock is wound.

☐ CORE IDEA. The film maker's value judgment or intellectual premise with regard to the basic subject in a given film.

☐ COUNTERS. Devices for determining the cumulative number of frames photographed or increments moved in the operation of the animation stand.

☐ CREDITS. Acknowledgment by name of those film makers who have contributed to a film's production, presented at the beginning or the end of a film. *See* Titles; Labels.

☐ CROSS DISSOLVE. *See* Dissolve.

☐ CROW QUILL. The trade name for a type of pen point commonly used in inking cels.

☐ CURVATURE OF FIELD. An optical aberration in which the aspects of the subject are brought into focus on a curved surface instead of a plane.

☐ CUT. In motion pictures, an instantaneous change from one scene to the next.

☐ CUTOUT. *See* Animation, Cutout.

☐ CUTTING COPY. British term referring to "workprint."

☐ CYCLE. A short series of drawings or cels which may be photographed over and over to create the illusion of continuing, repeated action.

☐ DAILIES. *See* Rushes.

☐ DEGRADATION. A loss of photographic fidelity as a consequence of duplication.

☐ DENSITY. The relative opacity of developed photographic emulsion.

☐ DEPTH OF FIELD. The range of distances before a camera within which the subject can be reproduced photographically with acceptably sharp focus.

☐ DEPTH OF FOCUS.** That range of possible plane positions perpendicular to the optical axis of a lens, lying in front of,

at, and behind the plane of the minimum circle of confusion (optimum focus), which will yield an acceptably small circle of confusion. For maximum image definition the emulsion of the film should lie in the plane of the minimum circle of confusion. The term is often mistakenly used when "depth of field" is meant.

☐ DEVELOPER. A solution in which the development of film emulsion takes place.

☐ DIALOGUE. Lip-synchronous sound from a cartoon or live action subject.

☐ DIAPHRAGM, PRINTER. A variable aperture on certain types of printer, used for controlling the amount of light conveyed to the film.

☐ DIORAMA. A semicircular painted setting which serves as a background for three-dimensional subjects in the foreground.

☐ DIRECTOR. The person who is responsible for transmuting a script into a motion picture and supervises all aspects of its production.

☐ DISSOLVE. A fade-in superimposed over a fade-out so that the first scene on the screen gradually disappears as the succeeding scene replaces it.

☐ DISTORTION. *See* Astigmatism.

☐ DOPE SHEET. British term referring to "exposure sheet."

☐ DOUBLE EXPOSURE. A technique in which the same strip of film is exposed twice in the camera in order to combine images which cannot be photographed together during a single run.

☐ DOUBLE FRAME. British term referring to photographing in "twos."

☐ DOUBLE RUN. *See* Double Exposure.

☐ DOUBLE SYSTEM. A system in which picture and sound are recorded simultaneously, but are processed independently to permit greater latitude during the editing process.

☐ DRAWING DISC. A circular piece of metal containing an opal glass insert and pegbars, which is most often mounted on a wooden chassis; the disc is used while drawing or rendering animation and can be turned to suit the convenience of the film maker.

☐ DROPPED SHADOW. A dark shadow added to a white or colored title to enhance its legibility.

☐ DRY BRUSH. A form of rendering in which a brush is dipped into paint or ink and dragged nearly dry before rendering.

☐ DUBBING. A film jargon term referring to any of several processes of rerecording. *See* Re-Recording.

☐ DUBBING SESSION. *See* Re-Recording.

☐ DYE COUPLERS. Chemical ingredients added to film or to developer with the intention that it unite with a developer decomposition product, during film development, to render an image in color.

☐ EASE-IN, EASE-OUT. A progressive acceleration and deceleration of movement at the beginning and end of a pan, a zoom, or a compound move.

☐ EDGE FOG. Unwanted marginal exposure along one side of the film, caused either by insufficient darkness during loading or by a camera which is not adequately light sealed.

☐ EDGE NUMBERS. A series of numbers spaced one foot apart on the edge of raw film stock which are used for editing purposes.

☐ EDITING. The process of selecting those scenes and sound tracks to be used in a film and assembling them into a desirable relationship for a good motion picture.

☐ EDITOR. The person responsible for selecting the recorded scenes and sounds to be used in a motion picture and for arranging them in the most desirable relationship and tempo.

☐ EFFECTS. *See* Sound Effects; Special Effects.

☐ EMULSION. The light-sensitive coating of the film base, on which images are photographically recorded.

☐ EMULSION NUMBER. A classification assigned by a film manufacturer to each type of film it releases.

☐ EMULSION SPEED.** The photosensitivity of an emulsion, usually expressed as an index number based on the film manufacturer's recommendation for the use of the film under typical conditions of exposure and development.

☐ ENLARGEMENT PRINT. The enlargement of motion picture frames from a smaller film stock to a larger film stock, as from 16mm to 35mm by means of an optical printer.

☐ ETCHING ANIMATION. *See* Animation, Etching.

☐ EXPOSURE.* The process of subjecting a photographic film to light in such a manner that a latent image will be produced on the emulsion.

☐ EXPOSURE GUIDE. Instruction sheet for photographing a filmograph.

☐ EXPOSURE METER. An optical or photoelectrical device designed to ascertain the amount of light falling on a given subject for the purpose of determining the correct exposure of the film.

☐ EXPOSURE SHEET. A chart on which all the cels, backgrounds, zoom and pantograph charts, and computed pans are entered in order for photography at the animation stand.

☐ EXTREMES. Drawings made by the animator showing the animated subject at the critical moments of a given action. Drawings of the intermediate phases of the action are subsequently provided by in-betweeners.

☐ FADE. A fade-in is the gradual appearance of a scene from a darkened screen. A fade-out is the gradual darkening and disappearance of a scene to black on the screen.

☐ FADE SCALE. A measuring device mounted on a camera and used to control the progressive sector openings of a variable shutter.

☐ FAST FILM STOCK. *See* Emulsion Speed.

☐ FEATURE LENGTH. A film averaging 90 minutes or more in length and intended for theatrical distribution.

☐ FIELD. British term referring to the image area resolved by a lens.

☐ FIELD GUIDE. A transparent sheet printed with vertical, horizontal, and diagonal lines, used for planning and plotting moves and scenes to be photographed on the animation stand.

☐ FIELD MASK. A black piece of cardboard with a rectangular hole cut out of its center whose dimensions correspond to a given field size on a field guide. Field masks are used primarily for composition, and are customarily made in sets ranging in size from a 1 field to a 12 field.

☐ FIELD POSITION LEVEL. The height of an animation camera above the surface of the compound which will enable the camera to photograph an area of the subject corresponding to a given field size of the standard field guide.

☐ FIELD SIZE. A measure of the size of the area being photographed on the animation stand at a given moment. Field sizes range from a 1 field to a 12 field and are of a 36 to 50 proportional ratio.

☐ FIELD STEP. The distance between adjacent parallel lines on a field guide. This distance is equal to 36 increments between each of the N–S lines, and 50 increments between each of the E–W lines.

☐ FILM CLIP. A short strip of motion picture film.

☐ FILMOGRAPH. A technique in which movements of the camera and compound create the illusion of animation in still photographs and artwork.

☐ FILM, MOTION PICTURE. A long, thin, flexible ribbon of transparent material, most often made of cellulose triacetate or acetate propionate, bearing a surface of light-sensitive emulsion capable of reproducing images, and perforated along the edge.

☐ FILM PERFORATION. Holes punched at regular intervals for the length of motion picture film, intended to be engaged by pins, pegs, and sprockets as the film is transported through cameras, processors, and projectors.

☐ FILM REGISTRATION. *See* Pilot Pin Registration.

☐ FILM SPEED. *See* Emulsion Speed.

☐ FILTER, PHOTOGRAPHIC. A transparent optical element commonly used with a lens for the purpose of preventing unwanted portions of the spectrum from reaching the film emulsion.

☐ FINE GRAIN. Low-contrast positive image print of a negative with accurate registration. Also called Registration Print.

☐ FIXING (FIXATION).* The process of removing the residual sensitive silver halides from a developed film to render the developed image permanent. During the process of fixation, films are customarily treated to preserve and harden the developed image.

☐ FLATNESS OF FIELD. The variation of density across a frame of motion picture film which has been exposed to an evenly illuminated neutral gray card.

☐ FLIP. An effect whereby a still scene appears to revolve on its vertical axis and may introduce a new scene or a new title with each revolution.

☐ FLIP BOX. A device mounted over the photography area of the compound table, which is used to create the effect of a flip.

☐ FLIPPING. A technique of testing the approximate smoothness of an animation action by allowing several pencil drawings to fall down steadily in sequence.

☐ FLOATING PEGBARS. *See* Pegbars, Floating.

☐ FLOATING PLATEN. A platen affixed to a rollaway unit which enables the compound to be moved independently while the platen remains stationary, and which can be moved out of the photography area when three-dimensional objects are being animated.

☐ FLOW. British term referring to the smoothness of animated action.

☐ FLUORESCENT ANIMATION. *See* Animation, Fluorescent.

☐ F-NUMBER (STOP). A designation expressing the ratio of the opening in the iris to the focal length of a given lens.

☐ FOCAL LENGTH.** For any lens, or combination of lens elements such as a photographic objective, the focal length is the distance from either principal focus to the corresponding principal point. The "principal points" are two positions on the optical axis, separated from each other by a distance variable with the characteristics of the individual lens or combination of lenses, and under ordinary conditions they coincide with the conjugate points for unit magnification, in this context being known as "nodal points."

☐ FOCAL PLANE. The area in space on which parallel rays of light refracted through a given lens focus to form sharp images.

☐ FOCUS. (1) The point where parallel rays of light refracted by a given lens appear to meet. (2) The degree of clarity of an image refracted through a lens onto a screen or a film emulsion.

☐ FOLLOW FOCUS. Changes in the focal setting of a lens to maintain focus as the animation camera advances toward or retreats from the subject. *See* Follow-Focus Cam.

☐ FOLLOW-FOCUS CAM. A mechanical device used on an animation stand, with a linkage between the column and the lens of the camera, which keeps the lens focused on the surface of the compound tabletop regardless of the height of the camera above the subject.

☐ FOOT. A unit of measure in film length. One foot of 35mm film is equal to 16 frames; of 16mm, to 40 frames.

☐ FOOT CANDLE. A measure of illumination equal to the amount of light falling on a surface one square foot in area each point of which is one foot distant from a light source of one standard candle intensity.

☐ FOOTAGE. A given length of motion picture film.

☐ FOOTAGE COUNTER. A mechanical device used to measure the number of feet of film passed through the camera.

☐ FOREGROUND. The part of a scene which is nearest the viewer. In animation, the foreground refers to those cels and artwork which represent the equivalent of a live-action foreground.

☐ FOURS. The exposure of a given image on four frames of film.

☐ FRAME. A single picture in a motion picture film.

☐ FRAME COUNTER. An indicator mounted with a camera which specifies how many frames of film have been exposed.

☐ FRAME GLASS. British term referring to "platen glass."

☐ FRAME MASK. British term referring to "field size."

☐ FREEZE-FRAME. An effect whereby the same frame of motion picture film is held on the screen by repeated printing of that frame in the optical printer.

☐ GHOSTING. A technique for creating translucent images by means of double exposure or double printing.

☐ GRAININESS. A term used to describe the quality of a projected motion picture image having discernible particles ''boiling'' on the screen, instead of grains too small to be perceived.

☐ GREEN PRINT. A projection print having excessive surface friction as a consequence of inadequate hardening during processing, or insufficient drying time after processing.

☐ GUIDE LINES. Lightly drawn pencil lines used to control and direct the movements of animated cutouts and objects.

☐ HELD CEL (Or HOLD CEL). A cel retained in place for repeated photography while other cels are changed.

☐ HOT SPOT. Any part of the photography area which is overilluminated, resulting in overexposure of film emulsion in the corresponding image area.

☐ ID. An abbreviation of identification, referring to a television commercial which also carries the television station's call letters.

☐ IMAGE PLANE. See Focal Plane.

☐ IN-BETWEEN BREAKDOWN. Instructions from the animator to the in-betweener with regard to the treatment of in-between drawings.

☐ IN-BETWEEN DRAWINGS. Those animation drawings between the extreme drawings which are used to create a smooth flow of animation.

☐ IN-BETWEENER. An assistant to the animator; one who sketches the animation drawings in between the extreme drawings made by the animator to create a convincing flow of action.

☐ INCIDENT LIGHT. The light from all sources falling upon a subject.

☐ INCREMENT. A unit of measure for moves to be implemented on the animation stand. Moves on the animation stand are calibrated at 100 increments to an inch.

☐ INKER. An artist who specializes in rendering animation drawings on cels in ink.

☐ INKING. The process of tracing the animation drawings on cels in ink.

☐ INTERLOCK. Any mechanical system which permits the synchronous presentation of picture and sound recorded on separate lengths of motion picture film.

☐ INTERMITTENT. A mechanical device designed to alternately move and then hold successive frames of film as they are transported through a camera, stepup-printer or projector.

☐ INTER-NEGATIVE. A print reproduced from an original film photographed on reversal film stock, and used to print duplicates and release prints.

☐ INVERTED PANTOGRAPH. See Pantograph, Inverted.

☐ JITTER. A British term referring to ''strobing.''

☐ KELVIN SCALE. A temperature scale calibrated in the same degrees as the Centigrade scale, but starting with absolute zero. A given Kelvin temperature is obtained by adding 273° to the temperature in degrees Centigrade. See Color Temperature.

☐ KEY DRAWING. See Extremes.

☐ KEYS. A British term referring to ''extremes.''

☐ KEY-TO-FILL RATIO. The proportionate amount of foot candles of illumination spilled upon a subject from different directions. See Lighting.

☐ LABELS. Names of objects, superimposed on the photographic image. See Titles; Credits.

☐ LABORATORY. A system equipped to process motion picture film and produce duplicates for distribution.

☐ LAP DISSOLVE. See Dissolve.

☐ LAYOUT. In animation work this refers to the design and relation of the cartoons to the backgrounds, and to the visual concept of the film as a whole.

☐ LAYOUT SKETCHES. British term referring to storyboard sketches.

☐ LEAD SHEETS. See Bar Sheets.

☐ LEADER. A length of clear film used at the head and tail of a motion picture for protection and threading purposes; a leader is also used for a variety of purposes in editing. See Academy Leader.

☐ LENS.** (1) In optics, any transparent system by which images may be formed through the light-refracting properties of the curved surfaces of translucent objects. Photographic objectives usually are made up of a number of individual units, each having a combination of positive and/or negative spherical section surfaces. In some instances the unit combination includes a neutral, or plane surface. The several units are mounted in a specific relationship to each other in a cylindrical mounting, a barrel, which usually also includes an iris diaphragm with its calibrated external scale, and a mechanical device to permit refocusing. Glass of an appropriate index of refraction is used for each of the unit elements, some combinations of which may be cemented together with an optical cement such as Canada Balsam. Other combinations may include an air space, as dictated by the specific lens design.

(2) Commonly, any optical system complete with barrel, focusing ring, and so on.

☐ LEWIS PANTOGRAPH. A variant of the conventional pantograph unit in which a plastic sheet, scribed with intersecting North–South and East–West lines, is used in lieu of a steel pointer over the pantograph field guide or chart.

☐ LIGHT BOX. A glass surface lighted from below.

☐ LIGHT METER. *See* Exposure Meter.

☐ LIGHTING. The illumination of a subject to permit photographic reproduction.

☐ LIMITED ANIMATION. *See* Animation, Limited.

☐ LINE-TEST. British term referring to "pencil test."

☐ LIP SYNCHRONIZATION. A relationship which exists when the sounds of an image's voice coincide with the movements of its lips.

☐ LIVE-ACTION PHOTOGRAPHY. The use of the motion picture camera to record events taking place before the camera.

☐ LOG, ANIMATION. A written record of the activities of making an animated motion picture.

☐ LOG, CAMERA. A written record of the optimum exposures achieved on the animation stand with various types of films under differing lighting conditions.

☐ LOG, LIVE-ACTION. A written record of the camera and sound activities of making a motion picture.

☐ LOGO. The symbol or trademark identifying an organization.

☐ MACHINE LEADER. Clear, transparent film stock.

☐ MAGAZINE. A chamber for holding rolled motion picture film, usually designed with the dual capacity to supply the film for exposure and then reroll it, used with certain types of cameras and printers.

☐ MAGNETIC FILM. Perforated film coated with a magnetic recording medium.

☐ MAGNETIC RECORDING. The recording of the sequential sound waves of the audio subject, on a film, tape, or wire which has been coated with a magnetic recording medium.

☐ MARRIED PRINT. *See* Composite Print.

☐ MASK. A cover used to eliminate or reduce the exposure of film emulsion in one area of a given frame while permitting exposure of another area. *See* Matte Rolls.

☐ MASTER SCENE (ANIMATION). A photograph of a picture at its maximum size on the animation stand.

☐ MASTER SCENE (LIVE-ACTION). A wide angle view of a scene which orients the audience to the context, mood, and environment in which the following film story will take place.

☐ MATTE. Any opaque material used to prevent the exposure of film emulsion. *See* Matte Rolls.

☐ MATTE BLEED. A conspicuous, hard "line" around a subject which has been combined with a context from another film through multiple exposure matte techniques. Matte bleed is caused by slight variations in the registration of the mattes.

☐ MATTE ROLLS (TRAVELING MASKS).* Matte rolls (traveling masks) are a pair of film rolls used as light modulators. Matte rolls are complementary in that where one roll is clear, the other is effectively opaque. They are usually matched to rolls of original black and white, or of color reversal positives in the printing of black and white or color duplicates.

☐ MIX. American: The combining of voices, music, and sound effects into desirable proportions on a single sound track.

☐ MIX. British term referring to "dissolve."

☐ MIXER. The director of a sound-recording crew who is in charge of combining voices, music, and sound effects into desirable proportions on a single sound track.

☐ MIXING. The process of rerecording and combining separate sound tracks into a desired balance on a single sound track.

☐ MODEL SHEET. A sheet of drawings in which all the characters are shown in their relative sizes and proportions, numbered for color, to which all the persons concerned with production can refer.

☐ MONTAGE. European: Synonymous with editing.

☐ MONTAGE. American: A series of short scenes with a stream-of-consciousness effect.

☐ MOTION PICTURE FILM.* A thin, flexible ribbon of transparent material having perforations along one or both edges and bearing a sensitized layer or other coating capable of producing photographic images. The term "film" may be applied to unexposed film, to exposed but unprocessed film, and to exposed and processed film.

☐ MOVIOLA. Trade name for a motion picture viewing device containing facilities for viewing the film while simultaneously listening to sounds from one or more magnetic or optical sound tracks.

☐ MULTICEL LEVELS. The practice of using many cels at the same time, one on top of another, for the purpose of combining separate images in animation photography.

☐ MULTIHEAD PROJECTION. A British term referring to synchronized projection of picture and sound tracks from separate projectors.

☐ MULTIPLANE. A technique of enhancing the feeling of

depth in animation photography by presenting different units of artwork at more than one place in the film field.

☐ MULTIPLE-IMAGE EFFECTS. *See* Multiple Exposure.

☐ MULTIPLE EXPOSURE. A technique in which the same strip of film is exposed more than once in the camera in order to combine images which cannot be photographed together.

☐ NARRATION. Words heard from the sound track without the speaker being seen by the viewer of the film.

☐ NEGATIVE IMAGE.* A photographic image in which the values of light and shade of the original photographed subject are inverted. Light objects of the original subject are represented by high densities and dark objects are represented by low densities.

☐ NEGATIVE PERFORATION. Used for 35mm film for making original negatives or registration duplicates. Has a flat top and bottom which accurately fits the locating pins on a registration film movement. *See* Position Perforation.

☐ OBJECT ANIMATION. *See* Animation, Object.

☐ OFF REGISTER. Off-center positioning of the compound to achieve such effects as vibrations.

☐ ONES. The exposure of only one frame of motion picture film to a given image.

☐ OPAQUEING. The process of applying opaque paint to an animation cel.

☐ OPAQUER. An artist who specializes in applying opaque paint to animation cels.

☐ OPTICAL EFFECTS. Any modification or alteration of a motion picture subject by means of adaptive lens, matte, or mirror at the time of original photography or during processing or duplication.

☐ OPTICAL PRINTER.** Any printer in which an image-forming optical system lies between the film bearing the image to be transferred and the film onto which the image is to be printed. May be either a step printer or a continuous printer. The arrangement is versatile, in that alterations of image may be introduced to produce optical effects, or enlargement or reduction of image size.

☐ OPTICAL SOUND TRACK. A narrow band which carries the sound record, photographically printed, and running on one side of the pictorial images for the length of a sound motion picture. Variations of width or density in the sound track of a film modulate the amount of light projected through it to a photoelectric cell, which in turn converts the recorded variations of light to electrical energy, which is transmuted and amplified to the sounds of voice, music, and sound effects.

☐ OPTICALS. British term referring to "optical effects."

☐ ORIGINAL. An initial recorded impression of a photographic image, or of audio patterns recorded on a disc or a magnetic recording medium.

☐ OVERAGE. A computational method for determining the progressive changes in increment distances during the plotting of eases in and out.

☐ OVERLAY. Cel containing a foreground which overlaps the subject being animated.

☐ PAN (ANIMATION). The horizontal or vertical movement of the animation compound, bearing the animation artwork, while being photographed.

☐ PAN BACKGROUND. *See* Background, Pan.

☐ PAN (LIVE-ACTION). A horizontal scanning movement by the camera usually from the pivotal point of a tripod.

☐ PANNING GEAR. British term referring to traveling pegbars.

☐ PANTOGRAPH CHART. A semitransparent overlay containing the central path and increment distances of a pan. Pantograph charts are mounted over the field guide of the pantograph unit; the move is implemented by aligning the point of the pantograph needle with each increment mark along the central path for each exposure of the pan.

☐ PANTOGRAPH, CORRECTED. A relationship of the photography area to the pantograph unit in which the photography area and the pantograph field guide are both right side up.

☐ PANTOGRAPH, INVERTED. A relationship of the photography area to the pantograph unit in which either the photography area or the pantograph field guide is right side up, while the other is upside down.

☐ PANTOGRAPH UNIT. A flat metal surface with a field guide mounted on it and an iron pointer suspended over it. This unit is affixed to the right side of the animation compound; each movement of the compound is accompanied by an equivalent move of the pantograph needle over the pantograph field guide to the center of the area being photographed.

☐ PAPIER MÂCHÉ. A paper pulp used for spreading over wire or wood frames in the construction of puppets and their backgrounds.

☐ PASTEL ANIMATION. *See* Animation, Pastel.

☐ PEGBARS, FLOATING. A mechanical device bearing a set of pegs which lies on top of the compound tabletop and functions independently of the compound and its controls.

☐ PEGBARS, TRAVELING. Two sets of pegs mounted on separate mobile tracks embedded in the surface of the animation table.

☐ PENCIL TEST. The process of photographing and projecting the penciled animation drawings to determine the smoothness of the animation before proceeding to the inking and painting of cels.

☐ PERSISTENCE OF VISION. A characteristic of the human eye in which the retina retains the image of a viewed subject for an instant after the subject has been removed.

☐ PERSPECTIVE. In art, a method of creating the illusion of three-dimensional form and distance on a two-dimensional surface.

☐ PHOTOGRAPHY AREA. That portion of the surface of the compound tabletop of an animation stand which is within the photographic scope of the animation camera.

☐ PICTURE NEGATIVE.* Any negative film which, after exposure to a subject or positive image and subsequent processing, produces a negative picture image on the film.

☐ PICTURE PRINT.* Any positive printed from a picture negative.

☐ PICTURE WORK PRINT.* A positive print consisting of intercut picture daily prints, picture library prints, prints of dissolves, montages, titles, and so on, constantly synchronized with the corresponding sound work print. Used in editing and combining the various scenes of a motion picture into the desired form.

☐ PILOT-PIN REGISTRATION. Part of a transport and positioning system, used in some cameras and optical printers to hold each successive frame of motion picture film firmly in the same plane for each exposure by providing a pin over which the film perforations fit in an exact relationship.

☐ PIN REGISTRATION. See Pilot Pin Registration.

☐ PINHEAD SHADOW ANIMATION. See Animation, Pinhead Shadow.

☐ PLATEN. A sheet of water-white glass used to press down and hold flat any animation artwork placed under the camera for photography. Also the mechanical devices used to hold, raise, and lower the glass; used generically "platen" refers both to the device and to the glass as a single unit.

☐ PLOT. The computation of moves to be implemented on the animation stand.

☐ PLOT. The storyline of a dramatic film.

☐ POP-ON (POP-IN). The instantaneous appearance of a new image within a scene already on the screen.

☐ POSITIVE IMAGE.* A photographic replica in which the values of light and shade of the original photographed subject are represented in their original order. The light objects of the original subject are represented by low densities and the dark objects are represented by high densities.

☐ POST-SYNCHRONIZED SOUND. A sound track recorded to match the already completed portion of the film.

☐ POSITIVE PERFORATION. A perforation system designed for 35mm theater projection. See Negative Perforation.

☐ PRESSURE PLATE. A flat metal plate placed in a camera or projector for the purpose of holding the film firmly in place behind the aperture.

☐ PRESSURE PLATE PAD. British term referring to platen glass and to the underlying pad in the photography area.

☐ PRE-SYNCHRONIZED SOUND. Recording of the sound track prior to photographing a motion picture.

☐ PRINT. (Used interchangeably with "positive.") A term used to designate: (1) A processed film bearing a positive image. (2) Exposed but unprocessed film stock. (3) Unexposed film stock designed for positive images.

☐ PRINTING.* The process of exposing raw stock by using the image of another film as a light moderator. Through printing, one may produce a negative film from a positive film; or, if the reversal process is employed, printing may be used to produce positives from positives or negatives from negatives. When the verb "to print" is used, any of the above processes may be implied.

☐ PRODUCTION.* Production is the general term used to describe the processes involved in making all the original material that is the basis for the finished motion picture.

☐ PROJECTION.* Projection is the process of presenting a film for either visual or aural review, or both.

☐ PROJECTION PRINTING (OPTICAL PRINTING).* Printing accomplished by projecting the image to be copied on the raw stock. The image being copied may be enlarged, reduced, or made the same size.

☐ PROJECTION SYNCHRONISM.* The time relation between the picture and the corresponding sound in a projection print. Correct projection synchronism is indicated by exact coincidence of picture and sound as seen and heard. To attain this result, it is necessary to place the sound track 20 frames ahead of the corresponding picture for 35mm film and 26 frames ahead of the corresponding picture for 16mm film, since sound motion picture projection equipment is designed to produce correct projection synchronism when this relationship exists between the locations of the projected picture and the corresponding sound.

☐ PROJECTOR. A mechanical device commonly used for throwing the images of processed film onto a large screen for viewing. In television broadcasting, the device which transmits the images of a film to a television unit.

☐ PULL-DOWN CLAW. A device within a live-action camera which advances the film after each exposure by engaging its perforations and pulling the unexposed film down to the camera aperture for the succeeding exposure.

☐ PUNCH. Mechanical device used to punch registration holes in cels and paper.

☐ PUPPET ANIMATION. *See* Animation, Puppet.

☐ PUSH-OFF. *See* Wipe.

☐ RAW STOCK. Film with unexposed emulsion.

☐ REAR PROJECTION. Motion picture images projected onto the desired screen surface, usually translucent glass, from behind the surface instead of from the front.

☐ REDUCTION PRINTING.* The process of producing and recording photographically a smaller image, usually on a smaller film, from a larger image. Commonly used in making 16mm negatives or prints from 35mm originals. Film thus made is referred to as a reduction negative or reduction print, as the case may be.

☐ REEL. A metal or plastic spool around which a length of motion picture film is wound.

☐ REFLECTED LIGHT. The light from an external source which strikes an object and is not absorbed, but instead is thrown back.

☐ REGISTER PINS. British term referring to pilot pins.

☐ REGISTRATION. A correct relationship between the positions of the animation artwork and the camera.

☐ REGISTRATION HOLES. Holes punched in animation drawings, cels, and background to assure correct alignment when fitted over registration pegs.

☐ REGISTRATION PEGS. A set of projecting pins used on animation drawing discs and the compound of the animation stand to assure correct positioning in both areas.

☐ RELEASE PRINT.* A composite print made for general distribution and exhibition after the final trial or composite or sample print has been approved. It is in projection synchronism.

☐ REPEAT. *See* Cycle.

☐ RERECORDING. The electrical process of transferring sound patterns from tapes, discs, or magnetic films to one of these media, for the purpose of combining or modifying them in some way. In film jargon this process is known as ''dubbing.''

RETAKE. Photographing the same scene again.

☐ REVERSAL FILM.* Film which after exposure is processed to produce a positive image rather than the customary negative image. If exposure is made by printing from a negative, a negative image is produced. Reversal films may be black and white, or color, and either sound or picture or both; usually 16mm films.

☐ REVERSAL MASTER PRINT,* 16MM. A 16mm reversal print made specifically for use in producing other prints. Sometimes referred to as a first generation dupe. Prints from it will then be referred to as second generation dupes.

☐ REVERSAL ORIGINAL.* The film which is originally exposed in a camera or recorder and processed by reversal to produce a positive image. This positive image is not the same as a print from a negative inasmuch as right and left are transposed. A reversal original may be black and white or color film.

☐ REVERSAL PRINT.* A print, usually a positive, which is made on reversal film and developed by the reversal process.

☐ REVERSAL PROCESS.* Process in which a latent image of a reversal film is developed to a silver image by primary development, destroyed by a chemical bleach, and the remaining sensitized material exposed and developed in a second developer bath before fixing and washing.

☐ REWIND. A support for reels of film, used in pairs to roll lengths of film from one reel to another.

☐ ROSTRUM. British term referring to the animation stand, and to its components. For example, a rostrum camera is an animation camera.

☐ ROTARY UNIT. A circular unit supporting an animation compound by means of which the entire compound may be turned to any angle or rotated in a complete 360° circle.

☐ ROTOSCOPE. A piece of equipment which fits into the camera and is used to project motion picture images down from the camera to the compound table for the purposes of making layouts or traveling mattes.

☐ ROTOSCOPE WIGGLE. Variations in the rendering of animation drawings resulting when mattes are hand drawn, frame by frame during the process of rotoscoping, to match slow or tight moves, or irregular shapes.

☐ ROTOSCOPING. The tracing of images projected down from the camera to the compound tabletop for the purposes of making layouts or traveling mattes.

☐ ROUGH CUT. The first, tentatively edited form of the film.

☐ RUSHES. The first positive prints from the original film.

☐ SCENE. The exposed film which extends from the beginning to the end of one continuous roll of the camera.

☐ SCRATCHOFF. A technique in which inked or opaqued lines on a cel are removed, a small bit at a time, while the camera photographs the process with the film direction reversed. When the processed film is projected the lines appear to grow and advance across the screen.

☐ SCRIPT. A written statement of content and cinematic techniques to be used as a blueprint for producing a motion picture.

☐ SELF-LINE. An ink line which is the same color as the subject instead of the customary black.

☐ SEQUENCE. Complete dramatic action within a film; usually a series of scenes.

☐ SET-UP. British term referring to field size, and position.

☐ SET-UP KEY. British term referring to drawings given to the animation cameraman, instructing him with regard to field size, and position of the camera in relation to the compound.

☐ SHOT. A single frame of exposed motion picture film.

☐ SHOW PRINT. British term referring to ''release print.''

☐ SHUTTER CONTROL. A mechanism for controlling the degree of sector opening in a variable shutter, usually calibrated by degrees in a fade scale.

☐ SHUTTER, ROTARY. A flat circular metal disc, with a sector removed, which revolves once between the lens and the film for each frame of film exposed. The removed sector permits exposure of the film emulsion while a frame is being held in place behind the lens. The opacity of the disc prevents exposure of film emulsion while the next frame of film is being moved into place behind the lens for the next exposure.

☐ SHUTTER, VARIABLE OPENING. A shutter whose sector opening can be varied by degrees from 0° to the maximum opening of a given shutter, normally 170°.

☐ SILENT SPEED. The minimum rate of film projection at which the projected images can be fused by the persistence of vision into a continuous image; considered to be 16 frames per second.

☐ SINGLE-FRAME EXPOSURE. The exposure of one frame of motion picture film at a time, in the manner of still photography. Commonly used in animation because of the need to make changes of cels or in the relationship of the compound to the camera.

☐ SINGLE SYSTEM. A system whereby the sound is recorded optically while the picture is being photographed and when processed both will appear on the same length of motion picture film.

☐ SKIP-FRAME. A technique of periodically deleting a given number of frames from a motion picture film in order to shorten the film or to lessen its projection speed.

☐ SLIDES. Transparencies mounted between two pieces of glass, most often used for projection.

☐ SLOW FILM STOCK. *See* Emulsion Speed.

☐ SOCIALIST REALISM. A doctrine propounded by Socialist and Communist states which maintains that all forms of pictorial art should be expressed in realistic forms so they may be understood and appreciated by the greatest possible number of persons.

☐ SOUND CHART. British term referring to bar sheets.

☐ SOUND EFFECTS. Sounds from any source other than voice or music.

☐ SOUND, HAND-DRAWN. A technique in which music and effects are created by an animator who renders an optical sound track with inks or paints, bypassing conventional sound recording.

☐ SOUND READER. A playback device for listening to magnetic or optical sound tracks during the editing phase of film production.

☐ SOUND SPEED. The standard rate of projection for 16mm sound motion pictures is 24 frames per second or 36 feet per minute. The comparable rate of projection for 35mm sound film is 24 frames per second, 90 feet per minute.

☐ SPACING GUIDE. A chart given by an animator to an in-betweener to indicate how far each succeeding drawing between the extremes should be animated beyond its predecessor in order to portray a smooth, lifelike flow of action.

☐ SPECIAL EFFECT. Any motion picture effect unobtainable by conventional cinematography techniques; e.g., combining live-action footage with animation.

☐ SPEECH CHART. British term referring to the bar sheets for individual syllables, which are used by animators to assure lip synchronization.

☐ SPEED LINES. Lines drawn in the direction taken by an animated subject in order to emphasize its speed.

☐ SPHERICAL DISTORTION. An optical aberration in which the rays of light coming through the central portion of the lens and the rays coming through the outer areas do not converge at the same distance from the lens, resulting in a blurred image.

☐ SPIN. A movement in which a scene or title rotates around its own center point.

☐ SPLICE. The technique of uniting two lengths of film, end to end, by means of staples, film cement, or hot-splice welding. The term also refers to the welded picture itself.

☐ SPLICER. A mechanical device for holding two pieces of film in correct alignment to make a splice.

☐ SQUASH. A technique in animation drawing in which the subject is shown greatly compressed in order to endow it with dramatic vitality and to compensate for the lack of three-dimensional form.

☐ STANDARD ASPECT RATIO. The width-to-height ratio of a motion picture frame, broadly expressed as four to three. In the two widths most widely used by professional film producers, this ratio is 0.410 to 0.294 for 16mm film and .868 to .631 for 35mm film. These figures are determined by the camera apertures which define the area of each frame exposed. In animation work, this ratio is 50 to 36.

☐ STEP PRINTER. An optical or contact printer in which a motion picture film is printed by stopping each frame in the print aperture.

☐ STEREOSCOPIC ANIMATION. Animated films which achieve a three-dimensional effect by presenting multiple images to the spectator, but require the viewer to wear spectacles in order to resolve the images. Vectographic film, which produces a stereoscopic effect without the need of viewing glasses, proved too thick to be feasible in commercial processing.

☐ STIPPLE. A form of rendering using areas of dots.

☐ STOP MOTION. *See* Single Frame Exposure.

☐ STOP MOTION PRINTING. *See* Freeze Frame.

☐ STORYBOARD. A visual presentation in the form of sketches of the ideas and pictorial continuity of the script.

☐ STRETCH. Elongated distortion of an animated action.

☐ STROBING. An effect whereby the successive images of a progressive movement are not fused by the persistence of vision, but appear to move as a series of short, staccato jumps.

☐ SUBJECTIVE CAMERA. A camera technique in which the camera assumes the point of view of the audience in order to gain greater viewer involvement.

☐ SUPERIMPOSURE. The combining of separate discrete images into a given frame of film either within the camera or within an optical printer.

☐ SYMPATHETIC MOVEMENT. Any pan across a subject, or movement by a subject, which the eye perceives as continuous. For unsympathetic movement, see Strobing.

☐ SYNCHRONISM. A picture-sound relationship whereby the projected image appears in correct correlation to the desired sounds of words, music, and sound effects.

☐ SYNCHRONIZER. A multichannel mechanical device used for maintaining frame-for-frame registration between live-action footage and its accompanying sound tracks of narration, music, and sound effects.

☐ SYNCHRONOUS PULSE. An electronic device used in some tape recorders to time the material being recorded by impressing inaudible electronic beats at regular intervals on the tape.

☐ SYNOPSIS. A one-page outline stating the essential concept of a proposed film in terms of its target audience, purpose, subject, core idea, plot, identification, and cinematic form.

☐ TABLETOP. *See* Compound Table.

☐ TAKE. *See* Scene.

☐ TAP. *See* Beat.

☐ TARGET AUDIENCE. The people intended to view a given motion picture.

☐ TASK ANALYSIS. The process of deciding in advance of production what objectives a given film will be designed to achieve.

☐ TELEVISION ANIMATION. Animated films intended for broadcast distribution differ from the traditional form in that their subjects must be more carefully centered to preclude any amputation of key images by ''television cutoff.''

☐ TELEVISION CUT-OFF. The area around the edges of each frame of film which is masked off by television projection.

☐ THREES. The exposure of three frames of film to a given image.

☐ TILT. In live-action motion pictures, a vertical, pivotal camera move while a scene is being photographed.

☐ TIME-LAPSE PHOTOGRAPHY. A single-frame motion picture technique by which normally slow processes are photographically speeded up by allowing a long interval of time to elapse between each exposure of frame of film.

☐ TITLE. The name given to a motion picture. *See* Credits; Labels.

☐ T-NUMBER.** A number used in calibrating lenses by a uniform system which takes into account variations of optical efficiency. Calibrated by this system, any lens set to a specific t-number should produce the same central image illumination, for a given scene, as any other lens so calibrated and set. *See* F-Number.

☐ TORQUE MOTOR. A motor which can increase or decrease its pull in proportion to the amount of tension present. Reversible torque motors are often used in pairs in camera magazines.

☐ TRACKING. British term referring to trucking in live-action cinematography, and a zoom in animation.

☐ TRACK-LAYING. British term referring to editing of synchronous picture and sound tracks.

☐ TRAVELING PEGBARS. *See* Pegbars, Traveling.

☐ TRUCK. *See* Zoom.

☐ TREATMENT. A prose description of a proposed motion picture, setting forth its essential content and cinematic approach.

☐ TRIPOD. A supporting stand for a live-action camera, usually consisting of three legs adjustable for height, and a head containing some means of firmly mounting the camera.

☐ TRUCK. *See* Zoom.

☐ TWOS. The exposure of two frames of motion picture film to a given image.

☐ UNIT ''I'' SYSTEM. A shuttle film movement with a pilot pin registration system developed by the Bell & Howell Company.

☐ VALUE. The shade of light or dark in a subject.

☐ VIEWER. A device for enlarging the images of motion picture film, usually for the purpose of editing.

☐ VIEWFINDER. A device which permits the cameraman to view the subject by means of a mirror or prism located between the camera film plane and the taking lens.

☐ VIEWFINDER, RACKOVER. A camera viewfinder which requires that the main body of the camera be moved to one side, bringing an off-center viewing device into alignment with the taking lens. After the scene is composed and the lens focused, the camera body is returned to its former position for actual photography.

☐ VISUAL SQUEEZE. A technique in which images, not necessarily related, are flashed in rapid succession before the viewer.

☐ WIPE.** An optical effect used as a transition from one scene to another. In its commonest form scene A appears to be ''wiped'' off the screen by the progressive revelation of scene B, as a vertical dividing line separating the two advances across the screen from left to right. Many modifications of this basic form have been used, such as vertical, diagonal, iris, spiral, and even ''atomic bomb'' wipes.

☐ WORK BOOK. *See* Log, Animation.

☐ WORKPRINT. A duplicate positive motion picture print used for editing purposes.

☐ ZOOM CHART. A chart marked with the progressive distances an animation camera should be moved during each phase of a zoom. A zoom chart is mounted on the column of the animation stand, with the ends of the chart matching the beginning and end points of the zoom.

☐ ZOOM COUNTER. A mechanical device for cumulatively recording the movements of the camera carriage up or down the column of an animation stand. It may be calibrated in hundreths of an inch or tenths of a field.

☐ ZOOM-IN. A continuous approach by the camera to the animation artwork which gradually narrows down the area of the picture being photographed, giving the effect of continuously enlarging the subject.

☐ ZOOM LENS. A lens whose focal length is variable within given limits, and is capable of simulating the effect of the camera's movement toward or away from a subject.

☐ ZOOM-OUT. A progressive retreat from the subject which gradually enlarges the area being photographed, giving the effect of a continuously diminishing subject.

☐ ZOOM, SUBJECT. A zoom in which the camera does *not* move toward or away from the subject, but in which the subject is progressively enlarged or reduced in a series of drawings or still photographic reproductions which are then photographed on the animation stand.

INDEX

Italic numbers indicate art.

A NOTE ON THE BOOK

This book is set in Galaxy light and medium. Galaxy is the Harris-Intertype Fototronic cut of Univers, a type face designed in 1957 by Adrian Frutiger for Deberny et Peignot, Paris.

Text and binding design by Ben Kann

The line illustrations were drawn by Visual Direction, Massepequa, New York

Composed by Graphic Services, Inc., York, Pennsylvania

Printed by Halliday Lithograph Corp., West Hanover, Massachusetts

Bound by J. F. Tapley Company, Moonachie, New Jersey